lies
phy

f Habeas Corpus

Movement: A Study of Antebellum

Revolutionary Paris

908–1940

the Founding Fathers: A Study in

An Administrative and Legal History
he Stuarts

nial Legal History

can Business Corporation, 1784–1855:
f Public Service During Industrialization

The Politics and Diplomacy of Punishing
t World War

State Supreme Courts and State Security

ontrol: The Role of Men and Manipulation
rafficking

olicymakers in the Federal System
d G. Alan Tarr, editors

Contributions in Legal Stu
Series Editor: *Paul L. Mur*

A Constitutional History o
William F. Duker

The American Codificatio
Legal Reform
Charles M. Cook

Crime and Punishment in
Antoinette Wills

American Legal Culture, 1
John W. Johnson

Governmental Secrecy and
Constitutional Controls
Daniel N. Hoffman

Torture and English Law:
from the Plantagenets to t
James Heath

Essays on New York Colo
Herbert S. Johnson

The Origins of the Ameri
Broadening the Concept o
Ronald E. Seavoy

Prologue to Nuremberg:
War Criminals of the Firs
James F. Willis

The Network of Control:
Statutes, 1920–1970
Carol E. Jenson

Drugs and Information C
in the Control of Drug T
Jerald W. Cloyd

State Supreme Courts: P
Mary Cornelia Porter an

The Future of Our Liberties

Perspectives on the Bill of Rights

Edited by Stephen C. Halpern

CONTRIBUTIONS IN LEGAL STUDIES, NUMBER 25

Greenwood Press
Westport, Connecticut
London, England

Library of Congress Cataloging in Publication Data
Main entry under title:

The Future of our liberties.

(Contributions in legal studies, ISSN 0147-1074; no. 25)
Bibliography: p.
Includes index.
1. Civil rights—California. I. Halpern, Stephen C.
II. Series.
KF4749.F87 342.794'0085 81-13430
ISBN 0-313-22366-1 (lib. bdg.) 347.940285 AACR2

Library of Congress Catalog Card Number: 81-13430
ISBN: 0-313-22366-1
ISSN: 0147-1074

First published in 1982

Greenwood Press
A division of Congressional Information Service, Inc.
88 Post Road West
Westport, Connecticut 06881

Printed in the United States of America

10 9 8 7 6 5 4 3 2 1

For Jake and G. R. for the very special light they bring to my life.

Contents

NORMAN DORSEN

Preface

It is less than twenty years to 2000 A.D., not a long time in the history of nations or their institutions. But momentous changes can occur in that span.

Look back a little more than two decades to 1960, the last year of the Eisenhower era. Although the discerning could detect subsurface stirrings, the period epitomizes normalcy. International tranquility and a stable economy, presided over by an avuncular and much-loved leader, were the chief ingredients of what has been called a country club society.

Since 1960 an undeclared war tested the power of the presidency and the rights of individuals to protest and resist that war and the military conscription on which it fed; a lawless president was almost impeached; the civil rights movement prospered, waned, and altered; the feminist movement was reborn; the homosexual community began to challenge age-old taboos; and previously silent groups pressed for legal rights—students, prisoners, mental patients, the physically disabled, persons of illegitimate birth, others. The Bill of Rights was transformed in the hands of the most libertarian Supreme Court in American history; and then came the Burger Court.

Of only one thing am I certain—that in the year 2000 government will continue to infringe upon the civil liberties of Americans. Some of these attempts will be blatant, others subtle; some will succeed, others fail. And the judicial reaction to some of these attempts will mold and alter the Bill of Rights.

Which constitutional trends will continue, which will end, and what new doctrines will develop? The answer will turn, in large measure, on what happens to our society and social structure. It is necessary to be a seer. This book is a welcome and manysided effort to confront the central questions and to hazard some answers.

In his article that predicts the place of the First Amendment in 2000 A.D., Thomas Emerson provides his assumptions about the shape of American society. I agree with many: economic expansion will end; and a sharp decline in the economy may follow; economic and political pressures from abroad will heighten; new technologies with new risks will emerge. Emerson's other predictions are less sure. It is questionable whether society will be "primarily collective" with "widespread government planning and direct control of major industry, and an end of private enterprise on any substantial scale." It is even more doubtful that "there will be some alteration in the basic ethic of the ordinary citizen from a set of values based on personal gain or profit to one based upon a greater sense of social obligation."

Economic difficulties could as easily lead to a loosening of community, sharper competition, and intense individualism. Lines could increasingly be drawn among racial, religious, and ethnic groups. Rampant and persistent inflation may breed a sense of outrage and injustice even among those who are moderately comfortable. A fear of social disintegration, already a major premise of conservatives such as Irving Kristol and Norman Podhoretz, would in such circumstances haunt the comfortable classes.

International tensions likewise will lead to civil liberty violations. Just as World War II witnessed the internal exile of Japanese-American citizens, and just as the barbaric seizure of American hostages in Iran led to illegal government attempts to deport Iranian students, so will future crises provoke responses that threaten vulnerable groups. International events will also occasion more systemic dangers to civil liberty, such as the administration's requests for military registration and a Central Intelligence Agency (CIA) charter that would permit resumption of forms of covert action that were recently thought inimical to a government of laws.

These developments could lead to greater pressure on minorities, women, and poor people; less tolerance for social deviance; impatience with protest movements and the press; undue deference to national security concerns; a harsher criminal justice system; and a lessening of individual privacy. In such circumstances the people would be forced to display courage, stamina, and inner resources, even while vast new technologies presented unpredictable threats.

This is a bleak scenario. But it is not inevitable. In place will be tested institutions and a long American tradition of dedication to individual liberty. Judges will be asked to curb government when it seeks to achieve goals, however laudable, by cutting constitutional corners. Some will be skeptical of this means of protecting individual rights. They will rest on Learned Hand's theorem that courts cannot save liberty if it dies in the hearts of the people. Even if ultimately true, this belief should not be an invitation to judicial inaction. Courts sensitive to the constant need to protect minorities against majoritarian excesses should do what they can even if they cannot do everything. That is what they are there for.

Two other unfathomable but important questions remain. The first is whether the Bill of Rights, which was designed to protect the people from government, will provide redress to people victimized by private entities such as huge corporations, labor unions, or universities. Realistically, the power and pervasiveness of these institutions is vast and increasing; are they not—from the point of view of affected individuals—private governments?

A second question is whether the national government or the states and local governments are the securer bulwark—or perhaps the greater threat—to civil liberty. The arguments are well balanced, and the contributors to this book differ on this point. Local units are closer to the people but offer more opportunity for undetected discrimination and repression. The national government acts more visibly and with more formal regard for minority interests, but its vast power is a civil liberties time bomb that in this century has brought us the Palmer Raids, McCarthyism, and Watergate. We will probably continue to rely on all levels of government for what protection we can obtain while fearing these same governments for the damage they are capable of inflicting.

In sum, it seems that under different guise and in different circumstances we will confront civil liberties problems that in their essentials are not very different from those that we face today. And institutions exist that are capable of protecting us if there is a public will to defend a strong Bill of Rights. We are indebted to the Buffalo Citizens Forum, the New York Council for the Humanities, and the authors of this book for enabling us to see the future more clearly . . . and perhaps be better prepared for it.

STEPHEN C. HALPERN

Introduction

The study of the future has in recent years become the subject of serious scholarly inquiry. Despite the proliferation of futurist research by scholars of many academic disciplines, there has been little research examining how future conditions and changes in the United States may affect traditional constitutional liberties. A few thoughtful scholars have treated the subject in an indirect way and have reached pessimistic conclusions about our future capacity to retain many freedoms that have long been part of our political tradition. Political scientist William Ophuls in *Ecology and the Politics of Scarcity*, economist Robert Heilbroner in *An Inquiry into the Human Prospect*, and biologist Garrett Hardin in *Exploring New Ethics for Survival* all conclude, for surprisingly similar reasons, that within our children's lifetime we will be compelled simultaneously to expand considerably the powers of the state while reducing drastically the scope of individual liberties.

As one who writes and teaches about civil liberties, I had not, until very recently, thought much about the future of personal freedoms and what useful observations scholars could make on such matters. Reading Robert Heilbroner's elegant and profound book changed that. Heilbroner's pessimistic prognosis launched my interest in scholarly attempts to analyze how circumstances likely to prevail in the near future may affect the scope and character of individual freedom. I hoped that a conference devoted to that subject would prompt original scholarly research and enliven public discussion of what, for me at least, were very grave concerns about the future of individual liberties in our society. The New York Council for the Humanities and the State University of New York at Buffalo provided the financial support necessary to realize that hope. This book is an outgrowth of the papers prepared for the conference and follows the format and organization of those meetings.

Participating scholars were asked to write "think" pieces in which they explored issues that they anticipated would emerge as civil liberties problems within roughly the next two decades. I asked them to gear their work to a general and not scholarly audience in order to achieve the widest possible dissemination of their thoughts.

There is a rich scholarly literature and strong traditional support for the study of individual freedom within the academic community because of the intimate connection between personal liberty and intellectual activity. While there may appear to be a notable attachment and commitment to individual freedom within the academy, intellectuals should recognize that academic freedom cannot flourish in institutions of higher education if personal freedoms generally are trammelled and threatened in the larger society. Indeed, because of the profession they are in, academics bear a special public as well as scholarly responsibility to safeguard the moral and legal traditions that protect individual freedom in our nation. The conference out of which this volume grew was intended in a small way to contribute to that end.

The conference and this volume were organized around a keynote address and seven topics. Those topics focused on historical perspectives on the Bill of Rights; freedom of speech, press, and association; freedom of religion; mental illness and state power; economic liberty; governmental benevolence and social control; and the protection of racial minorities.

HISTORICAL PERSPECTIVES ON THE BILL OF RIGHTS

Although all the other pieces in the volume focus on problems or trends we may experience in the future, the two articles in this section provide an analysis of the place of the Bill of Rights in our national history. We cannot intelligently evaluate the future of the principles in the first ten amendments if we do not have a sense of their roots and evolution in our society. Paul Murphy and Alpheus Mason bring their considerable wisdom to that effort.

THE FIRST AMENDMENT

The provisions of the First Amendment may be viewed as the indispensable fundamentals for virtually all other freedoms. In section II, Thomas Emerson and Henry Abraham examine the first part of the amendment focusing on freedom of speech, press, assembly, and association. Leo Pfeffer and Sister Marie Augusta Neal, in section III, analyze offshoots of those clauses of the First Amendment that deal with the place of religion and religious freedom in American life.

MENTAL ILLNESS AND STATE POWER

The protection afforded individuals and groups that the mainstream may view as deviant and in need of control provides one important indicator of a society's tolerance and concern for individual liberty. David Rothman and Alan Stone, in section III, examine one specific and fascinating aspect of that dilemma—the public policies controlling the mentally ill.

ECONOMIC FREEDOMS

Notions of economic liberty have deep roots in Western history and philosophy and have enjoyed a special prominence in the American capitalist experience. In section V economists Herman Daly and Gerald Sirkin bring to bear widely divergent views of the role that public authority and power should play in regulating the economic order.

BENEFICENT SOCIAL CONTROL

Here Christopher Lasch and Frances Fox Piven expand upon the themes implicit in the more limited terrain covered earlier by Stone and Rothman. In section VI Lasch and Piven suggest that wide ranging and powerful social control by public authorities may operate in subtle ways and be effectively disguised by the state as benevolent in character.

RACIAL MINORITIES

Charles Hamilton's brief concluding essay on the civil rights of racial minorities suggests the ways in which the nation's agenda on minority rights will differ and likely become more vexatious in the decades ahead. Hamilton's comments on the impact of economic difficulties on racial justice touch upon a broad theme in scholarly writing on the future which emphasizes the social consequences that may result from what William Ophuls called the "politics of scarcity." It is a theme worth pondering for what light it may shed generally on the economic requisites necessary to sustain a broad range of individual freedoms in our society.

This volume is an attempt to stimulate preliminary but informed discussion about the future of individual liberties in our society. It will make its largest contribution if it prompts further inquiry by scholars and others concerned about that subject.

The Future of Our Liberties

1

HENRY STEELE COMMAGER

Keynote Statement

In the most memorable of all American documents, Thomas Jefferson asserted the "self-evident truth" that "all men are created equal." Equality was and perhaps still is the mainspring of American philosophy and history. Yet the word "equal" does not appear in the Constitution of 1787, nor was equality included in that Bill of Rights which was, for all practical purposes, part of the original Constitution. Not until 1868 was the word incorporated into the Constitution. That year the Fourteenth Amendment—which revolutionized our constitutional system by making the federal government, rather than the states, the guardian of the rights of men—provided that:

> No State . . . shall deprive any person of life, liberty or property, without due process of law; nor deny to any person within its jurisdiction the equal protection of the laws.

What did the word "equal" mean in the Declaration of Independence? What did it mean in the Fourteenth Amendment? That, as Robert Frost said, in one of his aphoristic poems, is a hard question that each age will have to reconsider. It is perhaps less hard, however, when addressed to Thomas Jefferson than when addressed to the authors of the Fourteenth Amendment. There can be little doubt that Jefferson used the term "created equal" in a quite literal sense: namely, that in the eyes of Nature (and doubtless, too, of Nature's God) every child was *born* equal. All subsequent inequalities—those of race, sex, color, class, wealth, even of talents, for the most part, were derived not from Nature but from society, government, or law. Nature did not decree the inequality of blacks

This address was delivered before the *Bakke* decision and subsequent equal protection decisions dealing with race and sex discrimination.

to whites, or of females to males. Nature did not impose class, political, economic, or social distinctions; it was not even clear—certainly it was not to Jefferson—that Nature imposed even physical or intellectual distinctions. Doubtless Jefferson meant, too, that if all men were not equal they *ought* to be. This was the exact interpretation that Lincoln put upon the phrase in his famous speech at Springfield, Illinois, in 1857, when he stated that the Framers

> "meant to set up a standard maxim for a free society, which should be familiar to all and revered by all; constantly looked to, constantly labored for. . . . They meant it to be a stumbling block to all those who in after time might seek to turn a free people back into the hateful paths of despotism."[1]

The meaning of the phrase "equal protection" in the Fourteenth Amendment is more elusive. We do not know with any certainty what those who wrote it into the Constitution meant—perhaps they did not know themselves. The ultimate meaning of this phrase—as with so many others in history—was to be defined by use, events, and circumstances; perhaps by necessity. "Words," as Justice Oliver Wendell Holmes observed, "have a life of their own." Certainly the term "equality" has had a life of its own, a life that has responded to the vicissitudes of history. It is fashioned by society; it, in turn, infuses society with new life.

In his monumental study of the *American Commonwealth*, published almost a century ago, Lord James Bryce compared the American written and the British unwritten constitutions, and asked, "How can a country whose very name suggests to us movement and progress be governed by a system and under an instrument which remains the same from year to year and from century to century?"[2] He implied, if he did not clearly conclude, that the British "flexible" constitution was in many respects superior to the American "rigid" constitution. To this question Americans might have answered as Henry James answered a similar query about American culture in his essay on Hawthorne at about the same time: "That is our private joke." But in fact the alleged rigidity of the American Constitution was an illusion. For while the Founding Fathers yearned for "a standing law to live by" and sought to establish one by a written Constitution which was "supreme law" and which was designed to prevent government from exercising tyranny over men, they at the same time yearned for a constitution which would preside over an effective federal system and would enable a group of independent states to function as a single nation. These were paradoxical but not incompatible ends. Thanks to the political resourcefulness and ingenuity of Americans, they were able to adapt their written constitution to the exigencies of events just as well as the British did. In one of his great judicial opinions, Chief Justice John Marshall called for a Constitution designed "to endure for ages to come, and, consequently, to be adapted to the various crises of human affairs."[3] And that is what the American people developed, not only for their Constitution, but for their entire political system. Within a short time, they had contrived an astonishing number of ways in which to carry through that adaptation—a process which is still going on.

First, they used a provision in the Constitution itself for formal amendment. It was a slow and difficult process and not readily effective: although an overwhelming majority of the people approve the equal rights amendment, it is after many years on the verge of defeat. Second, the people themselves invented new political institutions, and put them to work: the political party, for example, unknown to the formal constitution. Third, they abandoned such parts of the constitutional system as were no longer relevant or useful: thus the cumbersome machinery of the electoral college, which has been reduced to "innocuous desuetude." Fourth, presidents and legislatures adopted (when necessary) that "broad" interpretation of the Constitution which Alexander Hamilton had originally advocated and which has by now become almost standard in American politics: it can be seen in the continuous enlargement of legislative power which made possible the creation of a welfare state and in the frequent enhancement of executive power through a broad interpretation of the authority of presidents in the realm of foreign affairs and in time of war. A fifth method of accommodation, if not amendment, has developed rapidly in recent years: the growth and ramification of administrative regulations which, for all practical purposes, have the force of laws and which increasingly concentrate effective power in Washington. And, sixth, the institution of judicial review has developed: a practice which makes the judiciary not only a quasi-legislative body but a constitution-making body.

Each of these methods and practices of constitutional amendment has played a role in adapting an eighteenth-century constitution to the needs of a twentieth-century economy and society; each has contributed to the reinterpretation of the concept of equality. It is with the last and most interesting of these—judicial review—that I am primarily concerned. It is the most interesting for a variety of reasons. First, because it is unique. In no other country does the judiciary exercise such far-reaching legislative and constitutional roles. Second, because it is the most effective—it operates as a mandate throughout the union and is customarily not only enforced, but obeyed. And third, because it is, on the surface, so stunningly paradoxical. In a democracy it is the one nondemocratic process used to make fundamental decisions on great social, economic, and even moral issues.

We turn, next, to what is now the most controversial and promises to be the most consequential clause in the Constitution: "nor shall any State deny to any person within its jurisdiction *the equal protection of the laws*" (emphasis added).

It is only within recent years that the Courts—and belatedly the Congress—have resurrected this clause to achieve not only racial justice (its original purpose) but justice in the broad area of social welfare. For almost a century, the Congress ignored the obvious potentialities of the phrase, and the Courts, through the narrowest possible interpretation, drained it of meaning. Beginning with the Warren Court (1953–1969) came a decisive, indeed, revolutionary change. Within one year of his accession to the chief justiceship, Earl Warren was able to give a unanimous opinion that reversed the century-long practice of racial segregation in the public schools. "Separate educational facilities," wrote Justice Warren in *Brown v. Board of Education of Topeka*, "are inherently unequal," and children subjected to such segregation are "deprived of their equal protection of the laws guaranteed by the Fourteenth Amendment."[4] It was a simple and brief opinion, but its implications were nothing less than revolutionary. By a stroke of the judicial pen, practices and malpractices, rationalized by over a century of history, were repudiated and outlawed.

Brown v. Topeka opened the floodgates. There had, of course, been antecedents in a series of cases dealing with the denial of admission of blacks to law schools. If a denial of equality in education through racial discrimination was unconstitutional, was there not, then, an obligation not only to strike down discrimination but also to provide real equality? So the Court held a few years later in *Swann v. Charlotte-Mecklenburg Board of Education*,[5] which ordered a North Carolina county to inaugurate a program of busing children to neighboring schools in order to achieve a racial balance. Thereafter came a series of judicial and legislative interventions designed to equalize educational facilities among poor and rich school districts and to prevent what might appear to be overt racial or sexual discrimination in the admission of students to colleges and professional schools throughout the land.

The new interpretation of equal protection spread rapidly to other areas of American life. In 1962 it was invoked to put an end to radically disproportionate representation in state legislatures from one election district to another—an intervention designed to establish the democratic principle of "one-man, one-vote."[6]

The application of equal protection to the areas of education and voting was logical enough, for the nexus between these institutions and an effective democracy was clear and even irrefutable. Education was designed to help create an intelligent citizenry; voting to insure that all citizens might participate equally in politics.

More controversial was the application of this new concept of equal protection to areas outside education or politics—that is, outside those areas that had an undeniable relationship to citizenship. Soon Courts were inundated with appeals from special interest groups (environmental and employment, for example), which felt that their interests were being neglected or that they were being discriminated against, and thus being denied equal protection. These groups insisted that there was a positive obligation on the part of the state to abolish all discrimination. To these appeals the Courts responded with both ambiguous and inconsistent rulings. They readily supported protests against discrimination based on color, race, or sex (all of which were traditionally suspect) but showed somewhat less enthusiasm in embracing those based on broad claims of social and economic justice. Yet over the years there were significant advances that promised to bring about something of a revolution in American government, economy, and society. Thus in 1972 the Court struck down capital punishment, in part on the ground that it constituted "cruel and unusual punishment," but more decisively because in the past its application had long been grossly discriminatory against blacks and the poor, and it thus constituted a clear denial of equal protection. The following year the Court voided a law of Texas (and of many other States) making abortion illegal on the grounds that such laws unduly invaded the privacy of women, that they denied to many women equal protection available to them in other states, and that they denied to the poor rights available to the rich. The Court intervened also, to protect the rights of minorities in employment and in military service, and of the poor in access to welfare, health care, and housing. Increasingly, personal rights and economic rights were intermixed and distinctions between them blurred. As Justice Potter Stewart said:

> The right to enjoy property without unlawful deprivation, no less than the right to speak or the right to travel, is in truth a personal right, whether the property in question be a welfare check, a house, or a savings account.[7]

And he added, prophetically, that the right to liberty and the right to property are fundamentally interdependent.

The quest for equality and for justice have been intertwined throughout the whole of American history. Jefferson connected life and liberty with the pursuit of happiness; the preamble to the Constitution specified the establishment of justice and the promotion of the general welfare as purposes of the Constitution; Lincoln exalted liberty and equality as the chief characteristics of the new nation; Wilson asserted, in his first inaugural address, that "the firm basis of government is justice," and called for "equality of opportunity" as its essential ingredient; and, Franklin Roosevelt included "freedom from want" among his Four Freedoms. All of these were moral objectives, as well as political objectives. Have we come, in the past two decades, to embrace the possibility that these are legal objectives as well? And, if so, is the achievement of this end properly the function of the Courts?

These are the issues agitating the Court, and the country, today—the obligation of government to bring about a more just society by enlarging the concept and broadening the scope of equality, and the procedural question (no less important for democracy) of whether the Courts are the proper instruments to carry through such a revolution.

The first of these was inconclusively fought out in the historic case of *San Antonio School District v. Rodriguez*,[8] which challenged the Texas system of financing public education on the ground that gross disparities from one school district to another deprived some children of the equal protection of the laws. The Supreme Court rejected this challenge, but only by a narrow vote of five to four. Clearly the issue is not yet settled. Rejecting the challenge to the Texas system, the majority invoked the argument of the "entering wedge": if equal protection requires equal appropriations to all school districts, where do we stop? "The logical limitations on [this] theory," wrote Justice Lewis Powell, "are difficult to perceive. How, for instance, is education to be distinguished from the significant personal interests in the basics of decent food and shelter? Empirical examination might well buttress an assumption that the ill-fed, ill-clothed, ill-housed are among the most ineffective participants in the political process."[9]

Powell was right in pointing out that the logic extending the reach of equal protection from those rights that seemed fundamental to effective citizenship, such as voting, education, and travel, might also be extended almost ad infinitum to public health, prison and penal conditions, housing, and employment. And why not? we may ask. After all, these concerns are clearly within the original objectives of the Constitution as set forth in its preamble: "to form a more perfect Union, establish Justice, insure domestic Tranquillity, provide for the common defense, promote the general Welfare, and secure the blessings of Liberty." They are, therefore, the proper objectives of government, and the national Constitution provides that no state may deny their protection. If states do deny their protection or fail to provide such protection, the Courts therefore have the authority to intervene. This argument is clearly implicit in what Justice William Brennan said in his address celebrating the centennial of the Fourteenth Amendment (1968):

Society's overriding concern today is with providing freedom and equality of rights and opportunities, in a realistic and not merely a formal sense, to all the people of this nation. We know that social realities do not yet fully correspond to the law of the Fourteenth Amendment. We do not yet have justice, equal and practical, for the poor, for the members of minority groups, for the criminally accused, for the displaced persons of the technological revolution, for alienated youth, for the urban masses, for the unrepresented consumer—for all, in short, who do not partake of the abundance of American life. . . . Who will deny that despite great progress we have made in recent decades toward universal equality, freedom, and prosperity, the goal is far from won and ugly inequalities continue to mar the national promise?[10]

That, under a broad reading of the Constitution, the national government does have a right to legislate in the arena of social justice, cannot be denied. Does it, then, have a right to sweep away state barriers to what may be considered social justice and to require states positively to provide equal protection of these rights? And, is it the function of the Courts to preside over this constitutional requirement?

The most famous footnote in American legal history—I refer, of course, to footnote four of *U.S. v. Carolene Products*—launched a debate, in and outside the courts, whose echoes have not yet died down. We need do no more than recite the essence of that footnote: "That there is a narrower scope for the presumption of legislative constitutionality when legislation appears on its face to be within a specific prohibition of the first ten amendments, and particularly of legislation which restricts those political processes which might be expected to bring about repeal of undesirable legislation or to curtail the operation of those political processes which can be relied on to protect minorities."[11]

The difficulty of detecting or determining with any degree of accuracy such legislation did not discourage more enterprising members of the Stone and Warren Courts from assigning a "preferred position" to the guarantees of the First Amendment. The Burger Court has pretty well abandoned any flirtation with a "preferred position," and neither Justices Brennan nor Marshall any longer advance it with any urgency.

Yet might not the Carolene Products standard, not so much rejected as subordinated by the present court, take on new and affirmative significance by application to the Equal Protection Clause, just as the Due Process Clause was earlier given an affirmative significance? Both of these considerations were implicit in *Brown v. Topeka* and in *Baker v. Carr*: the readiness to adopt a closer scrutiny of legislation or regulations that might weaken or curtail "political processes ordinarily relied on to protect minorities," and the obligation to remedy injustices by positive legislative and even judicial actions. The first (*Brown v. Topeka*) not only ended the scandal of segregation but mandated positive rearrangements such as busing; the second (*Baker v. Carr*) not only ended the scandal of ignoring state constitutional provisions for reapportionment but, by positive requirements, mandated "one-man/one-vote." Thus, by analogy, might we not apply the equal protection requirement where states frustrate equality by permitting wide variations in the quantity or quality of education, health, and psychiatric care, or of other services, that may be presumed to weaken the fulfillment of the obligations of citizenship—including military service. Should not the courts be under an obligation—even a constitutional obligation—to require states to repair inequalities and deficiencies that threaten the well-being of sister states, given the mobility of people from state to state?

Footnote four of Carolene Products referred specifically to "prejudice against discrete and insular minorities . . . which tends seriously to curtail the operation of those political processes ordinarily to be relied upon to protect minorities." But "curtailment" can be passive as well as active, can emerge from covert neglect as well as from overt discrimination. "Separate but Equal" did not work in education or in access to public facilities or jobs. Yet the same kind of logic that thought up that formula in *Plessey v. Ferguson*[12] in 1896 is still at work: witness Justice William Rehnquist's opinion in *General Electric Company v. Gilbert* just six years ago.[13] In that case the Court managed, by a feat of intellectual dexterity rarely surpassed in our judicial history, to ignore the clear intention of the Congress, guidelines of the Equal Employment Opportunity Commission of HEW, and the verdicts of seven appellate courts, and to find that pregnancy was not a sex-related disability and thus did not qualify female employees for disability compensation during the time lost from work.

That case, which belongs in the archeological museum as the cases that fabricated the concept of "liberty of contract," reminds us that equal rights have not yet been achieved for a major segment of our population—women—they have not even achieved the elementary requirement of equal protection of the laws. Whether this goal should be achieved through the judicial rather than the political process is another matter.

We are in the presence here of what is the oldest and perhaps the most perplexing philosophical problem of American constitutionalism: the propriety and wisdom of judicial review in a democratic government. It is the conflict implicit in the paradox of Jefferson's First Inaugural Address:

> All, too, will bear in mind this sacred principle, that though the will of the majority is in all cases to prevail, that will, to be rightful, must be reasonable; that the minority possess their equal rights, which equal law must protect, and to violate which would be oppression.

It is the conflict implicit, too, in Chief Justice Marshall's statement that "it is emphatically the province and duty of the judiciary department to say what the law is. . . . If two laws conflict with each other the Courts must decide on the operations of each."[14] In the solemn admonition of the illustrious Judge Learned Hand, "If an independent judiciary seeks to fill [its moral adjurations] from its own bosom, in the end it will cease to be independent. And its independence will be well lost, for that bosom is not ample enough for the hopes and fears of all sorts and conditions of men, nor will its answers be theirs; it must be content to stand aside from these fateful battles."[15]

Ideally the philosophy of "judicial abstinence" formulated by Justice Oliver Wendell Holmes and embraced in our own time by Justice Felix Frankfurter, would seem to be sound: ultimately the safest depository of freedom is the people themselves, not the Courts. Again, the words of Learned Hand:

> A society so riven that the spirit of moderation is gone, no court *can* save; a society where that spirit flourishes, no court *need* save; in a society which evades its responsibility by thrusting upon the courts the nurture of that spirit, that spirit will in the end perish.[16]

But, in Emerson's wonderful phrase, "history has baked our cake." We have come to take judicial review for granted as an essential part of our constitutional system. On the whole, it has served us well.

Certainly, we continue to depend on the judiciary to preserve both the federal system and essential liberties. The first of these responsibilities was assigned to the Courts by the Constitution itself in Article VI. Historically, the chief function of judicial review has been, precisely, to harmonize the federal system: the alternative to a single, authoritative interpretation of the meaning of the federal constitution would be chaos.

The second function—the preservation of essential liberties—has emerged largely in the past half century. This has been due in part to the broad interpretation given to the guarantees of the Bill of Rights, and particularly of the First and Fifth Amendments, and in part to an application of the restrictions which the Bill of Rights originally imposed on the United States, to the States themselves—a development made not only possible but perhaps mandatory by the Fourteenth Amendment. For the Court to abandon the practice of reviewing (and where necessary nullifying) state legislation that might be in violation of the Constitution or of the Bill of Rights would send a profound shock through the whole of our constitutional system. This conclusion is supported by history. When, in 1937, Franklin Roosevelt, the most popular of all American Presidents and at the height of his power and popularity, proposed a mild and perfectly legal reform of the federal judiciary, the response of the people was almost convulsive. A vast majority looked upon the proposal as a threat to the independence of the Court and rallied to its defense. The president was forced to withdraw his bill. That response, and the acquiescence of the people to the continuation of judicial review in the forty years thereafter, has in a sense foreclosed the question. However undemocratic it may appear to be in theory, it has the support of the American people.

The problem of accommodating a constitution designed to embody eighteenth-century principles of the nature of government and the relations of men to government to the exigencies of future generations of history was logically left by the framers to the political branches of the government and to the processes of democracy. But, as Alexis de Tocqueville saw a century and a half ago, America was greatly blessed with pluralism and diversity, and these in turn contributed richly to experimentation and to liberty. So resilient and flexible is our constitutional system that, over the years, it has permitted and encouraged resort to the judiciary for the solution of large political, social, and economic problems when the legislative and political branches have failed.

Instead of deploring this violation of the abstract principle of separation of powers—or what might appear to be this challenge to the traditional processes of democracy—should not Americans embrace this development as yet another illustration of the resourcefulness of a people not bemused by political theory and also as an indication of the potentialities of a Constitution which could display at once the advantages of constancy and growth, the static and the organic? In the nineteenth century, judicial review often contributed more to the enhancement of national power and even of economic power, than to the enlargement of liberty and equality. In the past half century, with the problem of national supremacy largely solved,* the Court has contributed more to the protection of liberty and the enhancement of equality than the other branches of our government. We should not allow commitment to the principle of separation of powers or to the anachronism "that government is best which governs least," to seduce us into opposition when the Court, whose constitutional obligation is to justice, finds new ways to advance it.

NOTES

1. John Nicolay and John Hay, eds., *Complete Works of Abraham Lincoln* (New York: Lamb, 1905), 2:5 331.
2. James Bryce, *The American Commonwealth* (New York: Macmillan, 1888), 1:350.
3. *McCulloch v. Maryland*, 4 Wheaton 316 at 415 (1819).
4. *Brown v. Board of Education of Topeka*, 347 U.S. 483 at 495 (1954).
5. *Swann v. Charlotte-Mecklenburg Board of Education*, 402 U.S. 1 (1971).
6. *Baker v. Carr*, 369 U.S. 186 (1962).
7. *Lynch v. Household Finance Corporation*, 405 U.S. 538 at 552 (1972).
8. *San Antonio School District v. Rodriguez*, 411 U.S. 1 (1973).

*This was written before the advent of Ronald Reagan to the presidency.

9. 411 U.S. 1 at 37 (1973).

10. William J. Brennan, "The Responsibilities of the Legal Profession," *American Bar Association Journal* 54 (February 1968):122.

11. *U.S. v. Carolene Products*, 304 U.S. 144 at 152–53 (1938).

12. *Plessey v. Ferguson*, 163 U.S. 537 (1896).

13. *General Electric Company v. Gilbert*, 429 U.S. 125 (1976).

14. *Marbury v. Madison*, 1 Cranch 137 at 177 (1803).

15. Learned Hand, *The Spirit of Liberty* (New York: Knopf, 1963), p. 163.

16. Ibid., p. 164.

SECTION I

Historical Perspectives on the Bill of Rights

2

PAUL L. MURPHY

The Bill of Rights in our Historical Development

In order to understand and to appreciate fully the role that the Bill of Rights has played in American History, it is necessary to understand the American people's perception of that document, the purpose that they saw it fulfilling, and the values that they hoped it would preserve. The Bill of Rights was, from the outset, a symbol; it was an aspect of a state of mind and represented a means to ends generally embraced by a majority of citizens. The fact that it is still at the core of our constitutional system today and the fact that "liberty" is still the central value in that system suggests that it gets to the heart of what Americans feel to be the government's central commitment and in many ways its central obligation.[1]

Let me be more specific. The United States was born on a wave of virulent localism. It grew out of a widely shared consensus that the European centralized state of the eighteenth century was an agency for the destruction of human dignity and human individuality. The Americans of 1776 were convinced both that liberty, that is, personal freedom and individual self-determination, was not only central, but was their birthright. Further, the key to that liberty was personal independence—the ability of individuals to control their own lives and their own destinies on their own terms. Central to the thinking and expression of leaders of the Revolutionary generation on this issue was a broadly held consensus that a rational or free state would be a state governed by such laws as all rational men would freely accept—such laws, in other words, as they would themselves have enacted had they been asked what, as rational beings, they demanded. The boundary of the permissible limitations on the use of freedom would, therefore, be such as all rational men would consider to be the right frontiers for rational beings. The operation of the Bill of Rights, in other words, would flow from public commitments to see that its guarantees would be extended when it made sense to do so. A further assumption was that the burden of proof fell on those who would restrict liberty, to first convincingly demonstrate why society would be served by so doing.[2]

The British legal system, which somewhat ironically Americans brought to this country and largely retained, accepting most of its fundamental assumptions at face value, was not working for them in 1776.[3] Americans had no vote that could alter British imperial policy. They were certainly not placated by the suggestion that their political wishes were taken care of by the British Parliament. The British legal system, due to its centralized nature, had become concerned with little other than the monolithic application of royal authority. The basic rights of individuals that conflicted with such authority were clearly expendable, if not in England, certainly within the empire, and especially within the colonies themselves. It was all well and good to have a pious statement in the British Petition of Rights that no troops would be quartered in private homes, but the flimsiness of such a guarantee was seen in America the first time the British found it convenient to abrogate that principle (incidentally, a principle that was later incorporated into the Third Amendment of our Bill of Rights).[4] Few school children need to be told that one way the British, seemingly chronically in financial crisis, saved money after the failure of the Stamp Act was to quarter troops in homes and in public buildings in Boston, leaving the householders to pick up the bill, to say nothing of dealing with the physical and emotional carnage that such occupation inevitably produced. In similar fashion, during the Revolutionary years the colonists got lessons in the fragility of such guarantees as free speech and press, with the King proclaiming criticism of the crown seditious libel and calling for the arrest of editors who had had the temerity to speak out against his policies.[5]

Thus, to a Revolutionary generation, a monolithic centralized state was not the means to achieve personal dignity, and to protect life, liberty, happiness, and equal justice under law. Rather it tended to prevent the achievement of any of these ends, and reaffirmed the colonists' firm convictions that the best means for their attainment was localism—tightly controlled self-government at the local level—that is, state sovereignty in all its manifestations. The republic principle, in other words (that men could and should govern themselves through representatives of their own choosing who would be close to them and sensitive to their needs and demands), could best be realized through keeping maximum governmental power in the hands of local leaders and in the hands of local units of government. This would, in turn, insure proper representation: a fair and equitable legal system; and the optimum of freedom of speech, press, assembly, and religion. Therefore, it is easy to agree with a modern political scientist when he contends that the American Revolution was fought "to maintain the civil liberties and civil rights of Americans—which meant further, the right of Americans to define their rights for themselves."[6]

Yet from the outset some questions arose. The newly freed American communities were charged now with protecting the civil liberties of their citizens from any perversion by the state, but who was to protect the dissenters within those communities who did not subscribe to all of the norms that the community leaders set down? One of the first things the newly freed Americans did, after proclaiming their commitment to their own civil rights, was to assail any remaining British Loyalists in the community who disagreed with them, closing down their publications, confiscating their property, and in extreme cases, sending them hiking off to Canada as a place of refuge. So from the outset there was some concern that civil liberties now existed for those in agreement with the militant majority but that they were not conspicuously available for those who did not so agree.[7]

Certain of the more creative of the Founding Fathers saw this problem and hoped for more meaningful standards. The new federal constitution was to hopefully expand the republican principle to a large area through the agency of a strengthened federal government. Hopefully also such a government might be an instrument to temper certain negative aspects of localism that had so plagued citizens in the Confederation era. Yet, many Americans saw the civil rights implications of such a move only negatively. And protests against the new Constitution were widespread and loud. The antipathy of a group of vigorous Pennsylvania anti-Federalists was typical of early opposition. "We dissent," one of their resolutions proclaimed, "because the powers vested in Congress by this constitution must necessarily annihilate and absorb the legislative, executive, and judicial powers of the several States, and produce from their ruins one consolidated government, which from the nature of things will be an iron handed despotism, as nothing short of the supremacy of despotic sway could connect and govern these United States under one government."[8]

Such protest continued even after adoption. The minimum condition for the acquiescence of many Americans to the new government's authority was a set of iron-clad guarantees to limit that government's authority over the individual. Further, in the fifteen or so years since the Declaration, Americans had had a history lesson of their own—experiential learning, we now call it. They now realized fully that tyranny was possible on the part of any branch of government—executive, legislative, judicial, and especially on the part of such divisions within the states. In fact, the Constitution really embodied a new view of liberty from that of 1776—the protection of individual rights against *all* governmental encroachment but particularly by legislative bodies, those units that leaders in 1776 had confidently assumed would be the surest instrument to defend their individual liberties.[9] Indeed, by 1789, Madison argued, as the demands for a Bill of Rights was being responded to, that "the most valuable amendment" to add, would be one prohibiting the *States* from infringing on freedom of conscience, speech, press, and jury trial.[10] Such an amendment was not added however, and, in final analysis, the key to the protection of liberty came to lie in federalism. The abuse of power, as Madison argued in the Federalist Papers, would best be prevented "by so contriving the interior structure of the government as that its several constituent parts may, by their mutual relations, be the means of keeping each other in their proper places."[11] Further, in what is undoubtedly the key to the political thinking underlying the creation of the Constitution, Madison went on to contend that the partitioning of power in America would be intensified by "the extent of country, and number of people comprehended under the same government" so that "the society itself would be broken into so many parts, interests, and classes of citizens, that the rights of individuals, or of the minority will be in little danger from interested combinations of the majority."[12]

However, note the interesting assumptions underlying this statement. The system that was being created, in a sense, depended upon the people to make it work. Government would play the role of the neutral umpire (the "armed neutrality")[13] encouraging mass participation from all sides in the process, but keeping the government off the backs of people in terms of imposing arbitrary restrictions upon them. But the people were at the core in terms of liberty. They had to want to use this government for that end, and to make it work in such a way as to achieve that end. There was nothing automatic in the process of the way the government operated.

The Bill of Rights was, then, a means to liberty—a way for the people to achieve individual freedom. Yet, to quote a familiar bromide, "eternal vigilance was the price of freedom," a vigilance which the people, accepting then the general republic principle of representation, had to insist that their representatives respect and preserve.

The first American war promptly changed the picture. Less than a decade after the adoption of the Bill of Rights by Congress, the same body, now in strongly partisan hands, passed a series of laws—the Alien and Sedition Acts—which violated directly the First Amendment guarantees of freedom of speech and press in the name of national security. One law even authorized the President summarily to deport aliens whose views he deemed dangerous to the peace and safety of the United States. Further, the Federalist administration of John Adams set out to enforce these laws rigidly, with the rights of critics of the government turning out to be less respected than had been those of critics of the King under the colonial system. Over two dozen Jeffersonian newspaper editors were rounded up and jailed by federal officials for printing editorials critical of the Adams administration, and the damage from intimidation was impossible to measure. Jefferson, who was at the time leader of the opposition and by a strange quirk of the initial electoral system, also Vice President, found himself, even though in a position of high authority, unable to protect even his own supporters in the country. He could initially only fulminate: "under the Sedition Law, if a man believes that human affairs are susceptible to improvement . . . this makes him an anarchist, disorganizer, atheist, and enemy of government." The law, he contended, "was worthy of the eighth or ninth century."[14] The frailties of Bill of Rights protections were thus illustrated in practice in ways disturbing to victims and general citizens alike, with Federalist excesses in this area an important factor in the party's being voted out of power in the subsequent election of 1800.[15]

It is significant that the first formal theory of states rights enunciated after the Constitution was ratified was set forth as a means to protect freedom against encroachment and abrogation by the federal government. For Jefferson was finally pushed to act and wrote, with James Madison, the famed Kentucky and Virginia Resolutions to oppose this repressive federal policy. In so doing, both he and his fellow Virginian turned to the states, setting forth a vigorous philosophy of state sovereignty with mechanisms for ultimately nullifying federal laws that affected people's rights adversely. This was done as a means of affording concrete protection of the individual, his life, liberty, and claim to equal justice. The underlying assumption was that it was the federal government that was the threat to these personal rights and that the people were to turn to their local units of government, principally the states, as the agencies for insuring the proper preservation and protection of their rights.

Thus the concept of states rights in the United States was born out of a need to find new ways of protecting Bill of Rights freedoms, and the two were instinctively linked in a complementary union. But an abstraction such as states rights can be altered and perverted to different ends. Thus the next question the historian instinctively asks is: did local sovereignty work to produce such desired ends? Did it become an instrument for gaining protection for the individual for his personal rights? The answer is that by and large it did not. But this reality turns on the fact that as the nineteenth century progressed, many local leaders turned sharply away from the Jeffersonian states rights conception and turned the principle into a device for protecting the behavior of the local majority from federal interference—a majority, incidentally, that was frequently more concerned with preserving the integrity and the standards, good or bad, of the local community rather than respecting the rights of the individual. Yet the story is not simply one of going from states rights to insure freedom to states rights to insure conformity. Let us look at specific developments.

The federal government, during virtually the remainder of the nineteenth century, and, in fact, well into the twentieth, continued to be looked at by many Americans as an instrument for potential tyranny over the free individual. The program of the Radical Republicans of the 1860s and 1870s comes to mind. Here national leaders set out to create a federal policy of positive civil rights not unlike that enacted into law in the 1950s and 1960s. The central thrust of the program was to enforce the Bill of Rights within the states through federal action.[16] More specifically, the intent was to insure free Black Americans their full rights of citizenship through federal guarantee and enforcement of those rights. But the vast majority of nineteenth century Americans had trouble conceiving of the federal government as an agency able to serve the positive cause of civil rights. Federal coerciveness, even if it was in the name of guaranteeing the freedman his vote, or guaranteeing him access to public facilities, or guaranteeing him fair trial in the courts, was nonetheless coerciveness, and its threat to the freedom of local citizens and to localism generally was too dangerous and too great to accept, even if its purposes might have been the advancement of human dignity and the rights of the freed slave. A further test of this fact came when women demanded new federally protected rights under the post-Civil War amendments.[17] Their claim was denied. If rights were to be extended to women, they were to come from the largesse of the local community.

Such a philosophy did not exist merely among state and local leaders at the time. Seven members of the Supreme Court in 1884 agreed that the decision was pretty much up to the local judges when deciding what ingredients made up a fair trial at the state court level.[18] Certainly it was not a subject on which federal authorities could or should dictate. Again uniform national standards threatened the integrity of creative local justice designed to fit local community standards, but the justices carefully did not spend much time probing such integrity even in flagrant cases on appeal. A dozen years later in 1896, eight of the nine Supreme Court members went along with the contention of southern-oriented Justice Brown when he insisted that the handling of race relations was best and most constructively left to local authorities.[19]

Such a position assumed that the states were continuing to serve the initial function of protecting individual freedom; and the simple truth was that few were. Local leaders continually conjured up the spectre of a massive national government ominously ready to destroy individual rights. But such an image was frequently set forth for the purpose of keeping what few federal officials there were in the nineteenth century from looking too closely at the kind of local repression that went on and could not stand the scrutiny of federal supervision. The dissenting, or offbeat individual or organization in the average community of the nineteenth century was hardly secure in his or its rights because of the absence of national power. On the contrary, the absence of any effective national protection left the individual at the mercy of the local community. In practice it was the local community that effectively set the limits of his free speech, established proper thresholds of tolerance in religious matters, and set down patterns of justice for dealing with local citizens when they got too far out of line in any of the above areas. Civil rights in the nineteenth century constituted, as Mark Twain once wrote, "free speech, free press, and the good sense not to use either."[20]

Nineteenth-century America was caught in a dilemma of loyalty—whether to be loyal to a symbol (the Bill of Rights) or loyal to a social system, wherein the local community handled its problems in ways acceptable to the local majority. The resolution was to publicly proclaim loyalty to the symbol, but, in practice, to accept loyalty to local majorities. Thus, the concept of individual rights enforceable against the community (which only certain of the abolitionists had advocated) was never really embraced in nineteenth-century America. It would have meant placing loyalty to abstract values above loyalty to an established and accepted social system that kept order, maintained stability by keeping dissident minorities in their place, whether those were blacks, Indians, assertive women, militant farmers, or rebellious factory workers, or for that matter, simply troublesome have-nots—the poor, the "criminal class," who were generally factored out of the system, put in ghettoes, or more forcibly in reservations, asylums, places of detention, or otherwise isolated, with certainly no thought that such people might have rights which legitimately could be respected under any formal legal structure.[21]

In practice, the mobility of nineteenth-century America tended to ameliorate the situation somewhat. If one did not subscribe to or generally embrace local standards one could move on in the hopes of finding a community in which standards were more in conformity with one's views, religious, political, or otherwise. The treatment of the Mormons by a variety of communities in which they found themselves affords a good example of nineteenth-century processes and values. To their claims of the right to multiple wives as an aspect of free exercise of their religion, local judges and juries uniformly replied that bigamy was a crime in their communities, and not a religious practice protected by the First Amendment.[22] But finally having been forced to move on until they reached the remote semi-isolation of Utah and Idaho, the Mormons themselves quickly embraced nineteenth-century American values and began exercising the prerogatives of local community control themselves. Here the Mormon majority dominated governmental institutions, and a new orthodoxy prevailed. Twelve Mormon jurors had little trouble acquitting fellow Mormons charged with the identical earlier crime of bigamy. When outsiders, federal government officials, attempted to interfere with this kind of local social control, they met with little success and on occasion with violent assault and physical eviction. Now that they were the local majority, the Mormons reasoned that they should be able to utilize against those who would interfere with their freedom, the same kinds of sanctions that had been imposed so ruthlessly against them from New York to Utah.

Similarly, nonconformist citizens in a small town in the nineteenth century who publicly advocated things as shocking as birth control frequently found themselves in court charged with "lewd behavior," and "breach of the peace." People could think whatever they wanted to but could not behave lewdly.[23] In certain settings lewd behavior apparently included the mere expression of opinion. However, the picture was not entirely one-sided. Different communities had different levels of tolerance and very different patterns of local orthodoxy. A story is told of a conservative economics professor at a western state university who was fired in 1896 as a "gold bug," who, however, promptly swapped jobs with an economics professor at a New England school who had been dismissed for his advocacy of "free silver."

Thus, in some ways what existed in nineteenth-century America was a type of pragmatic decentralized authoritarianism with local communities setting up their own standards often with the desire of preserving local things as they had always been in the face of outside dangers. Through much of such behavior ran the old Puritan values of "good works," and "stewardship." Those within the community who had economic power were respected as its natural leaders. Unwarranted challenges to such power were inevitably suspect and, if they became too raucous and insistent, were censored quietly but effectively by those operating the instruments of local social control.

The situation shifted only slightly as the twentieth century opened. As huge national corporations grew, many became economic feudalities and functioned as virtually private governments. This was especially true well into the 1930s in industries like steel and coal. The New York Central Railroad, the United States Steel Corporation, and the Rockefeller and Morgan interests exercised virtually all aspects of sovereignty over their minions except issuing postage stamps; they exacted a required degree of loyalty and essential conformity, which frequently destroyed human individuality and oftentimes human freedom, fully as effectively as any centralized European governmental tyranny had done in the eighteenth century. Further, such dispensers of economic sovereignty played in many ways the same games with civil rights as did the holders of local sovereignty in any state or community. They also maintained that the real threat to personal freedom and civil rights came from excessive centralized government. Again the classic threat of the Hobbesian Leviathan state was conjured up. Federal activism, it was contended, sometimes almost hysterically, would only result in choking out local differences, destroying salutary local control, and interfering unwarrantedly with the freedom of the local community to deal with its members in its own way. Further, in a period when local law and law enforcement was the principal means of social control, it was argued that any questioning of the local legal system was a first step toward social chaos and anarchy.[24]

The results were not pretty. In their ultimate form, they meant virtually total destruction of civil liberties and civil rights for the have-nots and nonconformists within society in the rather ironic name of states rights and local self-determination. States rights, in other words, came, in the early years of the twentieth century to be the principal instrument for the suppression of civil rights and civil liberties, quite in contrast with the purpose for which states rights theory was initially set forth by Jefferson and Madison. Blacks in the south and in the north were effectively disenfranchised, segregated, and denied almost totally the guarantees of a fair trial, under the banner of preserving the local social system. Immigrant workers and militant laborers seeking reform found themselves constantly harassed by a great battery of state criminal syndicalism and criminal anarchy laws, their leaders jailed on trumped up charges and, in extreme cases, deported; their headquarters raided without warrants by overaggressive law-enforcement officials, and the ability of their organizations to meet, strike, and picket regularly denied by the tyranny of local judges.[25]

The earlier twentieth century utilization of community standards as a shield for the exercise of personal-liberty-denying localism also took other forms. Few major cities in America were without local censorship boards or official censors. The only true American religion was Protestantism; and Americans displayed their tolerance by statements such as that of the hero of Sinclair Lewis's novel *Babbitt*, who assured a friend that "he didn't mind Jews, as long as they went to a good Christian church." Religious fundamentalists sought vigorously to enact legislation and to enforce it, denying the right of any public schoolteacher or university professor to teach the theory of evolution in the classroom.[26]

Yet our revolutionary heritage hung on hard. The concept that the federal government might be an instrument for the revival and guarantee of personal freedom and civil rights was so foreign to Americans that the American Civil Liberties Union as late as the 1940s still was dubious that federal action could provide any relief and any meaningful protection in this area.

But for some sensitive Americans who had seen a great tradition corrupted, federal means to achieve the kinds of objectives for which the country was initially set up no longer seemed so unthinkable and out of the question. After some vigorous prodding by Justices John Marshall Harlan I, and Louis D. Brandeis, in 1925 the Supreme Court majority began exploring the possibilities of applying the Bill of Rights against the states and making the federal government the protector of its citizens when their rights were abrogated by local and state repression and their Bill of Rights freedoms were denied.[27]

For those of us who lived through that period, attentive to the growth of this development, it has been a highly revealing one. The statements of key Supreme Court Justices in several vital cases give a sense of what was happening at this time. Benjamin Cardozo, in a case in the late 1930s while expressing doubts as to whether the entire Bill of Rights should be categorically enforced by the federal government against the states, nonetheless suggested that the federal government had an obligation to protect those rights "implicit in the concept of ordered liberty."[28] While such a posture left to the Supreme Court the task of deciding which rights were "implicit," the implication was nonetheless clear that the Court should indeed take on this task and in the process modernize the Bill of Rights. Such a challenge encouraged the Justices to formulate new liberties, when they felt modern economic and social conditions necessitated their creation. Read by attorneys and civil liberties advocates, this was an open invitation to obtain for citizens more meaningful use of their liberties arguing that those freedoms were clearly part of ordered liberty.

Attorney General Frank Murphy, however, was not convinced that such a task should be simply left to the Justices. In 1939, therefore, he set up a small Civil Liberties Unit in the Justice Department, an agency that over time developed into an aggressive and active Civil Rights division prepared to intervene directly in behalf of citizens being denied their rights.[29] Even more startling was the fact that such a move tended to challenge state and local officials and government units, to whom the federal government was no longer prepared to give automatic free rein to handle local citizens' liberties and rights as they saw fit.

Further, in a case during the war, Murphy, now a Justice of the Supreme Court, took another dramatic step.[30] Throughout nineteenth-century America the assumption had been that not only did "bad men have no rights," but that people generally considered by the majority to be incapable of utilizing their rights responsibly—blacks, native Americans, women, the poor, minors— should not be afforded those rights, at least until such time as they became respected and responsible members of the community. Such a view, Murphy argued in 1944 was incompatible with the true meaning of Bill of Rights freedoms. In stopping the deportation of a naturalized citizen charged with having criticized the government, Murphy made clear that "American citizenship is not granted on a condition that the naturalized citizen refrain in the future from uttering any remark or adopting an attitude distasteful to the majority.[31] Any American, he inferred, should not only be free to utilize his civil liberties fully, but must be assured that the government would protect him fully in that use. The opinion followed by less than a year a popular and frequently quoted statement by Justice Robert Jackson, in the famous flag-salute reversal case, exempting Jehovah's Witness children from the compulsory flag salute exercise in the public school. Jackson, in denouncing the narrowness of prior orthodoxy, attempted to establish a new pluralism. "If there is any fixed star in our constitutional constellation," he wrote, "it is that no official, high or petty, can prescribe what shall be orthodox in politics, nationalism, religion, or other matters of opinion, or force citizens to confess by word, or act, their faith therein."[32]

The capstone of this massive switch of assumptions regarding where citizens should turn for aid in securing their Bill of Rights freedoms came in the Report of President Truman's Civil Rights Committee in 1947. That report made clear that the entire government had an obligation to see to it that rights were guaranteed and, as the committee stated:

> It is clear that in modern democratic society, a man's freedom . . . is not and cannot be absolute—nor does it exist in a vacuum—but instead is hedged about by the competing rights of others and the demands of the social welfare. In this context it is government which must referee the clashes which arise among the freedoms of citizens, and protect each citizen in the enjoyment of the maximum freedom to which he is entitled.

"There is no essential conflict between freedom and government," the report went on:

> Bills of rights restrain government from abridging individual civil liberties, while government itself by sound legislative policies protects citizens against the aggressions of others seeking to push their freedoms too far.[33]

Federal intervention in behalf of civil rights and civil liberties and a variety of other forms then became a growing feature of the constitutional law of the United States. John F. Kennedy, in his inaugural address stated: "Ask not what America will do for you; but what together we can do for the freedom of man."[34] The Democratic platform on which he ran had placed a major focus on the achievement of civil rights and civil liberties for *all*, "too often disregarded by previous administrations."[35] Such professions were followed by active executive branch agencies pushing for compliance with new federal rules, regulations, and statutes, generally geared to seeing that individual freedom was protected not only from the government, but from those individuals and groups within the society that sought to deny it.

The results have proved to be controversial. Many Americans were apprehensive at the outset about this increasing federal intervention. While they might grudgingly acknowledge that it could serve to extend the rights of individuals, they were still persuaded that it could also turn into central statism, and just as well deny civil liberties—a concern that was validated thoroughly and somewhat appallingly as revelations of the Watergate days showed. Big government could and would use agencies from the FBI to the CIA not only in surveillance of citizens' private lives, but to restrain their ideas, their behavior, and their associations.[36]

Leaving aside the regrettable abuse, even the positive side of federal intervention in behalf of people's rights and liberties represented a troubling development for many. It seemed to place loyalty to the symbol of the Bill of Rights and its literal application above loyalty to a social system and to local community control. Further, the policies coming from the President, from Congress, and from the courts also seemed all too often to place the rights and wishes of the minority above those of the majority. Hence, bitter opposition developed to the programs of racial integration, supported with federal coercion; the elimination of prayer, Bible reading, and other religious services in the public schools; federally mandated reapportionment of local legislatures and elective bodies; and federal demands that local patterns of criminal justice enforcement conform to uniform national standards.[37]

The opposition went even deeper on the plane of proper priorities in public values. If literal and rigid enforcement of the Bill of Rights, complete with agencies assigned to assure full compliance, meant preferential treatment for those less favored than oneself rather than equality between oneself and those previously disadvantaged, many were reluctant to support such policies. Federally enforced or condoned reverse discrimination, even if used to compensate for decades of past denial of basic Bill of Rights freedoms, was a policy troubling to large numbers of Americans, not because it placed the rights of the individual above those demanding the priority of community standards, but because it seemed to penalize innocent Americans, not themselves responsible for Bill of Rights denials, as a way of compensating for the sins of the biased application of past community standards throughout the country.[38] Further, there seemed no end to the claims of discrimination for which some Americans were prepared to seek remedies. In North Carolina two career marines charged that the Marine Corps unconstitutionally discriminated when it discharged them for being chronically overweight. In Kentucky a left-handed postal clerk charged that the U.S. Postal Service discriminated against him by setting up its filing cases for the convenience of right-handed clerks. In Colorado, a twenty-four-year old man sued his mother and father for "parental malpractice," asking for $350,000 in damages. Cases such as these prompted one observer to write: "There must be some sensible bounds—no matter how elusive—to the claims that can be made in the name of nondiscrimination. . . ."[39]

One wonders if there is a way out of such a dilemma. The federal government cannot legislate tolerance, liberty, or for that matter, true total equality or justice. Further, as Harvard Professor Thomas Reed Powell once said: "Nine men in Washington cannot hold a nation to ideals which it is determined to betray."[40]

The answer, if there is one, has to go back, in some ways, to James Madison and has to constitute a vigorous revitalization of federalism in this country. It was never anticipated that the federal government would be the only agency that would be responsible for seeing that the provisions of the Bill of Rights were respected. This was a job for the people through all of their governmental instrumentalities. The federal government can certainly play a role. It can set forth minimal universal norms and work to see that local units adhere to those norms. But by and large that adherence has to come from people across the country in various kinds of local communities, working to turn government into a pragmatic, problem-solving instrument, seeking constructively and creatively, as individuals and in groups, to evolve appropriate solutions for the unique local problems that each of those communities confronts. Judge Learned Hand once wrote: "Liberty lies in the hearts of men and women; when it dies there, no constitution, no law, no court can save it; no constitution, no law, no courts can even do much to help it. While it lies there, it needs no constitution, no law, and no court to save it."[41] In this sense the values inherent in the Bill of Rights can really best be attained through local citizen participation. Such localism, constructively working toward the values the Bill of Rights sets forth, obviates the need for massive federal solutions to local problems and, if it could work successfully, should relieve the federal government from the necessity of taking actions that could best be handled at the local level.

Constructive federalism is, after all, the major contribution of the United States to political science. It has been and hopefully will continue to be a model for other countries. But the thing that makes it constructive is the free individuals who breathe into it the spirit of liberty, justice, and concern for human rights that we are currently trying to persuade the world is one of our highest commitments. Federalism can serve as an instrument for channelling the energies of individual citizens into the most constructive paths possible in the achievement of these ends and in actually squaring the symbolic meaning of Bill of Rights freedoms with their practice, something ultimately essential if an open society is to still exist in this segment of North America.

NOTES

1. See Austin Sarat, "Studying American Legal Culture: An Assessment of Survey Evidence," *Law and Society Review* 11 (Winter 1977): 441–45; and Donald J. Devine, *The Political Culture of the United States* (Boston: Little, Brown, 1972), pp. 135, 190–200.
2. See Isaiah Berlin, *Two Concepts of Liberty* (Oxford: Clarendon Press, 1958), p. 30.
3. On aspects of the "reception" of English law in America, see David H. Flaherty, *Essays in the History of Early American Law* (Chapel Hill: University of North Carolina, 1969).
4. Richard L. Perry and John C. Cooper, *Sources of Our Liberties* (New York: American Bar Foundation, 1959), pp. 71–72.
5. Irving Brant, *The Bill of Rights: Its Origin and Meaning* (New York: New American Library, 1965), p. 197; Leonard Levy, *Freedom of Speech and Press in Early American History* (New York: Harper and Row, 1963), p. 145.
6. William H. Riker, *Democracy in the United States* (New York: Macmillan, 1953), pp. 101–2.
7. John P. Roche, "American Liberty: An Examination of the 'Tradi-

tion' of Freedom,'' in *Aspects of Liberty*, eds. Milton R. Konvitz and Clinton Rossiter (Ithaca: Cornell University, 1958), pp. 139–40. See also Robert Calhoon, *The Loyalists in Revolutionary America* (New York: Harcourt Brace Jovanovich, 1973).

8. John B. McMaster and Frederick D. Stone, eds., *Pennsylvania and the Federal Constitution, 1787–1788* (Philadelphia: J. B. Lippincott, 1888), p. 478.

9. Gordon S. Wood, ''Freedom and the Constitution,'' in *Freedom in America: A 200-Year Perspective*, ed. Norman A. Graebner (University Park: Pennsylvania State University Press, 1977), pp. 48–49.

10. Marvin Meyers, ed., *The Mind of the Founder: Sources of the Political Thought of James Madison* (Indianapolis: Bobbs-Merrill, 1973), pp. 207–8.

11. Federalist, Number 10, in *Liberty and Justice*, ed. James M. Smith and Paul L. Murphy (New York: Knopf, 1965), p. 74.

12. Ibid., p. 75.

13. Roche, ''American Liberty,'' p. 143.

14. James M. Smith, *Freedom's Fetters: The Alien and Sedition Laws and American Civil Liberties* (Ithaca: Cornell University, 1956), p. 101.

15. Daniel Sisson, *The American Revolution of 1800* (New York: Knopf, 1974).

16. On this ''nationalist'' view of Reconstruction see Robert J. Kaczorowski, ''The Nationalization of Civil Rights: Constitutional Theory and Practice in a Racist Society, 1866–1883,'' (Ph.D. diss., University of Minnesota, 1971). See also Herman Belz, *Emancipation and Equal Rights: Politics and Constitutionalism in the Civil War Era* (New York: Norton, 1978), pp. 117–37, 160–61.

17. *Minor v. Happersett*, 21 Wallace 162 (1875).

18. *Hurtado v. California*, 110 U.S. 516 (1884).

19. *Plessey v. Ferguson*, 163 U.S. 537 (1896).

20. Quoted in Paul L. Murphy, *The Meaning of Freedom of Speech* (Westport, Ct.: Greenwood, 1976), p. 15. See also Stephen W. Gard, ''The First Amendment Prior to 1919: 140 Years of Silence'' (Master of Law Thesis, University of Chicago, 1972); and Alexis J. Anderson, ''State Courts and Free Speech during the Formative Period of First Amendment Theory'' (Paper at the Organization of American Historians Annual Meeting, April 1979).

21. The literature here is extensive. See especially, John P. Roche, *Sentenced to Life* (New York: Macmillan, 1974), pp. 269–308; and David J. Rothman, *The Discovery of the Asylum: Social Order and Disorder in the New Republic* (Boston: Little, Brown, 1971).

22. Orma Linford, ''The Mormons and the Law: The Polygamy

Cases," *Utah Law Review* 9 (1964, 1965), pp. 308–70, 543–91. See also Philip B. Kurland, *Religion and the Law of Church and State and the Supreme Court* (Chicago: Aldine, 1961), pp. 21–25.

23. See David J. Pivar, *Purity Crusade: Sexual Morality and Social Control, 1868–1900* (Westport, Ct.: Greenwood, 1973). On aspects of censorship in the same era and following see Paul S. Boyer, *Purity in Print* (New York: Scribner, 1968), ch. 1.

24. Robert H. Wiebe, *The Search for Order, 1877–1920* (New York: Hill and Wang, 1967), p. 76.

25. Paul L. Murphy, *World War I and the Origin of Civil Liberties in the United States* (New York: Norton, 1979), ch. 2–3.

26. Norman F. Furniss, *The Fundamentalist Controversy* (New Haven: Yale University, 1954).

27. *Gitlow v. New York*, 258 U.S. 652 (1925).

28. *Palko v. Connecticut*, 302 U.S. 319 (1937).

29. Robert K. Carr, *Federal Protection of Civil Rights: Quest for a Sword* (Ithaca: Cornell University, 1947), pp. 1–32.

30. *Baumgartner v. U.S.*, 322 U.S. 665 (1944).

31. 322 U.S. 665 at 679.

32. *West Virginia State Board of Education v. Barnette*, 319 U.S. 624 (1943).

33. James M. Smith and Paul L. Murphy, *Liberty and Justice* (New York: Knopf, 1958), pp. 507–08; President's Committee on Civil Rights, *To Secure These Rights* (New York: Simon and Schuster, 1947), p. 5.

34. *U.S. Department of State Bulletin*, February 6, 1961, p. 3.

35. Kirk H. Porter and Donald B. Johnson, *National Party Platforms, 1840–1964* (Urbana, Ill.: University of Illinois, 1966), pp. 597–98.

36. Morton H. Halperin, *The Lawless State: The Crimes of the U.S. Intelligence Agencies* (New York: Penguin, 1976); Morton H. Halperin, *Freedom vs. National Security: Secrecy and Surveillance* (New York: Chelsea House, 1977); and Robert J. Goldstein, *Political Repression in Modern America* (Cambridge: Schenkman, 1978), pp. 430–545.

37. Paul L. Murphy, *The Constitution in Crisis Times, 1918–1969* (New York: Harper & Row, 1972), p. 461.

38. Barry R. Gross, ed., *Reverse Discrimination* (Buffalo: Prometheus Books, 1977); Robert M. O'Neil, *Discriminating Against Discrimination* (Bloomington: Indiana University, 1975); Allan P. Sindler, *Bakke, DeFunis and Minority Admissions: The Quest for Equal Opportunity* (New York: Longman, 1978).

39. "Is There a Limit to the Rights Revolution? *Minneapolis Tribune*, July 19, 1978, p. 5a.

40. Zachariah Chafee, Jr., *Free Speech in the United States* (Cambridge, Mass.: Harvard University, 1941), p. xiv.

41. Irving Dilliard, *The Spirit of Liberty: Papers and Addresses of Learned Hand* (New York: Knopf, 1959), pp. 143–44.

3

ALPHEUS THOMAS MASON

The Bill of Rights: An Almost Forgotten Appendage

What is the Bill of Rights? Nearly every American, including the proverbial man on the street, thinks he knows the answer. The question is not all that simple. Strictly speaking, the Bill of Rights consists of the Constitution's first eight amendments, all designed to protect personal liberties against governmental encroachment, except under certain prescribed procedures. The Ninth Amendment is precautionary. The possibility that listing individual rights might inadvertently omit other basic freedoms moved its framers to declare that the preceding amendments should not be construed "to deny or disparage other rights retained by the people." Concerned with states rights rather than freedom of the individual, the Tenth Amendment does not qualify for inclusion. Precautionary and redundant, it declares that powers not delegated to the national authority are reserved to the states or to the people, thus reiterating the substance of the Supremacy Clause, Article VI, paragraph 2, of the Constitution.

While it is literally correct to say that the original document contained no Bill of Rights, certain provisions of the unamended Constitution provide specific individual safeguards. Article I, Section 9 places limits on suspension of the writ of habeas corpus. Article I, Section 10 forbids ex post facto laws and bills of attainder. Article III, Section 2 requires trial by jury in federal criminal cases, specifying that trials be held in the jurisdiction where the crime was committed. Article III, Section 3 precisely defines conduct which constitutes treason.

Nor are these specific provisions the only security afforded individual rights in the original Constitution. The structure and organization of government, featuring separation of powers and federalism are mighty controls. In *Federalist* No. 28, Hamilton declared that "the State governments will, in all possible contingencies, afford complete security against invasions of the public liberty by the national authority."

In the 1960s, dissenting Justice Harlan deplored the Court's mad rush to bring an increasing number of natural rights provisions under the Fourteenth Amendment's due process clause at the expense of principles that "lie at the root of our constitutional system."[1] Spelling out his objections, he observed: "We are accustomed to speak of the Bill of Rights and the Fourteenth Amendment as the principal guarantees of personal liberty. Yet it would surely be shallow not to recognize that the structure of our political system accounts no less for the free society we have." The Founding Fathers "staked their faith that liberty would prosper in the nation not primarily upon the declaration of individual rights but upon the kind of government the Union was to have. . . . No view of the Bill of Rights or interpretation of any of its provisions which fails to take due account of [federalism and separation of powers] can be considered constitutionally sound."[2] Harlan sounded John Randolph's eighteenth century warning: "You may cover whole skins of parchment with limitations, but power alone can limit power."[3] There is more than a grain of truth in Hamilton's blanket observation in *Federalist* No. 84: "The Constitution is itself, in every rational sense, and to every useful purpose, a Bill of Rights."

In 1947, when Earl Warren, destined to become the fourteenth Chief Justice of the United States, identified a Bill of Rights as "the heart of any constitution," he had the first eight amendments in mind.[4] A few years later, he began a remarkable judicial career, translating this hierarchy of values into the law of the land, a latter-day development all the more noteworthy because in 1787 the narrowly conceived Bill of Rights was an almost forgotten appendage. How to explain this apparent oversight? What were the factors and forces leading to its proposal and prompt ratification?

The idea of "original, inherent, indefeasible natural rights" has ancient antecedents, dating from Magna Carta and earlier.[5] Seventeenth- and eighteenth-century Americans believed that certain principles of right and justice were "entitled to prevail of their own intrinsic merit."[6] Existing prior to the social compact, they did not depend on positive law.

Widespread recognition and acceptance of the natural rights philosophy, affirmed in the Declaration of Independence and rooted in the common law of England, had apparently led the Constitution's framers to omit specific mention of rights considered so obviously fundamental as not to need enumeration. Codification merely served, as Edmund Burke put it, "to fortify the fallible and feeble contrivances of reason with nature's unerring and powerful instincts."[7]

Another explanation for this apparent neglect was ambivalence concerning the freedoms that merited special consideration, making it difficult, even dangerous, to undertake a grouping of basic liberties. For whatever reason, the Constitution was drafted, submitted to the states, and ratified without a bill of rights.

On September 12, 1787, a few days before the Constitutional Convention completed its work, George Mason, author a decade earlier of Virginia's famous bill of rights, rose in the Convention to announce that he "wished the plan had been prefaced with a Bill of Rights." The reason Mason assigned for his last-minute proposal seems relaxed, almost an afterthought: "It would give great quiet to the people."[8] Although his motion was overwhelmingly defeated by a vote of ten to one, Mason, convinced that want of a bill of rights was "a fatal objection," returned to Virginia with a "fixed disposition to prevent adoption of the plan."[9]

What loomed before Mason as an insurmountable defect at the Philadelphia Convention seemed not to have occurred to other delegates at all. "I cannot say," James Wilson remarked in the Pennsylvania ratifying convention, "what were the reasons of every member of that convention, for not adding a bill of rights; I believe the truth is, that such an idea never entered the mind of many of them."[10] Mason's "fatal objection," James Madison noted impatiently, "surely was not brought forward in the Convention. . . . Were it allowed the weight which Col. Mason may suppose it deserves, it would remain to be decided whether it be candid to arraign the Convention for omissions which were never suggested to them. . . ."[11]

Mason's proposal came too late for effective consideration, lending weight to Wilson's observation that a bill of rights "would have been spurned with greatest indignation."[12]

Why did Mason wait until the closing days of the Convention to raise a question destined to become the crucial issue in the debates on ratification? The answer may be that antifederalist delegates were fully aroused only after the Convention approved two of the most nationalizing provisions of the Constitution: Article I, Section 8, paragraph 18, the "necessary and proper" clause and Article VI, paragraph 2, the Supremacy clause, adding a second and third dimension, respectively, to the enumerated powers granted Congress in Article I, Section 8. The former conferred on Congress a discretionary choice of means for carrying out its enumerated powers; the latter put the stamp of supremacy on congressional legislation passed in "pursuance of the Constitution." Dubbed "sweeping clauses," these two provisions reinforced opposition to ratification.

Slow to see the need for a bill of rights, the antifederalists, once aroused, exploded with fury. The framers had, they charged, belied their heritage. When America was in its youth, Patrick Henry commented caustically, "liberty was the primary object." It ranked high both in word and deed. This country had become "a great, mighty, and splendid nation" because liberty was "its direct end and foundation"[13] Having triumphed in the War of Independence, Americans had stored away, along with their muskets, earlier convictions about natural rights. Writing Thomas Jefferson in Paris, Madison suggested that the Constitution's critics "fancied that the Convention . . . had entered into a conspiracy against the liberties of the people at large, in order to erect an aristocracy for the rich, the well-born, and the Men of Education."[14]

A formidable triumvirate in Virginia, Mason, Henry, and Richard Henry Lee, waged a relentless campaign. Under the proposed Constitution, the sovereignty of the states had, they argued, been "relinquished" and the "rights of conscience, trial by jury, liberty of the press . . . all pretensions to human rights and privileges were rendered uncertain."[15]

Luther Martin of Maryland sharpened these complaints: "The proposed Constitution being intended and empowered to act not only on states but also immediately on individuals . . . renders a recognition and stipulation in favor of the rights of both states and of men, not only proper, but . . . absolutely necessary." A Bill of Rights would, he argued, "serve as a barrier between the general government and the respective states and their citizens."[16]

Supporters of ratification minimized the nationalizing effect of the so-called sweeping clauses. Both, they contended, were tautologies. For James Iredell of North Carolina the supremacy clause meant only that "when congress passes a law consistent with the constitution, it is to be binding on the people." The national Constitution would, of course, supersede the state constitutions, but "the latter must yield to the former, only in those cases where power is given by it." "If congress under pretence of executing one power, should in fact usurp another," Iredell explained, "they will violate the constitution." Article VI, paragraph 2 was "merely a general clause," which always raised the question of whether Congress had exceeded its authority. It granted no power itself and made supreme no laws lacking constitutional authority.[17]

The necessary-and-proper clause, likewise, was "only a superfluity." It gave "no supplementary power," Madison declared; it merely enabled Congress "to execute the delegated powers."[18] For James Wilson in Pennsylvania, the "necessary and proper" clause meant only that powers "already particularly given, shall be effectually carried into execution."[19]

Federalist effort to play down the nationalizing significance of the supremacy and necessary and proper clauses was not convincing. Unsuccessful in their attempts to render "the sweeping clauses" mere truisms, supporters of ratification tried to meet the challenge by recourse to history. Wilson argued that bills of rights, being hangovers from the era of kings, did not fit the American situation. The ratifying conventions were voting on a government of enumerated powers. Any transgression of these bounds would be recognized as *ultra vires*. Why make exception to power not granted? "In a government possessed of enumerated powers," Wilson declared, "such a measure would be not only unnecessary, but preposterous and dangerous."[20] A Bill of Rights would also be "impracticable—for who will be bold enough to undertake to enumerate all the rights of the people?" "Enumerate all the rights of men!" Wilson exclaimed. "I am sure that no gentleman in the late convention would have attempted such a thing."[21] Sharing Wilson's doubts, Madison considered "a solemn declaration of our essential rights both unnecessary and dangerous."[22]

Refusing to budge, the opposition drew ammunition from the well-stocked federalist arsenal. If enumeration of rights beyond the reach of government endangered other equally basic rights, that risk had already been incurred by a partial listing in the Constitution itself. "No satisfactory reason has yet been offered for the omission of a bill of rights," John Whitehill of Pennsylvania charged.[23] Whitehill's compatriot, John Smilie, was equally blunt. The presence of a partial bill of rights, he argued, reinforced the antifederalist case. "It seems that the members of the federal convention were themselves convinced, in some degree, of the expediency and propriety of a bill of rights, for we find them expressly declaring that the writ of habeas corpus and the trial by jury in criminal cases shall not be suspended or infringed."[24]

Federalists distrusted express safeguards for the rights of states and individuals lest they sap the energy needed to achieve the Preamble's great national objectives. Furthermore, bills of rights in the various state constitutions had been ineffective. The people continually clamored that trial by jury, secured in the bill of rights of Pennsylvania, "OUGHT to be kept sacred." But "what is the consequence? There have been more violations of this right in Pennsylvania, since the revolution, than are to be found in England, in the course of a century."[25] "In Virginia," Madison wrote Jefferson on October 17, 1788, "I have seen the bill of rights violated in every instance where it has been exposed to a popular current."[26] Repeated infringements of these parchment barriers had been committed by overbearing legislative majorities in every state. Necessary safeguards must therefore be found elsewhere.

Federalist delegates in various state ratifying conventions ran the gamut of institutional checks—federalism, separation of powers, and popular elections—that presumably would secure freedom against abuse of national power.[27] Slow to emerge was judicial review, destined to become intimately linked with protection of individual rights. Conspicuous among the states stressing this peculiarly American control were Virginia and Connecticut.

To Patrick Henry's query, who is to determine the extent of national power, George Nicholas of Virginia retorted: "I say, the same power which in all well regulated communities determines the extent of legislative powers. If they exceed these powers, the judiciary will declare it void."[28] Edmund Randolph, taking up the cudgels in behalf of the Constitution he had declined to sign, also looked to the federal judiciary for protection. "Can it be believed," he asked, "that the federal judiciary would not be independent enough to prevent such oppressive practices?"[29]

The most forceful supporter of judicial review was Virginia delegate John Marshall, later fourth Chief Justice of the United States. Marshall called the federal judiciary "a great improvement." A tribunal had been established for "*the decision of controversies*, [author's emphasis] which were before, either not at all, or improperly provided for." The supremacy clause, he admitted, made the laws of the United States paramount, but any fear that "there is no case but what this will extend to" was unwarranted. Congress did not have power to make laws on every conceivable subject. "If they were to make a law not warranted by any of the powers enumerated, it would be considered by the judges as an infringement of the constitution which they are to guard; they would not consider such a law as coming under their jurisdiction. They would declare it void."

"Is it not necessary," Marshall asked, "that the federal courts should have cognizance of cases arising under the constitution, and the laws of the United States?" "To what quarter will you look for a protection from an infringement on the constitution," Marshall demanded, "if you will not give the power to the judiciary? There is no other body that can afford such a protection."[30] Chief among the guardians of individual rights would be the federal judiciary. It would exercise this authority even in the absence of paper guarantees.

Oliver Ellsworth of Connecticut, third Chief Justice of the United States, was no less firm: "If the general legislature should at any time overleap their limits, the judicial department is a constitutional check."[31] Under the new Constitution, future Supreme Court Justice James Wilson declared, "the legislature may be restrained and kept within its prescribed bounds by the interposition of the judicial department."[32]

To critics of the proposed Constitution, federalist pledges that courts would protect individual rights were persuasive only if judicial review were tied to a bill of rights. Fueling the fires of opposition was an outsider—Thomas Jefferson. From Paris, Jefferson wrote Madison: "A bill of rights is what the people are entitled to against every government on earth, general or particular, and what no just government should refuse, or rest on inference."[33] Around this "polar star, and great support of American liberty"[34] fierce battles were fought in New York, Virginia, and Massachusetts.

The constitution first encountered powerful opposition in the Bay State. For a while it seemed doubtful that enough votes in favor could be mustered. Samuel Adams, whose democratic convictions had highlighted the prerevolutionary years, noted signs of reaction against "the Natural Rights of Man" developing even before the conclusion of that struggle.[35] John Hancock, initially inclined to be negative, finally supplied the formula that won Adams's acquiescence: "I give my assent to the Constitution, in full confidence that the amendments proposed will soon become a part of the system."[36] Recommendatory, not "conditional amendments" was the price exacted. For Madison the outcome in Massachusetts created "a blemish," but one "least offensive" in form. The size of the minority, 187 to 168, was, he admitted, disagreeably large; but its temper supplied "some atonement."[37]

George Wythe of Virginia had taken a decisive step on June 24, 1788, when he admitted the Constitution's imperfections, and "the propriety of some amendments." Wythe then proposed "that whatsoever amendments might be deemed necessary, should be recommended to consideration of the congress which should first assemble under the constitution."[38] Notwithstanding misgivings as to their efficacy, Madison finally acquiesced.

Jefferson was elated. Previously, a staunch, uncompromising advocate, he now took a more balanced view. Bills of rights were, he agreed, "like all other human blessings alloyed with some inconveniences." Their presence might, under some circumstances, "cramp government." Not all rights could ever be made secure, but it was better to protect some than none. Transcending all other considerations was his conviction that the inconveniences attending omission of a bill of rights would be "permanent, afflicting and irreparable . . . in constant progression from bad to worse." Almost as an afterthought, it seems, he alerted Madison to a crucial oversight: "In the arguments in favor of a declaration of rights, you omit one which has great weight with me, the legal check which it puts into the hands of the judiciary."[39]

In his campaign for a seat in the new Congress, Madison was charged with abandoning the cause of religious freedom. Now modifying his previous stand as to the wisdom of including a bill of rights, he took the position that ratification, without prior attempts at alteration, made amendments safe and proper. As a member of the First Congress, in the face of objections from federalist members inclined to delay "til the more pressing business is despatched,"[40] Madison felt "bound in honor and duty" to fulfill his campaign commitment.

On June 8, 1789, he submitted to the House seventeen amendments. In piloting them through Congress, Madison stressed the very point Jefferson had earlier called to his attention as a glaring omission: "If they [the Bill of Rights] are incorporated into the constitution, independent tribunals of justice will consider themselves in a peculiar manner the guardians of those rights; they will be an impenetrable bulwark against every assumption of power in the legislative or executive; they will be naturally led to resist every encroachment upon rights expressly stipulated for in the constitution by the declaration of rights."[41] "The great object in view," according to the now converted Madison, "is to limit the power of government, by excepting out of the grant of power those cases in which the Government ought not to act, or to act only in a particular mode."[42]

For antifederalists specific safeguards against government encroachment on individual rights, though of great importance, were not enough. Opponents of ratification, without a bill of rights, had conjured up the image of a national colossus, destined to swallow up or destroy the defenseless states. To quiet these fears, Madison proposed the Tenth Amendment: "The powers not delegated by this constitution, nor prohibited by it to the States, are reserved to the States respectively." In explanation he said:

> I find from looking into the amendments proposed by the State conventions, that several are particularly anxious that it should be declared in the Constitution, that the powers not therein delegated should be reserved to the several States. Perhaps words which may define this more precisely than the whole of the instrument now does. I admit they may be deemed unnecessary; but there can be no harm in making such a declaration, if gentlemen will allow that the fact is as stated. I am sure I understand it so, and do therefore propose it.[43]

Finally convinced that a bill of rights protecting individual liberties could acquire "the character of fundamental maxims of free government," Madison became an ardent sponsor. He firmly opposed amendments which might unduly restrict national power. On three occasions it was proposed that the word "expressly" be inserted before "delegated." Madison objected, arguing that "it was impossible to confine a Government to the exercise of express powers." Unless the Constitution descended to recount every minutia, there must be power by implication. He remembered that the word "expressly" had been "moved in the convention of Virginia by the opponents of ratification, and after full and fair discussion, was given up by them and the system allowed to retain its present form."[44] Madison's concern was realistic. Insertion of "expressly" before "delegated" would eliminate the second dimension of national power—choice of means for carrying enumerated grants into execution. Although Congressman Martin Tucker, joined by Elbridge Gerry, continued to press for its insertion, the proposal was defeated by a thirty-two to seventeen vote.[45]

Antifederalist motives are hard to disentangle.[46] The unavailing struggle to give substance to the Tenth Amendment suggests that for certain bill-of-rights advocates, states rights weighed more heavily than their concern for personal freedom. Critical reaction to the amendments Madison sought and finally procured indicates high priority for states rights. Writing Patrick Henry in June 1789, William Grayson objected to Madison's proposed amendments as greatly overemphasizing the protection of personal rights at the expense of states rights.[47] Pierce Butler had the same low regard for the Bill of Rights. Instead of "substantial amendments," Madison had proposed a "few *milk-and-water* [author's emphasis] amendments . . . such as liberty of conscience, a free press, and one or two general things already well secured."[48]

The framers of the Tenth Amendment, including Madison, interpreted it for what it was—a constitutional tranquillizer. It was framed, Chief Justice Marshall observed, "for the purpose of quieting the excessive state jealousies which had been excited."[49] In 1940, Justice Harlan Fiske Stone labeled the amendment "but a truism, that all is retained which has not been surrendered."[50] One of the ironies of American constitutional history is that the Supreme Court achieved through judicial decision what the framers failed to accomplish—insertion of the word "expressly" in the Tenth Amendment.[51]

For his contributions in the Convention that framed the Constitution, Madison was widely hailed "Father of the Constitution." Madison also played a unique role in the battle for a bill of rights. His remarkable insight is evident in failure no less than in success. Among the proposed amendments, the one he considered most important, approved by the House but rejected in the Senate, was Number 14. It provided: "No state shall infringe the right of trial by jury in criminal cases, nor the right of conscience, nor freedom of speech or press." Believing there was more danger of abuse of power from state governments than by the government of the United States, Madison rated ill-fated Number 14 "the most valuable amendment of the whole list. If there were any reason to restrain the government of the United States from infringing these essential rights, it was equally necessary that they should be secured against state governments."[52]

Although several state constitutions, adopted after 1776, contained either a bill of rights or other provisions presumably designed to achieve the same objective, these had not, as we have seen, proved effective. Even before the Convention assembled, Madison had deplored "injustice of the laws of the states," particularly those injurious to property and contract rights. For him, correction of these abuses was an object vying with the need for a more energetic central authority.[53] Indeed, these injustices had, he said, brought "into question the fundamental principle of republican government, that the majority who rule in such governments are the safest guardians of the public good and private rights."[54]

Madison's stress on the ill-fated amendment was prophetic. It anticipated adoption of the Civil War amendments nearly a century later. It also foreshadowed the latter-day drive of certain Supreme Court justices to apply the specific provisions of the Bill of Rights to state action under the Due Process Clause, a goal nearly realized.

Neither the Constitution nor the Bill of Rights has completely dispelled the notion that "the fundamental maxims of a free government seem to require that the rights of personal liberty and property should be held sacred."[55] Supreme Court justices, throughout our history, have debated this issue. In *Calder v. Bull*, Justice Salmon Chase argued that even in the absence of specific constitutional barriers, "certain vital principles in our free republican governments . . . will determine and overrule an apparent and flagrant abuse of legislative power."[56] In *Fletcher v. Peck*, Chief Justice Marshall suggested that a Georgia statute was invalid "either by general principles which are common to our free institutions or by the particular provisions of the constitution of the United States."[57] Justice Stephen Field, dissenting in *Munn v. Illinois*, declared that "the principles on which our republican government is founded," as well as the Constitution, barred the state legislature from placing the rights of property "at the mercy of a majority of its legislature."[58]

The stock judicial argument against the "natural justice" limitation was Justice James Iredell's reply to Chase in 1798: "The ideas of natural justice are regulated by no fixed standard: the ablest and the purest men have differed upon the subject."[59] In 1965, when the Court embellished certain provisions of the Bill of Rights with the penumbral right of privacy, Justice Hugo Black, echoing Iredell, complained that "natural justice" is "an uncontrolled standard for holding laws unconstitutional," enabling judges to enforce their personal predilections as law and "subjecting federal and state law to . . . an unrestrained and unrestrainable judicial control." Nor was this allegedly self-acquired judicial power any "less dangerous when used to enforce this Court's views about personal rights than those about economic rights."[60]

Justice Louis Brandeis and certain other Supreme Court justices seem inclined to elevate personal rights to a higher level than economic interests, claiming for courts a correspondingly higher responsibility for their protection. In *Olmstead v. U.S.*, Brandeis observed:

> The makers of our Constitution undertook to secure conditions favorable to the pursuit of happiness. They recognized the significance of man's spiritual nature, of his feelings and of his intellect. They knew that only a small part of the pain, pleasure and satisfactions of life are to be found in material things. They sought to protect Americans in their beliefs, their thoughts, their emotions and their sensations. They conferred, as against government, the right to be let alone—the most comprehensive of rights and the right most valued by civilized men.[61]

Although incorporation of the Bill of Rights under the Fourteenth Amendment's due process clause seems to preclude invoking "principles of natural justice," the Burger Court, speaking through Justice William Brennan in 1977, ruled that "unlike the property interests . . . the liberty interest in family privacy has its source . . . not in state law, but in intrinsic human rights, as they have been understood in this nation's history and tradition."[62]

The campaign for a Bill of Rights had begun as a seemingly partisan move, a strategic maneuver, some believed, to defeat ratification. In the end the goals sought were generally accepted by all. "[S]ecurity for liberty," through a Bill of Rights, was demanded "by the general voice of America."[63] Fundamental maxims of a free society gained no greater moral sanctity by incorporation into our basic law. The significant gain was that formerly natural rights became civil rights. Individuals could thereafter look to courts for their protection and to the Constitution for a relatively more precise standard than "principles of natural justice."

NOTES

1. Address at the American Bar Center, Chicago, August 13, 1963.

2. "The Bill of Rights and the Constitution," Address at the dedication of the Bill of Rights Room, U.S. Subtreasury Building, August 9, 1964. Similar sentiments were expressed in dissenting Supreme Court opinions.

3. William Bruce, *John Randolph of Roanoke* (New York: Octagon, 1970), vol. 2, p. 211.

4. Henry Christman, ed., *The Public Papers of Chief Justice Warren* (New York: Simon and Schuster, 1959), p. 7.

5. Bernard Bailyn, *Ideological Origins of the American Revolution* (Cambridge, Mass.: Belknap Press, 1967), p. 78.

6. Edward S. Corwin, "The 'Higher Law' Background of American Constitutional Law," *Harvard Law Review* 42, no. 2 (December 1928): 149, 365. See also Corwin, "Basic Doctrine of American Constitutional Law," *Michigan Law Review* 12, no. 4 (February 1914): 247.

7. H. Thomas, ed., *Reflections on the Revolution in France* (New York: Bobbs-Merrill, 1955), p. 16.

8. Max Farrand, ed., *The Records of the Federal Convention* (New Haven, Conn.: Yale University Press, 1911), vol. 2, p. 587.

9. Madison to Jefferson, October 24, 1787, Gaillard Hunt, ed., *The Writings of James Madison* (New York: Putnam's, 1904), vol. 5, p. 34.

10. Jonathan Elliot, ed., *The Debates in the Several State Conventions on the Adoption of the Federal Constitution* (Washington, D.C.: Taylor and Maury, 1836), vol. 2, pp. 401–9.

11. Madison to Washington, October 18, 1787, in Ferrand, *The Records of the Federal Convention*, vol. 3, p. 180.

12. Elliot, *The Debates in the Several State Conventions*, vol. 2, pp. 408–9.

13. Elliot, *The Debates in the Several State Conventions*, vol. 3, p. 80.

14. Madison to Jefferson, February 19, 1788, Hunt, *The Writings of James Madison*, vol. 5, p. 102.

15. Elliot, *The Debates in the Several State Conventions*, vol. 3, p. 72.

16. Farrand, *The Records of the Federal Convention*, vol. 3, p. 290.

17. Elliot, *The Debates in the Several State Conventions*, vol. 4, pp. 184–85. For similar views, see Dayton McKean in John McMaster and Frederick Stone, ed., *Pennsylvania and the Federal Constitution* (n.p., 1888), p. 277, p. 354. See also, Elliot, *The Debates in the Several State Conventions*, vol. 4, pp. 191–92.

18. Elliot, *The Debates in the Several State Conventions*, vol. 3, p. 405.

19. McMaster and Stone, *Pennsylvania and the Federal Constitution*, p. 330.

20. Elliot, *The Debates in the Several State Conventions*, vol. 4, p. 409.

21. McMaster and Stone, *Pennsylvania and the Federal Constitution*, p. 314.

22. Elliot, *The Debates in the Several State Conventions*, vol. 3, p. 560.

23. McMaster and Stone, *Pennsylvania and the Federal Constitution*, pp. 286–87.

24. Ibid., p. 255.

25. Ibid., pp. 353–54.

26. Hunt, *The Writings of James Madison*, vol. 5, p. 272.

27. For details, see Alpheus Mason, *The States Rights Debate: Antifederalism and the Constitution* (New York: Oxford, 1972), ch. 4.

28. Elliot, *The Debates in the Several State Conventions*, vol. 3, p. 409.

29. Ibid., p. 431.

30. Ibid., pp. 501–3.

31. Ibid., vol. 2, p. 198.

32. McMaster and Stone, *Pennsylvania and the Federal Constitution*, p. 304; Paul Leicester Ford, ed., *Pamphlets on the Constitution of the United States* (Brooklyn, N.Y.: n.p., 1888), p. 234.

33. Jefferson to Madison, December 2, 1787. Mason, *The States Rights Debate*, p. 171.

34. James Monroe's characterization of the projected Bill of Rights, in Elliot, *The Debate in the Several State Conventions*, vol. 3, p. 219.

35. Samuel Adams to Richard Henry Lee, December 3, 1787, in Harry Cushing, ed., *The Writings of Samuel Adams* (New York: Putnam's, 1908), vol. 4, p. 325.

36. Elliot, *The Debate in the Several State Conventions*, vol. 2, p. 179.

37. James Madison to George Washington, February 15, 1788. Hunt, *The Writings of James Madison*, vol. 5, p. 100.

38. Elliot, *The Debate in the Several State Conventions*, vol. 3, pp. 531, 532.

39. Quoted in Alpheus Mason, *Free Government in the Making* (New York: Oxford, 1965), p. 323. Much earlier, in his *Notes on Virginia*, Jefferson had implied the connection between judicial review and a Bill of Rights as a remedy "to render unnecessary an appeal to the people, or in other words a rebellion on every infraction of their rights." Mason, *Free Government in the Making*, p. 168.

40. *The Annals of Congress* (Washington, D.C.: Gales and Seaton, 1834), vol. 1, p. 445. (June 8, 1789).

41. *Annals of Congress*, vol. 1, p. 457. See also pp. 454–55.

42. *Annals of Congress*, vol. 1, p. 453.

43. Hunt, *The Writings of James Madison*, vol. 5, pp. 387–88. (June 8, 1789). See also Charles Lofgren, "*National League of Cities v. Usery*: Dual Federalism Reborn," *Claremont Journal of Public Affairs* 4 (Spring 1977): 19; Lofgren, "The Origins of the Tenth Amendment: History, Sovereignty and the Problem of Constitutional Intention," in *Constitutional Government in America*, ed. Ronald Collins (Durham, N.C.: Carolina Academic Press, 1980).

44. *Annals of Congress*, vol. 1, p. 790.

45. *Annals of Congress*, vol. 1, p. 797.

46. Leonard Levy considers the Bill of Rights as an historical accident, a sham battle, an unwanted victory: "Indeed the history of the framing and ratification of the First Amendment and the other nine scarcely manifests a passion on the part of anyone concerned with the process. Considering its immediate background, our precious Bill of Rights was in the main the chance result of certain Federalists having been reluctantly forced to capitalize for their own cause the propaganda that had been originated in vain by the Anti-Federalists for ulterior purposes. Thus the party that had first opposed a Bill of Rights inadvertently wound up with the responsibility of its framing and ratification, while the party that had at first professedly wanted it discovered too late that its framing and ratification were not only embarrassing but inexpedient." Leonard Levy, *Legacy of Suppression* (Cambridge, Mass.: Harvard University, 1960), p. 233.

From a variety of motives, antifederalists advocated a Bill of Rights as early as the final days of the Philadelphia Convention. In the state-ratifying conventions, passion was not, as we have seen, in short supply. From Paris, Jefferson's exertions were both passionate and persistent. His influence on Madison—the prime mover in the first Congress—was incalculable. Federalists and antifederalists did, in fact, switch positions. Madison himself switched. This not unusual political phenomenon does not dwarf the significance of the achievement.

47. Grayson to Henry, September 29, 1789, William Henry, *Patrick Henry* (New York: Scribner's, 1891), vol. 3, p. 406.

48. Pierce Butler to James Iredell, August 11, 1789, Griffith McRee, *Life and Correspondence of James Iredell* (New York: Appleton, 1857), vol. 2, p. 265.

49. *McCulloch v. Maryland*, 4 Wheaton 316 at 406 (1819).

50. *U.S. v. Darby Lumber Company*, 213 U.S. 100 at 124 (1941).

51. Many Supreme Court decisions document this assertion, the most conspicuous being Justice Day's opinion in *Hammer v. Dagenhart*, 247 U.S. 251 (1918), overruled in the Darby case.

52. *Annals of Congress*, vol. 1, p. 784 (August 17, 1789). Twelve amendments were submitted to the states for ratification; two failed adoption. One dealt with the ratio of population to representation, the other with compensation of members of Congress. Herman Ames, *The Proposed Amendments to the Constitution* (Philadelphia: University of Pennsylvania, 1896), pp. 184–85.

53. See the Madison-Roger Sherman colloquy on this subject at the Federal Convention of 1787, in Mason, *Free Government in the Making*, pp. 212–13.

54. Hunt, *The Writings of James Madison*, vol. 2, 366 (April 1787).

55. *Wilkinson v. Leland*, 2 Peters 627 at 657 (1829).

56. *Calder v. Bull*, 3 Dallas 386 at 388 (1798).

57. *Fletcher v. Peck*, 6 Cranch 87 at 139 (1810).

58. *Munn v. Illinois*, 94 U.S. 113 at 140 (1877).

59. *Calder v. Bull*, 3 Dallas 386 at 398 (1798).

60. *Griswold v. Connecticut*, 381 U.S. 479 at 537, 538 (1965).

61. *Olmstead v. U.S.*, 277 U.S. 438 at 478 (1928).

62. *Smith v. Organization of Foster Families*, 431 U.S. 816 at 845 (1977). See in this connection Mason and Beaney, *American Constitutional Law* (Englewood Cliffs, N.J.: Prentice-Hall, 1978), pp. 541–46. This is a controversial subject. The various viewpoints, including Mason, "The Warren Court and the Bill of Rights," are presented in *The Supreme Court in American Politics* ed. David Forte (Lexington, Mass.: Heath, 1972).

63. Jefferson to John Paul Jones, March 23, 1789. Julian Boyd, *The Papers of Thomas Jefferson* (Princeton, N.J.: Princeton University, 1950–), vol. 14, p. 689.

SECTION II

The First Amendment: Press, Speech, and Association

4

THOMAS I. EMERSON

The First Amendment in the Year 2000

The First Amendment declares: "Congress shall make no law . . . abridging the freedom of speech, or of the press; or the right of the people peaceably to assemble, and to petition the Government for a redress of grievances." It has been broadly interpreted to establish a comprehensive right to freedom of expression. That concept includes not only the right to communicate information and ideas, but to form and hold beliefs, to receive communications from others, to inquire and obtain information, to remain silent, and to form associations with others in order to facilitate any or all of these endeavors. The right extends to all methods of expression, whether it be through speech, writing, music, art, or symbolism.

The purpose of guaranteeing freedom of expression in our society is manifest. It assures the individual the right to express himself or herself; to realize one's character and potentialities as a human being. It provides, through discussion and debate, an important method for discovering the truth, or at least reaching a better judgment. It is essential for citizen participation in the governmental process and in other kinds of public decision making. And it provides a method by which conflicts in a society can be resolved without resort to force, thereby maintaining a healthy balance between stability and change. In serving these functions the right to freedom of expression is the cornerstone of all individual rights. Without freedom of expression all the other guarantees of the Bill of Rights would be meaningless or impossible of achievement.

The idea of freedom of expression goes back a long way in human history—at least to the Greek city states. Its present form took shape in the context of Adam Smith and laissez-faire. It has developed to its current point under a system of constitutional liberalism. As we move toward the year 2000, it must adjust to the conditions of a more complex and more collectivist society. The concept, however, is universal and not tied to any particular form of political or economic organization. It continues to be a vital instrument in mankind's search for achieving the proper balance between individual freedom and collective obligation.

In order to consider the status of the right to freedom of expression in the year 2000 it is first necessary to make some basic assumptions concerning the nature of our society at that time. Then the changes in the substantive doctrines of the First Amendment that may be required to adjust to the new conditions should be examined. Thirdly, we need to look at the institutions and other mechanisms that will be essential for realizing an effective system of freedom of expression in actual practice.

It should be noted at the outset that the suggestions to follow will not be so much prediction of things to come as perhaps hopelessly utopian prescriptions of what ought to happen.

ASSUMPTIONS

The assumptions made here deal primarily with those features of our society that have the most direct bearing upon the First Amendment. No attempt will be made to justify them; they will merely be stated.

In order to pose the issues sharply the assumptions are deliberately extreme. Society may not move that fast. The assumptions stated do represent, however, a judgment of the direction in which society is most likely to advance.

In general, the process of change probably will be one of gradual evolution rather than violent revolution. Beyond this, no attempt is made to outline the series of events by which the state of affairs assumed to exist in the year 2000 will be reached. Inevitably the circumstances of development will mould the conditions of the future.

The Political-Economic Structure

By the year 2000 our society will have become primarily collective rather than laissez-faire in character. This means there will be extensive government intervention in the economic structure, less reliance upon a free market as a method of social control, widespread government planning and direct control of major industry, and an end of free enterprise on any substantial scale. In short, the country will be at, or well advanced toward, some American form of socialism.

This economic structure involves a number of political changes that are directly related to maintaining a system of freedom of expression. Government powers will of course be vastly increased. The official bureaucracy will grow in size and, very likely, in rigidity, impersonality, and centralization. The economic base from which individuals and associations (mainly business corporations) have been in a position to control or oppose government will be greatly diminished. Pressures for efficiency in government, for making and implementing hard decisions, will be powerful. All of this entails both dangers and promises.

The Technology of Communication

Vast changes will take place in the technology of communication. These will include the development of satellite communication, cable systems, inexpensive computers for use in the home, linkage to computer networks, recording systems, facsimile, and various automation devices. The net effect will be an enormous increase in the facilities for communication and an unparalleled expansion of the forms and purposes of communication.

The new facilities will be available for citizen to citizen communication, not a monopoly of the few who own and operate the radio and television stations. Thus not only will access to traditional broadcasting be open to virtually every person or group, but community to community or group to group exchange and discussion will be possible. The facilities will also be available for the citizen to communicate with government and for government to communicate with the citizen. Thus public opinion on any issue will be rapidly obtained or an instant referendum will be conducted. Citizen complaints will be quickly registered. Moreover, communication will no longer be unilateral but will be two-way. Thus proposed government policies will be able to be sent down the ladder for citizen reaction, returned for revision, sent down again for further reaction, and returned to the top for final promulgation. Or the process could be the reverse, with the initiation of policy emanating from below. In short, unprecedented opportunities for citizen participation in the system of free expression will be available, as well as unprecedented opportunities for government participation.

Accompanying the expansion of facilities for communication will be an increase in the amount of information available. The new technology has already created a nationwide, even worldwide, system of data banks. The existence of this information can readily shift the balance of forces in a society, depending upon who has access to the information and who is qualified, by education or otherwise, to make use of it. The accumulation of information can enhance the effectiveness of citizen participation in the system of freedom of expression, and it can permit greater decentralization of power, but it can also lead to other results.

The Social Structure

Two changes in the social structure of society in the year 2000 are assumed. One pertains to the value system of the individual; the other to the value system of the collective.

There will be some alteration in the basic ethic of the ordinary citizen from a set of values based on personal gain or profit to one based upon a greater sense of social obligation. This does not mean that material incentives will be totally eliminated, but simply that a consciousness of social responsibility will play a primary rather than a distinctly secondary role. Such a state of affairs would bolster the element of toleration in the system of freedom of expression (and perhaps add to the element of rationality).

It is assumed that the state will rely for social control less on sheer coercion and the operations of the marketplace and more on education, propaganda, and other methods of persuasion. This entails the possibility of a less violent and more planned society, but also a more manipulative one. It would mean greater participation by government in the system of freedom of expression, but also greater reliance upon the system of free expression as a governing force.

Other Assumptions

A number of other trends in our society will have important effects, though perhaps more indirect ones, upon the operation of the system of freedom of expression in the year 2000. First of all, while the matter is subject to dispute, it seems likely that there will be an end to unlimited economic expansion, forced upon us by the need to limit population, the exhaustion of resources, the impact of technology upon the environment, and similar factors. This will mean that conflicts in our society can no longer be resolved through distribution of the same shares of an ever-increasing pool of material goods. Secondly, the same phenomenon will exist on a worldwide scale, thereby putting the relatively affluent nations under heavy pressure from the have-not nations. Thirdly, the development of nuclear power and the existence of nuclear weapons will create security problems that will tend to force us into a closed rather than an open society. All these factors could have serious adverse results for a system of freedom of expression.

On the other hand, some trends are favorable. Thus the increase in leisure time would seem to promote greater interest in, and greater use of, free expression, including more citizen participation in the conduct of public affairs.

CHANGES IN SUBSTANTIVE DOCTRINE

Taking into account the foregoing assumptions, what developments in the law of the First Amendment are likely to occur by the year 2000? The task will be to explore what changes are necessary in order to maintain a healthy system of freedom of expression under the conditions prevailing in the year 2000. What will be the major points of pressure on the system and the major new problems that will have to be faced?

Direct Prohibition of Expression

Under current First Amendment doctrine, where expression as distinct from action is involved, the government has no power (with a few narrow exceptions). This means specifically that, first, the government cannot punish expression that challenges even the basic fabric of society, no matter how obnoxious, dangerous, unethical, or irrational others may feel such expression to be. Thus expression that is totalitarian, racist, offensive, or stirs to anger is nevertheless protected. Only action is punishable. Second, the government may not prohibit expression that is critical of the government, its officials, or the way it is carrying on its duties, no matter how difficult such expression may make the conduct of government business. Third, the government may not censor literature, art, music, or other cultural activities (apart from obscenity or offensive words used on radio or television), no matter how distasteful or "subversive" they may seem. Fourth, the law must draw a careful boundary between expression that is protected by the First Amendment and conduct that involves violence or other violation of law. The current doctrine is that only speech that is designed to and likely to incite imminent lawless action may be restricted. These principles are not always adhered to in practice, but they nevertheless constitute the bedrock of the First Amendment's protection to freedom of expression.

In the year 2000 there will undoubtedly be serious pressures, greater than at any time in our history, to soften these basic principles. As to the first, powerful forces will surely seek to contract the outer boundaries of expression by prohibiting speech that challenges the underlying political, economic, or social structure, and by limiting protection to speech that deals with issues that are more immediate and local and more within the framework of accepted policy. Such has always been the natural tendency of government officials and, indeed, of all persons wielding power. There will be intensified demands for restraint in the year 2000 on the ground that unity and cooperation are essential in making and administering the difficult decisions necessary to solve the critical problems of the times. Efforts to limit freedom of expression to less far-reaching issues will also emanate from the purest of motives, such as the desire to develop a social consciousness to replace private gain and material incentives. Even the attempt by government to use persuasion rather than coercion in attaining its goals does not necessarily encourage popular participation in the determination of those goals or tolerance toward those who question or oppose them.

The rule against limiting expression that makes the conduct of government operations more difficult is likely also to come under attack. The more complex the system of government control gets, the more vulnerable it is to criticism. And the more bureaucratic the process becomes, the less likely are government officials to tolerate or allow such criticism.

As to cultural censorship, there is always a strong inclination to invoke it when the impact of cultural activities upon the attitudes and moods of a society stirs official concern. Moreover, the Supreme Court, in its obscenity decisions, has left a gaping hole in the system of freedom of expression through which censorship could readily be imposed on any expression not considered to have "redeeming social value."

The task of drawing the line between legitimate expression and conduct that involves violation of law is always a troublesome one. It becomes more difficult as the number of laws capable of violation increases and the structure of controls grows more complex. Here again the Supreme Court's concept of "incitement," which punishes some conduct that is still expression and has not reached the stage of action, leaves open a serious loophole. It may well be that, in order to maintain an effective system of free expression, the doctrine of "incitement" should at least be limited to situations where the violation of law consists of physical violence.

The pressures that will be generated by the year 2000 to relax these four foundation principles of the First Amendment must be resisted. Weakness at any point will destroy the system of freedom of expression. Hopefully supporters of the system will recognize the dangers and be prepared to avoid them.

Indirect Controls Over Expression

Government control of expression through indirect means, by imposing qualifications upon the right to obtain privileges or benefits from the government, has been a significant problem in the United States during the last several decades. At various times the right to be an officer of a labor union, to practice law, to obtain government employment, to receive tax or welfare benefits, and the like have been denied because of political beliefs, opinions, or associations. Such restrictions have a grave impact on freedom of expression; a person or group is theoretically free to exercise First Amendment rights but is punished for doing so. The courts have never resolved the First Amendment issues at stake in a satisfactory way. They have normally applied a balancing test under which the interests of the government in imposing the qualifications are weighed against the interests of the individual or group in engaging in political expression. In many cases the qualifications have been found invalid, but in some they have been upheld. The more ardent supporters of the First Amendment have contended that no such qualifications should be permitted where the effect is to discourage freedom of expression.

In the year 2000 this problem will undoubtedly be accentuated, and its solution will be more difficult. Greater government intervention will create more situations where individuals and groups are dependent upon government benefits or where government permission must be obtained. At the same time these individuals and groups will be less able to carry on their affairs without meeting government requirements and will be less likely to possess an economic base independent of government power. A much larger proportion of the population will actually be in the employ of the government.

In general the principle adopted should be that government benefits or privileges cannot be withheld because of political ideas, opinions, associations, or activities, where such action would have a substantial adverse impact upon freedom of expansion. It would seem very likely, however, that in the application of this principle, there would be more situations in which political views and activities could legitimately be taken into account. In a collectivist society there could well be more occasions where social controls could not be effectively administered by persons holding completely unorthodox opinions pertaining to the job to be done. Thus a person having strong views in favor of returning to laissez-faire would not function well as director of a nationalized industry. Nor would refusal to put such a person in that position be considered a substantial infringement upon freedom of expression.

Clearly minimum rights to food, shelter, some type of employment, and the other necessities of life should not be conditioned in any way on political beliefs, opinions, associations, or activities. Nor should the right to education, although there might be some debate concerning certain specialized types of advanced education. But more positions in the public service, where important policies are made, might be subject to qualifications that would include political viewpoints. If the basic principle were accepted, and the lines carefully drawn in applying it, the system of freedom of expression would not suffer.

The Right of Association

Our present organization of society is distinctly pluralist. Numerous groups of different kinds are organized into associations designed to protect and advance their own interests. This is a vital feature of the system of freedom of expression. The lone individual in a complex world is often powerless. Under many circumstances the only method by which the single person can effectively exercise the right of expression is through combining with others of like mind.

Existing law protects this right of association. The individual has the right to form, join, and participate in an association. The association has the right to engage in various activities so long as they are otherwise lawful. Insofar as these activities constitute expression, the association has roughly the same rights under the First Amendment as the individual has. In practice, of course, these rights to freedom of association have not always been fully realized. Thus the doctrines of conspiracy and guilt by association have sometimes been used to curtail associational rights. In general, however, the right of association has been recognized by our law and plays a significant role in the democratic process.

The legal rights of an individual within the association, however, are relatively limited under present law. On the whole, constitutional protections do not apply; they are available only against "state action," not against nongovernmental centers of power. Some legislation to safeguard individual rights within associations has been enacted, such as the Labor Management Reporting and Disclosure Act. But the area of legal protection remains narrow.

Many people argue that a collectivist society cannot be a pluralist one. They point out that the private economic sector, which now supplies the principal base for pluralism, will be greatly diminished and many of its functions taken over by the public sector. They also assert that the difficulties of organizing a modern technological society—the needs of "mobilization for survival"—do not permit the luxury of multiple associations carrying on activities independent of the government.

There is no question that retention of the right of association does pose a major problem for a collectivist society. Pluralism is not conducive to efficient operations in the technological sense. Yet it is clear that the system of freedom of expression cannot function without recognition of the right of association. The individual citizen alone, pitted against the governing authorities, cannot maintain that balance of freedom and social obligation that is the mark of a democratic state. With the economic base for independence diminished in a collectivist society, the right of association becomes the principal foundation from which to maintain the individual's position against government power and the abuses of government bureaucracy. Moreover, in the long run a society that embraces pluralism, at least up to a point, is better prepared to adjust to change and to correct its mistakes, thereby becoming a more likely candidate for ultimate survival. It may be added that the end of unlimited economic expansion would, in this respect, support the system of free expression; for it would reduce the pressures for technical economic efficiency and perhaps allow other values to take on a higher priority than before. In any event, the right of association, in much its present form, must be maintained.

At the same time the rights of the individual within the association must be expanded. The association as a center of power may affect the life of an individual member to an even greater extent than the formal government does. The individual should therefore possess rights against the association in the same way he or she claims rights against the government. These rights, however, will not be identical. The relationship of a member to an organization is not quite the same as that of a citizen to the whole society, and the member's rights will be somewhat more circumscribed. Formulation of detailed rules of law in this area poses an important problem for our society as it moves toward the year 2000.

Government Secrecy and the Right to Know

The First Amendment embodies a right to know. The obverse of the right to communicate, the right to know includes the right to receive communications, the right to gather information for dissemination to others, and a limited right to obtain information in the possession of the government. This constitutional guarantee is still in embryonic form, particularly with respect to the right to compel disclosure of government information. It has been supplemented, however, by various kinds of legislation, the most important of which are the freedom of information acts, the sunshine laws, and the reporter's shield laws.

By the year 2000, the right to know should be further developed and its scope more broadly extended. The right to obtain information is crucial to citizen participation in a collectivist society. Thus the successful utilization of new techniques for two-way communication between citizen and government depends upon widespread dissemination of information, ideas, and opinions. Moreover, in order to forestall a government monopoly of information, severe limits must be placed upon government secrecy. Generally speaking, all government business should be public business. Any exceptions, such as may be necessary with respect to military tactics or diplomatic negotiations, should be very specific and very narrow.

Access to the Means of Communication

A major weakness in the present system of freedom of expression is the control of the mass media by a small group representing very much the same economic, political, and social interests. This monopoly of access to the most powerful facilities for communication is due in part to economic factors, as in the case of the large newspapers. As to radio and television, however, there is an additional factor, namely the physical limitations due to the lack of sufficient wavelengths or channels to accommodate all who wish to communicate. It is this scarcity of physical facilities that furnishes the constitutional basis for government regulation of the electronic media through licensing, the fairness doctrine, and other ways which would not be permissible in the case of the print media. Such regulation, however, has not reached the point of providing equal access for persons or groups who do not own or control broadcasting stations.

Technology will have eliminated the physical scarcity well before the year 2000. Hence there will no longer be any constitutional basis for government regulation of the content of communication by the electronic media; government control will be restricted to engineering problems. Equally important, the new technology will allow virtually unlimited access to all individuals and associations seeking to use the facilities. Both developments will greatly strengthen the system of freedom of expression. Newcomers will have to find or develop their own audience but, aside from that, there will be unfettered communication between citizens on a scale never before possible. Such a development will go a long way toward securing individual rights against government authority and toward countering government monopoly of the communication of information, ideas, and opinions.

Another important result of the new communications technology will be the creation of facilities for two-way communication between citizens and government. Citizens will be able more readily to inform the government of their needs and desires. And the government can more readily test out proposed policies and practices within the community itself. The result will be an unprecedented opportunity for citizen participation in public affairs. The two-way system, in which the citizen will exercise freedom of choice, could fulfill many of the functions now performed by the system of prices operating in a free market. It is conceivable that these changes in the methods of communication and the role of the citizen could reinvigorate the whole democratic process.

Affirmative Government Action

In general the system of freedom of expression is a laissez-faire system. Extensive government control over the system is a contradiction in terms. There are, of course, some points at which government intervention is necessary to keep the system in operation. Thus, some collective authority must protect those who wish to communicate from violence or disruption by those who oppose the speaker's views, must allocate scarce physical facilities, must regulate the time and place of demonstrations, and must perform similar functions. In addition, government action of a more affirmative nature, such as providing public funds for election campaigns or subsidies for cultural events, may be proper where it does not involve such a degree of control as to impair freedom of expression. Moreover, actual government participation in the system, consisting of government statements, reports, public education, and the like, already takes place on a large scale. At the present time there are few constitutional or other legal rules that regulate affirmative government actions pertaining to the system of freedom of expression.

In a collectivist society the system of freedom of expression will have to remain essentially a laissez-faire system. A greater degree of affirmative government support, however, can be expected as funds derived from the private economic sector diminish. Likewise, as the government turns from coercion and the free market to persuasion as a means of social control, increased participation by the government is inevitable. It will therefore be crucial that principles be developed to deal with the new situation. Such principles must be designed to make provision for government support of non-government expression that may be critical of the government itself; to prevent improper discrimination between beneficiaries of government support because of their ideas or opinions; and, in some situations where the government possesses a monopoly or near monopoly over an area of expression, as in the field of education, to require some balance in the presentation of information and opinion. Needless to say, this will be an enormously difficult task.

Freedom of Expression and Science

Under our present system of freedom of expression, scientific exploration and research have enjoyed a high degree of freedom. There have been indirect limitations imposed through government classification of information relating to national security and through the process of government funding. On the whole, however, there has been substantially more freedom for scientific than for political or even cultural expression.

This almost total freedom for science is now under attack. Questions are being raised concerning the responsibility of scientists for the impact of their discoveries upon the community and upon the world. Specifically, doubts have been raised about the operations of scientists in the area of recombinant DNA molecule research, psychosurgery, artificial insemination, cloning of humans, and research for warfare. Some regulations and guidelines are making their appearance.

By the year 2000 these problems will undoubtedly have become more acute. It is difficult to forecast what the results will be but some basic principles, as valid for 2000 as they are for 1982, can be stated. Under the First Amendment no limits should be placed upon the right to pursue knowledge and expound ideas in any field of science. The main issue then concerns scientific experimentation. Experimentation has always been an integral part of the development of new information and theory. In this aspect it must be considered expression and protected under the First Amendment. Yet at times experimentation has the effect of action and must be so treated. Certain kinds of experiments with nuclear materials would clearly pose a serious threat to the safety or health of the surrounding population. Other experiments may involve dangers to human subjects or an invasion of their privacy. Under these circumstances government controls are surely justified. The problem then becomes an appraisal of the facts and a decision upon where to draw the line.

Freedom of Expression and Privacy

One of the principal concerns with the growth of our technological society has been the threat to privacy. Increasing population, greater government intervention in formerly private affairs, collection and storage of data in computers, and many other features of modern life have made the quest for some protection against invasions of privacy a very urgent one. Here again the problem is bound to intensify by the year 2000. For example, the technology of two-way communication raises the specter of the government not only having a record of the votes and opinions of each citizen but also having the mechanism for constant surveillance of activities inside the home.

The function of privacy in a democratic society is to protect the dignity and autonomy of the individual citizen in his or her relations with the collective. In most respects the right of privacy is not incompatible with the right to freedom of expression. Both rights basically serve the same ends and both are indispensable features of a system of individual rights. Nevertheless at certain points conflict does exist. The two major issues concern the right to publish information about the private affairs of a person and the right to obtain data from the government that discloses information about such private affairs. The Supreme Court has never addressed these problems in full, and existing law is uncertain and confused.

The basic principles that should guide development of the law in this area are implicit in the nature of the two rights. The purpose of establishing a right to privacy is to protect the individual against intrusion by the collective, that is, to establish a zone in which the individual is autonomous and the outside world may not enter. It follows that the rules of the society for safeguarding freedom of expression, like other rules of the collective, may not be invoked to override claims to privacy. The problem therefore reduces itself to defining the concept of privacy; once it has been determined that a right of privacy exists then that right should be entitled to full protection. Thus far we have not made much progress in formulating a legal definition of privacy. But the task is not impossible, and by the year 2000 it may well have been successfully completed.

ADMINISTRATION OF THE SYSTEM

It is one thing to prescribe the substantive principles that should constitute the system of freedom of expression in the year 2000. It is more difficult to visualize the measures that need to be taken in order to assure realization of those principles in actual practice. It is unnecessary to emphasize the difficulties: Government will occupy a dominant position; the economic base from which to oppose the government will be curtailed; pressure for conformity will be enormous; and so on. Hope must be placed upon the traditions of our nation, a widely shared acceptance of the principles making up the system, and a pervading insistence upon the values that the system seeks to achieve. Almost certainly a basic shift from the ethic of personal profit to an ethic of social responsibility will be necessary for ultimate success.

Whether these conditions will prevail remains to be seen. It is not possible here to do more than note some of the institutions and methods that now exist or can be created to secure support for effective operation of the system.

Most important of all, an understanding of the principles underlying the system of freedom of expression must be incorporated into the socialization process. This means primarily that the values, the history, the concepts, and the procedures that constitute the system must be taught in the public schools, as well as in the family, church, and community. The system of freedom of expression is a sophisticated one. It must be learned. And it must be learned anew by each generation.

The major institutional support for the system of freedom of expression will undoubtedly continue to be the judicial branch of government. The judiciary is set up to be independent of the legislative and executive branches. It is headed by judges trained to deal with general principles and free from many of the political pressures of the day. It is staffed by persons experienced in the resolution of controversies. It is backed by a long tradition of applying constitutional principles to safeguard individual rights against government power. The judiciary, of course, often falls short of this ideal. Moreover, its usefulness is lessened by excessive delays, high costs, and other problems. Presumably some of these difficulties can be overcome by the year 2000. Certainly its role by then will be even more crucial than now.

In the year 2000 the principal institutional base for expressing dissent will most likely be voluntary, nonprofit associations organized around various economic, political, and cultural interests and issues. These associations will probably not have the support of large aggregates of private wealth. Rather, they will be financed by contributions of individual members who will be assured of their minimum material wants irrespective of their political or other views. Some of the associations might be funded, in whole or in part by public money, under rules that would leave them free to express dissenting opinions. The operations of the associations will be facilitated by ready two-way communication with their members and by access to the public at large.

The chief institution devoted to expressing criticism of society in its broadest aspects will probably be the universities. The universities inherit a tradition of scholarship going back to medieval times. They function as an academic community, subject to professional discipline. Through development of the principles of academic freedom, they have established a structure for individual and collective independence in the search for knowledge and truth. At the present time they constitute the principal institution receiving government funds under conditions that permit an appreciable degree of freedom from government orthodoxy. As in the case of the judiciary, the universities have by no means measured up to the standards that would be hoped for in the year 2000. They have not been sufficiently independent of government authority or private sources of funding, and at times they have been inordinately out of touch with the outside community. Nevertheless, they contain the potential to operate as the "fifth estate" in a future society.

A critical problem for the year 2000 will be to assure the continuance of the functions now performed by the privately owned mass media, namely the gathering and dissemination of worldwide news, investigative reporting, critical observation of government actions, and the like. Both the print and the electronic press will remain in the laissez-faire sector and continue to carry on much the same type of operation as before. But they will no longer be closely tied to private business interests, from which they now derive their major support in the form of advertising revenue, and they will probably not be able to function on their present scale. Their place might be taken in part by publications of voluntary, nonprofit associations.

Unfortunately, the objectivity of news reporting by private interest groups is not of the highest. Private news media could also be supplemented by publicly funded organizations controlled by public trustees. But this device clearly has severe limitations. Hopefully the capacity of the new technology to bring information into the home from many sources, including libraries, universities, and interest groups, will improve the amount, quality, and diversity of information available to the citizen.

Additional institutions and methods for maintaining an effective system of freedom of expression could be utilized. These include the public funding of election campaigns for those candidates who could show a minimum threshold of support, other kinds of public subsidies, and the development of an ombudsman system to give impartial consideration to citizens' complaints that freedom of expression has been infringed. Finally, by the year 2000 we will surely have invented new institutions and techniques we are not now able to envision.

CONCLUSION

Putting all this speculation together, the conclusion is that an effective system of freedom of expression, operating under the aegis of the First Amendment, is possible in the year 2000. Obviously the maintenance of a system of that sophistication, demanding that degree of consensus and social consciousness, will not be easy. It will require deliberate attention, full awareness, and constant effort.

5

HENRY J. ABRAHAM

The Future of First Amendment Protections for Freedom of Speech, Press, and Association

"Do keep in mind that the theme of this book is the *future* of the Bill of Rights in the year 2000," was the explicit admonition of the editor, Stephen C. Halpern. Fully intending to heed that entirely reasonable caveat, it seems to me that in order to protect whatever credibility I may have in the profession, and to cover my proverbial tracks, I might commence by advancing a few caveats of my own:

1. It would be presumptuous to endeavor to venture predictions on the subject a quarter of a century prior to the date at issue, be the putative clairvoyant a professional or layman, a legal expert, or merely an ordinary mortal interested in the abiding and evolving law and philosophy of the Constitution of the United States. But since we have been, in effect, charged with what, *de minimis*, is a very real measure of prognosis, I am prepared to try my hand at it.
2. While I have resolved to do so, although only up to a point, it will not be easy to segregate, let alone compartmentalize, the three nouns to be considered under First Amendment protections, that is, speech, press, and association. They do, and indeed should, run into one another in practical as well as theoretical terms, and what is crucial in the final analysis is their basic overall protection under the blanket provided by the covering concept of "freedom." This does not mean that there are no ascertainable differences of both a protective definition and the application of "speech," "press," and "association"—of course, there are. But I, for one, would hope that all three will always be part and parcel of the fundamental guarantees *cum*

protection of the umbrella of freedom of expression—and, frankly, I wish my assignment had been stated in that fashion. For the compartmentalized trifold subject matter may compel choices that could well be artificial. Yet, at the same time, I confess that the line-drawing inherent in the suggested distinctions is neither radical nor unknown. Many of our foremost libertarians have tried to create such lines, in one fashion or another, however one may judge their success. A poignant illustration is that of my own judicial hero, Justice Hugo Lafayette Black who, for much of the second third of this century (from 1937 to 1971)—or at least a healthy portion thereof—was committed to the proposition of forging and securing the First Amendment's hallowed mandates of freedom of expression, under which he subsumed all three components of this book's subject matter's charge—plus one or two others, depending upon one's count—into an identifiable line or distinction between "expression" and "conduct." Whereas "expression" was thus not only to be guaranteed, but to be guaranteed absolutely, against any interference or abridgment, "conduct" was to be societally proscribable under the tenets of due process of law. Justice Black dedicated much of his jurisprudential efforts toward creating and maintaining that line, often amidst catcalls and sniping, yet it represented a committed and an at least partly predictable approach to the kind of line-drawing that is simply unavoidable in the omnipresent clashes between individual and societal rights, either now or in the year 2000.

3. I shall view and treat the issues at hand from a national perspective, or, to be more precise, a nationwide one in both philosophical and constitutional terms. In other words, although I am not only aware of, but committed to, the federal nature of our governmental structure and process and do believe in the application of the Tenth Amendment's residual powers as tools available to the component states as long as these exist—I assume they will still be here in the year 2000, at least on paper—I regard the guarantees of the Bill of Rights, generally, and the First Amendment, in particular, as national responsibilities and commitments. One of America's foremost early political scientists, John W. Burgess, put the matter succinctly when in 1890 he thus wrote in his classic two-volume work, *Political Science and Comparative Law*:

> I say that if history has taught us anything . . . it is that *civil liberty is national in its origin, content and sanction* . . . if there is but a single lesson to be learned from the history of the United States, it is this: Seventy years of debate and four years of terrible war turn substantially upon this issue, in some part or other; and when the Nation triumphed in the great appeal to arms, and addressed itself to the work of readjusting the forms of law to the now undoubted condition of fact, it gave its first attention to *the nationalization in constitutional law of the domain of civil liberty.*[1]

There are still isolated disclaimers of the nationalization of the provisions of the Bill of Rights, but they have become derelicts on the constitutional ocean. In very considerable measure due to the assertive leadership on the issue by Justice Black, the Bill of Rights—with the exception of five minor provisions[2]—has been made applicable to the several states by judicial interpretation, and the earliest three to be so applied were speech, press, and assembly,[3] now approximately half a century ago. I cannot conceive a departure from that fundamental fact of our constitutional *cum* societal commitments in the year 2000—which is not to say, of course, that specific interpretations of some or all of these rights may not vary somewhat, sometimes, in different settings. For, after all, institutions of government are peopled by human beings, not automatons—and that emphatically applies as well to the judicial branch, which plays the key interpretative role here.

In order to determine where we might be in the year 2000, we must know, at least roughly speaking, where we are now. Hence, summarily and rather briefly, where do we stand on the fronts of protection of speech, press, and assembly? The state of these rights—recalling one of President Harry Truman's first "State of the Nation" addresses to Congress in 1946—is not only good, but very good. Since I am a teacher, if I were to assign grades to the three components—and I like to think of myself as a tough grader—I would assign the top letter grade of "A" to speech and press and "A –" to association, and if I had to rank them in order of protective success, I would place "press" first, "speech" second, and "association" third—again noting along the way my profound objection to the need to separate the three, and particularly speech and press. On the scale of statistics of pronounced and applied constitutional protections of all of the approximately twenty-five of our basic rights and/or liberties that are found in our 462-word Bill of Rights—our Constitution does not require a distinction between the nouns "rights" and "liberties," and I do not regard one as either helpful or desirable—those extended to the press are exceeded, if at all, only by those extended to the guarantee of the free exercise of religion (I am speaking here only of "free exercise," not of the more problematical, more complex, other aspect of the religion clauses of the First Amendment, that of separation of Church and State). Not all members of the press may agree, but it is patently clear on the record that, notwithstanding a host of assaults on it from high, medium, and low strata of society and its presumed servant, the state, and the latter's tool, government, press freedom is well protected. Thus its leading collegial organ, *Editor and Publisher*, in printing a list of 136 U.S. Supreme Court decisions adjudicating freedom of speech and press in 1976[4] could proudly point, in summary, to a plethora of victories, all of which—obviously in effect considering them essentially as "press" or at least "communication"—is pronounced as affirming the "guarantees of freedom of speech and press in the First Amendment [as] rights of national citizenship," listing them as follows:

- The liberty of circulating public information may not be infringed.
- Symbolic opposition to the government is protected.
- Courts shall not impose prior restraints on publication.
- A tax on advertising designed to penalize certain publications is illegal.
- Peaceful assembly to protest governmental actions is permissible.
- News writers are free to join unions.
- A license to distribute literature is void.
- An anti-litter ordinance directed against the distribution of reading matter is void.
- Pickets in a labor dispute may carry banners.
- Peaceful picketing in a labor dispute may not be enjoined.
- Commercial advertisements enjoy equal protection with other printed matter.
- Freedom of mind and conscience are protected.
- The Post Office Department shall not have the power of censorship.
- The press shall be free to criticize the Judiciary.

- Judges shall not suppress or edit what transpires at a public trial in court.
- A list of subscribers to a publication may be held confidential.
- Law-making inquiries are restricted.
- A loyalty oath shall not be required to qualify for a tax exemption.
- Anonymity may be safeguarded for peaceful discussion of public matters.
- Jurors need not be totally ignorant of the facts in a case.
- A paid ad expressing editorial opinion is protected.
- The public conduct of public officials is subject to press criticism.
- The press is free to report proceedings in open court.
- Newspapers may publish political editorials on Election Day.[5]

Although it is a far from complete coverage of the current constitutional law governing the freedom of the press, it is assuredly a manifest of its impressively broad and liberal range.

At the moment two aspects of press freedom provide concern and are by their very nature neither facilely analyzable nor lend themselves to that always incumbent line-drawing between individual and community rights and privileges. One is the realm of libel, the other that of finding accommodations between freedom of the press and fair trial. The former is not inevitably part and parcel of the formal concept of freedom of the press, for the publishing press is not necessarily always the conduit in libel cases, since a libel may be comprised in, say, a crude homemade handbill (although it, too, is not without constitutional protection as an element of free speech) and freedom of the press is not at all at issue in libel's oral relative, slander. But since libel, in order to be libel, ipso facto requires the publication of a printed statement or representation via such means as television or radio tapes, press freedom is involved in theory and in fact. He or she, who endeavors to pinpoint what the current status of the law of libel vis-à-vis freedom of the press is, is a brave soul, indeed. But broadly speaking, the Supreme Court now appears to be suggesting the following: a *public* official or even a public "figure"—although the 1976 *Firestone* decision[6] raised some doubt as to the "figure" coverage—is not entitled to damages unless he or she can prove "actual malice," that is, prove that the defamatory statement was made "with knowledge that it was false or with reckless disregard of whether it was false or not"—which, rather than simple truth or falsehood, thus becomes the test.[7] Furthermore, only those false statements made with a "high degree of awareness of their probative falsity," may be the subject of either civil or criminal sanction[8]—which, however, does not mean that in *no* circumstances will a public official be judicially found to have been libeled.[9] Although the test would seem to be less stringent in the case of private or quasi-private persons,[10] the line remains a somewhat ambiguous one.[11] The Court in 1971 did extend its free press doctrine to *news* "about private individuals involved in matters of public or general interest"[12]—which renders collection of damages extremely difficult—only to distinguish, probably even to overrule, that decision three years later when it narrowly held that an ordinary citizen "elevated to sudden prominence by news events" can sue any newspaper or radio or television station that circulated a false and defamatory account of his role in those events. Thus, by 1974 the Court had drawn a seemingly sharp distinction between an ordinary citizen libeled by a news account and "public officials and public figures [who] have voluntarily exposed themselves to incurring risk or injury from defamatory falsehoods."[13] The new doctrine raised doubts about such famed past (1967) decisions as *Time, Inc. v. Hill*,[14] in which "newsworthiness" had narrowly triumphed over "privacy." However, in 1975 an 8 to 1 majority, striking down a Georgia law that made it a misdemeanor to print or broadcast the name of a rape victim and barring the right of the victim or her parents to invoke "invasion of privacy" as a basis for a suit, held that the media cannot be subjected to either civil or criminal liability for disseminating accurately data that are available from public law enforcement records.[15] Moreover, the Court ruled five to three in 1976 that "reputation" is neither "liberty" nor "property" for purposes of an alleged civil rights violation.[16] Justices Black and William Douglas, of course, had no problems in the realm of libel: They considered an "unconditional right to say what one pleases about public affairs to be the *minimum* guarantee" under Amendments One and Fourteen.[17]

The second sector of freedom of the press that is, quite understandably, vexatious philosophically and extremely difficult in terms of finding a viable line-drawing solution, is that ubiquitous dichotomy of freedom of the press and the right to a fair trial. "The basis of our government being the opinion of the people, the first object shall be to keep that right; and were it left for me to decide whether we should have a government without newspapers or newspapers without government, I should not hesitate a moment to choose the latter." So wrote Thomas Jefferson in 1787.[18] But even the embrace of that noble statement by the revered sage of Monticello does not gainsay the need to face the reality of difficult and timely line-drawing. Thus, where *does* one draw the line between the right of a free press to comment and criticize and the duty of the judiciary to ensure a fair trial? A plethora of problems is involved here if the aim is, as it should be, to find a golden rule that will ascertain a fair trial to the accused and yet ascertain the presence and transmittal of the case's denouement to the public. Hence, to what extent and in what tenor may the press criticize a judge's conduct of a trial versus the presiding judge's prerogative of adjudging such criticisms to be contumacious? To what extent may a presiding judge enjoin the press from reporting aspects of an ongoing trial by imposing so-called "gag" orders in the interest of providing that trial's necessary fairness? Is there really a constitutionally protected right to conduct *ex parte* public trials in the press, on the radio, or on television? And, may reporters refuse to provide to a court for evidentiary use in a trial data gathered from confidential sources that are deemed vital to the proceedings to bring about a fair trial? These four questions—quite apart from such collateral ones as those presented in the 1978 police search case involving the *Stanford Daily*[19]—are just a few of the continuing uncertainties that surround what may be identified as the second area of still uncertain and unsolved, and perhaps unsolvable, components of freedom of press. How, briefly, has the judiciary pronounced the constitutional law in each of these four realms?

In the first of these, the Supreme Court, although rarely unanimous on the issue, has not had great difficulty in upholding the right of the organized press[20]—or, for that matter the right of any public or private commentator[21]—not only to be critical of the conduct of a trial but to be unfairly and even intemperately and inaccurately so.[22] But the Court has not hesitated to strike down convictions of accused individuals solely on the grounds of prejudicial pre-trial publicity—thus emphasizing the intriguing collateral question of the impact of broad press freedom on the individual on trial rather than its impact upon the tribunal itself.[23] As to the second issue in the free press/fair trial wrench, the matter of the right of presiding judges to impose "gag" orders as a means to assure fair trial: while appellate courts have encouraged and sanctioned reasonably imposed restraints[24] and while sundry American Bar Association-created or -supported committees have tried to establish rules of procedure that both the bar and the press could and would follow,[25] in the controlling case on the issue, a widely reported grisly multiple murder in which the Nebraska trial judge had imposed far-reaching gag orders, the U.S. Supreme Court ruled unanimously that, "in general" judges may not impose such orders on the press that forbid publication of information about criminal cases—even if, as here, Judge Stuart's considered opinion had been that his orders would bring about a fair trial by preventing prejudicial publicity.[26] But an indication of the cloudy future of the issue is that, although the Court was unanimous in overruling Judge Harold Stuart, the separate opinions written by five Supreme Court Justices in the case evinced considerable line-drawing difficulties, pointing to the obvious fact that there are no easy solutions here.

Regarding the third issue, that of the press going "whole hog," as it were, in conducting what, in effect constitutes the *ex parte* conduct of a trial in the public media, the Court, although again not without considerable difficulties in at least the first of two notorious cases,[27] made clear that the constitutional requirements of due process of law cannot be overridden by such freedom of press claims as those that attended the snake-pit television atmosphere which obtained during the pre-trial proceedings of Texas "wheeler-dealer" Billie Sol Estes[28] and the zoo-like courtroom conditions permitted to the press by an up-for-election trial judge in the sensational trial of Cleveland osteopath, Dr. Samuel H. Sheppard.[29] Yet in both cases that consistent champion of absolute press freedom, Justice Black, dissented from the reversals of the convictions—although in the Sheppard case he merely noted, "Mr. Justice Black dissents"—as if he had been almost embarrassed to be compelled to stick by his guns, given the facts of the proceedings.[30] Fourth and last, the delicate issue of reportorial claims of protected sources of information: although again severely divided[31] on the merits of the problem, the Court has repeatedly stuck to its seminal 5 to 4 decision, handed down in the 1976 case of a *New York Times* reporter who refused to divulge the identity of some confidential Black Panther sources to a grand jury, that is, that there is no such thing as a First Amendment freedom of the press prerogative to deny to properly constituted tribunals evidence needed in the judicial process to assure the conduct of a trial fair to both accused and accuser.[32] From 1972–1978 there were about forty contempt orders against reporters—highlighted by the case of *New York Times* reporter Myron A. Farber—resulting in more than a dozen actual jailings of reporters that lasted from just hours to weeks.[33]

Leaving freedom of the press until the later-to-be essayed prognostication stage of these ruminations, some words about the overarching parent issue of freedom of speech are in order. In an attempt to find out what its constitutional parameters are, where we stand, and where we might go, some basic concepts need to be advanced. In its overall concept, freedom of speech connotes the broad freedom to communicate—a concept that, with due respect to the specifications of my assignment's topical first noun, far transcends mere speech. For it embraces the prerogative of the free citizen to express himself verbally, visually, or on paper, without prior restraint, and, if the expression meets the test of truth, or at least nonmaliciousness, even to the postutterance period. Thus it is crucial to perceive that freedom of speech protection comprehends not only speaking and writing as speaking and writing but also, of course, the aforediscussed press sector; freedom of petition; of association (which is listed as a separate element in my essay's charge, and I shall try to treat it as such); of assembly, including lawful picketing and demonstrative protests; since 1976 apparently, too, of independent *spending* by and for a candidate for federal elective office, but not in the form of unlimited contributions;[34] to purely "commercial" speech;[35] to the right of professional association-rule-bound lawyers (and, by implication, other professions) to advertise their professional fees, at least on a limited, factual basis;[36] and, astonishingly, to the time-honored practice of dismissal of public employees, although only below the policymaking level, because of their political beliefs.[37] The Supreme Court's ruling in the latter case voided a patronage practice as old as the nation itself.

Yet, since none of these freedoms can be absolute, with due respect to Justice Black, any basic definition must consider the inevitability of limits—limits that recognize the rights of the minority in a majoritarian system, without, however, subscribing to a philosophy of the "tyranny of the minority." Thus, the Court has repeatedly pointed out that the First Amendment does not "afford the same kind of freedom" to communicate conduct as to that which it extends to "pure speech."[38] There is no doubt that picketing, for example, is a vital prerogative of the freedom of expression; mass picketing, however, or picketing that applies physical force to those who might wish to exercise their equal rights of freedom of expression by disregarding the picket line, is not.[39] Screaming "fire" in a crowded theater—to use the famed Holmesian illustration—upon discovery of a blaze is not only "freedom of speech" but a dutiful exercise of citizenship; yet if there is no fire, the call is not freedom of expression but license. Actual, overt incitement of the overthrow of the government of the United States by force and violence, accompanied by the language of direct incitement, is not freedom of expression, but a violation of Court-upheld legislative proscriptions; yet the theoretical advocacy of such overthrow on the other hand has been a judicially recognized protected freedom since 1957.[40] If a written work has "literary, artistic, scientific, or political value it is not proscribable as being" pornographic,[41] but this safeguard may be lost by virtue of its publisher's "pandering."[42] Publicly addressing someone as "damned Fascist" and "Goddamned racketeer" can hardly be considered as freedom of speech—in fact, those terms have been judicially held to be "fighting words" that are proscribable if (and it is a big "if") the proscribing statute is carefully and narrowly drawn[43]—but calling a duly convicted thief, "thief" or "crook" presumably can, at least until the epithet's target has paid his or her debt to society.

As a further illustration of the elusiveness of drawing the line for freedom of speech: petitioning and demonstrating against the draft are both bona fide manifestations of freedom of expression, but the burning of draft cards is not.[44] "We cannot accept the view," wrote Chief Justice Earl Warren in the leading case for his 7 to 1 Court, with only Justice Douglas in dissent, "that an apparently limitless variety of conduct can be labelled 'speech.' "[45] Justice Hugo Black, who drew the line at "conduct" rather than "expression," was in the majority here. And he strongly dissented from the Court's 7 to 2 holding, just a year later, that the wearing of black armbands by high school students constituted constitutionally protected "symbolic" free speech.[46] Only Justice Harlan sided with him in what they viewed as a matter of proscribable conduct. Again Black, this time joined in dissent by Justices Abe Fortas, Byron White, and Chief Justice Warren, saw as proscribable conduct rather than symbolic free speech the action of Sidney Street, a Brooklyn bus driver, who, while loudly cursing the American flag, burned it in outrage in 1966 after he had learned that James Meredith, the civil rights activist, had been shot and wounded in an ambush.[47] To compound the difficulties and unpredictabilities of this realm, the majority opinion was written by Justice Harlan who had dissented in the black armband case! (He was joined by Justices Douglas, William Brennan, Potter Stewart, and Marshall.) On the other hand, the Court found no difficulty at all and was in fact unanimous in declaring unconstitutional in 1970 a part of a federal law that barred theatrical performers from wearing a United States military uniform if their role was intended to discredit the armed forces,[48] the law had permitted performances that were laudatory! Appropriately, that classic symbolic freedom of expression opinion was written by Justice Black. But it was by a mere one-vote margin that the Court ruled in 1971 that the display on a jacket of the epithetical phrase "F— the draft" in a corridor of the Los Angeles courthouse is constitutionally protected speech and may not be made a criminal offense[49]—with the Court for the first time spelling out that Chaucerian term (Justice Harlan, of all people!, writing for the Court). Justice Black was one of three dissenters who saw "mainly conduct" and very little "expression" in the display. As he frequently did, Black here evidently drew the line based on his belief that "a law which primarily regulates conduct but which might also indirectly affect speech can be upheld if the effect on speech is minor in relation to the need for control of the conduct."[50]

Throughout our history, law-making and judicial authorities have had to wrestle with these and similar questions—including such, perhaps less than earthshaking, ones (although they do, of course, involve matters of privacy), as the right of public school boards and other public agencies to prescribe the length of the hair sported by those under their aegis[51]—and a welter of both common and statutory law is the result. Limitations, today almost entirely of a statutory nature, are thus present on both the national and state levels of government—a phenomenon almost unknown prior to World War I. Thus, there is scant doubt that Congress has the authority to guard against sedition and subversion[52] and it has asserted it rather widely, especially in periods of national emergency and throughout the Cold War. For example, between 1940 and 1954 it enacted three significant pieces of legislation: the Smith Act of 1940, the Internal Security Act of 1950 (passed over President Truman's veto), and the Communist Control Act of 1954—none of which, to all intents and purposes remains as an active statute today. The problem implicit in this legislation is, of course, where to draw the line between the individual's cherished right to espouse and express unpopular causes and the right of the community to protect itself against the overthrow of government. As the courts have ultimately been called upon to demonstrate time and again—as, for instance, in granting to members of the armed forces a significantly lower degree of protection against the "chilling effect" which broad and vague regulations would normally be viewed as imposing upon the exercise of free speech[53]—democratic society has the right and duty to maintain concurrently both freedom of speech and national security.

To reallude briefly to another area, one in which the states have predominated, what of the matter of prohibiting the sale and dissemination of "obscene" literature? Statutes abound, yet many of these quickly run afoul of First and Fourteenth Amendments safeguards of freedom of expression. To what extent then, may the community protect itself against "obscenity"? Do particular publications possess the "redeeming social value" which presumably underlies the exercise of responsible freedom? Is demonstrable obscenity a "civil right"? The anticipated negative chorus to those rhetorical questions must be discounted at least in part because of hypocrisy and the fiendishly difficult definition of the "obscene." Hence, here again the judicial branch has had to endeavor to draw lines—which it has done more than once by reading the allegedly "obscene" book, and, especially, by viewing the allegedly "obscene" film.[54] Some members of the Court, as was ever true of Justices Black and Douglas, have no problem here. Not only did they not go to those movies—cordially loathing them—but they do not have to. For any prior censorship of the visual (or the written) is a *prima facie* violation of freedom of expression.

Demonstrably, freedom of speech and its protection represent rich analytical fare—it is, as I have suggested, and am convinced, in healthy condition in terms of constitutional protection—which, needless to say, is not the same as saying that every member of society in his or her private capacity feels similarly. Indeed, there are areas in which a majority of the public would be willing to see repressive governmental action, even while conceivably winking at constitutional imperatives. Usually and rather naturally included in these areas are noisy as well as some quiet public demonstrations, especially by unpopular segments of society; zealously proselytizing religious groups that are highly and sometimes annoyingly visible in public places; conscientious military objectors; visible, let alone covert, activities of extremist political groups; what many of us, depending a bit on one's age and broad-mindedness, may regard as pornography, wherein we sometimes differentiate between the "hard-core" (bad) and "soft-core" (not-so-bad) kind; and foul-mouthing and similarly offensive public displays of a lack of civility.

The above allusion to political groups brings us to the third component of the trilogy under discussion, namely the First Amendment's protective mandate for freedom of association. Perhaps oddly, it is not specifically mentioned as one of the sextet of explicitly catalogued First Amendment guarantees—which, in the (slightly paraphrased) order of their enumeration in that primary constitutional mandate, are: nonestablishment of religion, free exercise of religion, freedom of speech, freedom of the press, the right peaceably to assemble, and that same right to petition the government for a redress of grievances. But freedom of association is obviously very much implicit in the several guarantees inherent in that First Amendment, generally, and is most closely derivative from the freedom of speech, assembly, and petition. However, by assigning or leaving the overt actions taken by identifiable associations, such as picketing and demonstrating, to the speech and assembly sectors, it is relatively feasible to find and treat separately the protected freedom of association, with a mere quick approving nod toward the right to petition. For the latter is so obviously accepted, understood, and practiced that governmental interference therewith is simply inconceivable, always assuming, of course, that what is being practiced is indeed the right of petitioning and not, for example, an impermissible verbal or written assault on a judicial body or a resort to libel or slander—as the above treatment of freedom of the press endeavored to elucidate.

In theory, at least, voluntary association and its formalization in a myriad of groups, is a veritable way of life in the United States. Indeed it has been just that ever since the dawn of our Republic, and it represented one of the cardinal stipulations of the raison d'être of the burgeoning American democracy in the eyes of its most articulate and most prescient early observer and commentator, Alexis de Tocqueville. His magnificent *Democracy in America*—which is just as pertinent today, 150 years after he wrote it—dubbed us as "joiners" of groups and associations, and we have not only assuredly retained that designation, but we have usually vigorously combatted certain periodic assaults upon the exercise of that freedom of association. Yet there have been problems, and particularly so as the result of the world's experience with extremist political movements that, sooner or later, inevitably touched our lives and have brought into focus questions of associational choice and freedom. A good many of these movements had their genesis abroad; for example, communism, socialism, fascism, nazism, Maoism, but others were indigenous to our own policy, for example, the Ku Klux Klan, the Know Nothings, and others. Indeed, the fact and concept of subversive activity and how to meet it have concerned the nation sporadically since its birth. From the hated Alien and Sedition Acts of 1798 through the trying eras of the Civil War, World War I, the "red scare" of the 1920s, post-World War II, McCarthyism, and the Cold War, the legislative and administrative remedies adopted to deal with the problem of national security have often been dominant concerns. And the resultant statutes, executive orders, and legislative investigations have almost all, sooner or later, found themselves in judicial hot water, heated by the friction between freedom of speech and association and national security. Answers given by the judicial branch in this area have understandably been more cautious and more circumspect than for any other aspect of the freedom at issue. Nonetheless, as the McCarthy-tinged 1950s turned into the 1960s, the courts became increasingly generous toward the individual's constitutional claims of associational prerogatives. Hence, while necessarily recognizing the right and duty of the legislative branch to keep itself informed in order to legislate more wisely, to keep an eye on the executive branch, and to inform the public, the Supreme Court has also recognized that there are and must be limits on the range and extent of the power to investigate. Among these are the witness's right to decline to respond by invoking the Fifth Amendment's privilege against compulsory self-incrimination, though in many areas he may be compelled to testify in return for immunity from prosecution,[55] to refuse to reply if the question is beyond the investigating committee's mandate,[56] and to have "explicit and clear" knowledge of the subject to which the interrogation is deemed pertinent.[57] Yet as other decisions of the Court have shown, great difficulties here are the matters of "pertinency"[58] and just what constitutes "exposure for the sake of exposure."[59]

Similarly troublesome has been the matter of "loyalty and security." Again, while recognizing the right and obligation of both legislative and executive authorities to ascertain the loyalty to the state of its employees and quasi-employees, the Court has been called upon repeatedly to draw lines between the rights of the individual under the Bill of Rights, which he or she assuredly does not surrender simply because he or she works for the government, and the rights of the state, which has a basic obligation to protect its citizenry from subversion by disloyal elements. Grave problems have surrounded the nature and meaning of the terms "loyalty" and "security," as well as the compatibility of such legislation and ordinances with the prerogatives of free citizens. Avoiding the constitutional issues whenever possible, the Court has handed down several significant guidelines, chiefly by statutory interpretation on the federal level, although it has been quite willing to reach the constitutional issues on the state level. Thus, federal employee loyalty-security regulations, which initially seemed to have a rather free rein, have found themselves increasingly confined in coverage and held to ever more strict requirements of procedural due process.[60] Indeed, at least one key aspect of the issue was more or less settled when a special three-judge federal court ruled in 1969 that the statute on which the then 25-year-old loyalty oath requirement for federal employees was based was "unconstitutionally vague." It was held to be not only a violation of the Fifth Amendment's due process of law clause, but also, in the ruling of the 2 to 1 majority opinion by Judges J. Skelly Wright and Harold Leventhal of the United States Court of Appeals for the District of Columbia, a violation of the strictures against "odious test oaths" inherent in Article VI of the Constitution.[61] When the U.S. Department of Justice decided not to appeal the decision to the Supreme Court, the Civil Service Commission quietly informed all federal departments and agencies that prospective employees would henceforth no longer have to sign the controversial affidavit stating that the applicant was neither a Communist nor a Fascist nor sought to overthrow the United States Government by force and violence.[62] Thus the Supreme Court did not have to rule on the delicate loyalty oath issue in ultimate constitutional terms.

On the other hand, the Warren Court did not duck the constitutional issue in a related matter—namely, the government's policy of barring employment to otherwise qualified individuals merely because of their beliefs and/or associations. While never having wavered from basic erstwhile, and entirely logical holdings that there is no ipso facto constitutional right to work for the government,[63] the Court nonetheless made clear in a series of cases in the late 1960s that the First Amendment is not vitiated simply because someone happens to be or aspires to be a governmental employee. Thus, in 1967, in the *Robel* case, speaking through Chief Justice Warren, the Court by a vote of 6 to 2 declared unconstitutional as a violation of First Amendment rights of freedom of association a provision of the Subversive Activities Control (McCarran) Act of 1950 that made it a crime for members of the Communist party to work in defense plants—regardless of the "quality and degree" of that membership.[64] And the Court extended the aforegone ruling to the maritime industry early in 1968, holding unanimously that Herbert Schneider, a Seattle marine engineer and former Communist party member who had applied for clearance in 1964, could not be barred from employment simply because of his beliefs or associations.[65] The government, wrote Justice Douglas for the Court, has every right to enact legislation to safeguard American shipping from subversive activity, but Congress had not, under the applicable statute—the Magnuson Act of 1950—given the executive branch the power "to ferret out the ideological strays."[66]

A host of state loyalty statutes and allied requirements have fallen on grounds of both substantive and procedural due process, often in concord with freedom of expression guarantees. Thus, while some practices have been upheld as valid exercises of the state policy power—particularly affirmative rather than disclaimer loyalty oaths[67]—others have fallen, more often than not because of the vice of vagueness: the sweeping implications of such terms as "subversive organizations," "subversive persons," or "sympathetic association with. . . ."[68] In fact, state loyalty oaths began to fall like veritable flies as of 1966, and by 1969 the vast majority of the disclaimer-type state oaths as well as "mixed" disclaimer-affirmative types[69] were a thing of the past.[70] And attacks, albeit unsuccessful,[71] have also been launched even against the simple "positive" type.

Here, again, the advocates of maximum security and those who believe that democratic society must take risks for the sake of freedom are at loggerheads. It is far easier to criticize than to solve. And it has been understandably rare for the Court to be unanimous in any cases where the restrictions involved were not clearly and patently unconstitutional.[72] As already indicated earlier, for all intents and purposes the three major federal antisubversive activity statutes of 1940, 1950, and 1954 are now dead letters. Although it took a generational span to write finis to their lives, they were rendered inapplicable or ineffective or both by virtue of political changes, but especially due to the assertiveness of the federal judiciary, with the Supreme Court at its apex, in siding with associational freedom against fear-ridden and often hysterical governmental as well as private "national security" and "antisubversive activity" syndromes. The Communist Control Act of 1954, a child of the height of the McCarthy period, which was written by a handful of liberal Democrats practically on the floor of the Senate in the forlorn hope of combatting the potent forays of the Senator from Wisconsin—who met his Waterloo at the hands of his colleagues in the Senate just a few months later—was never really utilized by the Department of Justice and did not figure in any major litigation, with the Supreme Court dealing with it only highly tangentially in three insignificant instances.[73]

The Subversive Activities Control Act of 1950, known as the McCarran Act after its author, long-time Senator and anti-Communist, Pat McCarran, was heavily involved at the bar of the judiciary. Thus the power of the Subversive Activities Control Board (SACB) to order the registration of Communist action and front groups was soon challenged on Fifth Amendment compulsory self-incrimination freedom of speech and freedom of association defense grounds. The provision's constitutionality was initially sustained by the Court in a 5 to 4 Justice Felix Frankfurter-written opinion that avoided the self-incrimination problem but held the statute not to be violative of the First Amendment. Justices Warren, Black, Douglas, and Brennan dissented vigorously, with Douglas pointing to the associational issue by exclaiming that "our Constitution protects all minorities, no matter how despised they are."[74] Three years later, however, the Court had changed its mind on the Fifth Amendment issue and, by siding with a lower tribunal, struck down the group registration requirement.[75] One year later it knocked out, 6 to 3, on "due process of law" Amendment grounds, the Act's provisions denying passports to members of the American Communist party and its "fronts,"[76] and in the same year it unanimously declared unenforceable the McCarran Act's "individual membership registration" requirements.[77] The SACB continued in existence, attempting to justify itself in a number of ineffective ways, until 1973 when even so staunch a Communist-battler as President Nixon totally denied all funds to it in his budget message to Congress. The McCarran Act itself is still on the books, but at most it is on the shelf in reserve, placed there because of its extreme assaults upon freedom of association without necessary regard for constitutional protection.

The oldest and most impactful of the three antisubversive activities laws, the Smith Act of 1940—initially written primarily to combat the budding internal Axis sympathy threat, but ultimately applied all but exclusively against real and alleged Communists—was repealed by Congress in 1978. But it figured in some memorable line-drawing battles, with its most notable victory coming in the famous 1951 case of *Dennis v. United States*,[78] in which, in a 6 to 2 opinion, written by Chief Justice Frederick Vinson (who based the gravamen of his holding on one issued by Judge Learned Hand of the U.S. Court of Appeals for the Second Circuit), the Smith Act's constitutionality was upheld against charges of infringement of First Amendment guarantees of speech and association (plus Fifth Amendment due process claims). Thus having been found guilty of statutorily-proscribed conspiratorial activities, with Justices Black and Douglas dissenting from the Court's decision, the eleven top leaders of the Communist Party-U.S.A. went to jail and stayed there. As a result of its victory, the Department of Justice proceeded to move to bring about a series of indictments against party members, and by 1957, it had obtained 145 indictments and 89 convictions. But then, a 6 to 1 majority of the Supreme Court, in a trail-blazing opinion by Justice John Marshall Harlan in *Yates v. United States*,[79] pronounced an important distinction to be inherent in the Smith Act: namely, between the statement of a philosophical belief and the advocacy of an illegal action; that, in other words, while it was constitutionally appropriate statutorily to forbid illegal action, that is, as Harlan put it, "to do something, now or in the future," associationally and expressionally protected was the right "merely to believe in something."[80] In effect, the Court, amidst widespread hostile public reaction—after all, the year was 1957, and the Cold War was still raging—had now drawn a line between "theoretical" and "actual" advocacy of hated and feared alien political philosophies, the former First Amendment-safeguarded, the latter not. The Smith Act of 1940 thus still stood, but most of its important teeth had been pulled by Dentist Judiciary. Twenty years later Congress pulled the remaining teeth—which does not mean that the United States retains no weapons against subversive activities. The arsenal exists.

So far, the bulk of this presentation has necessarily dealt with where we have been and/or where we now are on the First Amendment's frontiers of protective freedom of speech, press, and association. But the basic question posed for these thoughts was the future of these hallowed guarantees—specifically, what will they look like in the year 2000? Once again it is obviously vital to note that predictions are hazardous, and I am neither a quantifier nor a soothsayer—nor do I qualify as a behavioralist. Yet in order to proceed one must be prepared to stipulate certain basic future expectations for that year 2000—expectations that are crucial to that educated (I hope) guess as to the shape of things to come for the three freedoms at issue.

First, then, I must and do assume that this nation will still be dedicated to the same general constitutional constellation in which we now function—not, to be sure, in each and every detail, but assuredly in terms of the broad, fundamental commitment to what for want of a better descriptive concept we may style a liberal democratic society, with its dedication to majority rule with close regard for minority rights. Absent such an assumed commitment, we could hardly hope for a continued embrace of the tenets of our Bill of Rights and its philosophical firmament. Second, such a commitment implies and must insist upon a willingness on the part of the body politic to play the substantive as well as the procedural game of government and politics according to the rules, that is, there must be, and I assume that there will be—although I hold my breath a bit—an embrace of obedience to the law of the land; a firm spirit of recognition of the seminal principle that law is as the cement of society; that, in the trenchant comment by Abe Fortas: "Dissent and dissenters have no monopoly on freedom. They must tolerate opposition. They must accept dissent from their dissent."[81] There were times in the late 1960s and early 1970s—and there have been some recently (for example, the July 1977 New York City blackout looting)—when that commitment was missing. Although I have no doubt that the year 2000 may well see sporadic civil disobedience by members of the body politic, I would expect that to be within the framework of the rule, as J. A. Corry once put it so well, that it be "civil," not "uncivil," with the basic aim being persuasion, not violence,[82] and that those who invoke the tenets of civil disobedience be willing to pay the piper. Third, while I expect—and I do so with a heavy heart and considerable concern—ever-increasing bureaucratic, centripetal interference with our daily lives, I shall still assume, more or less confidently, that the American spirit of individualism and dedication to certain fundamental principles of local government will assert itself sufficiently even by the year 2000 to enforce at least some basic limits upon the reach of government, generally, and the central government, in particular.

With these three principal expectations in mind, what may one then predict for our three now amply and generously protected freedoms? Despite perhaps increasing assaults on the freedom of the press, I expect it to be not much different than it is today—and I include herein the press in its written and its representational, that is visual and verbal forms, to wit, radio and television. There will always be some pressure, of course, both of the official and unofficial kind, to include or exclude certain programming in the two last mentioned segments—for example, the "Seven Dirty Words" decision in 1978 affecting New York's radio station WBAI-FM[83]—but the combination of economic realities, discounted to some degree by certain laudatory idealistic commitments, will very likely continue to give us the sort of this-side-of-courageous but sporadically enterprising coverage by those still growing elements of the media. The daily press will almost certainly have shrunk even more in number and will, I fear, be concentrated even more in the hands of those few entrepreneurs who can afford to pay their enormous production costs (and I wish the unions would become more reasonable in the interim, but they are hardly likely to do so). Yet I confidently expect newspapers to be free from governmental censorship—although there is no question that bitter and sustained attacks upon the press will continue to issue from both the public and the private sectors.

As to the two aspects of freedom of the press that I identified as currently particularly troublesome and indeed vexatious in terms of any clear-cut line-drawing between individual and communal rights and responsibilities, the developing law of libel represents about as uncertain a prognosis as I could possibly imagine. For the judiciary has vacillated so grievously on the issue that, perhaps more than any other segment of the application of the tenets of the Bill of Rights, the approach to the libel syndrome depends upon the personnel on the bench. Since I do not intend to cop out on the issue, however, I would suggest that the year 2000 will see a continued dichotomy between alleged libelees in the public and the nonpublic realm, although I would hazard the expectation that the Supreme Court's recently charted, if less-than-crystal-clear, move away from a continuing expansion of the public sector will gradually grow apace. Indeed, while I do not necessarily predict it, I should think it within the realm of possibility, although not in that of probability, that even those who are demonstrably public figures may find a slightly more sympathetic hearing from the bench. Nonetheless, the days of the embrace of the hated concept of "seditious libel" is gone, as, of course, it should be.

On the current second trouble-sector of the press, namely, how to find viable constitutional and common-sense, if you please, accommodations between freedom of the press and the right to a fair trial, I suspect the difficulties more or less to continue in each of the four subdivisions thereof that I attempted to elucidate earlier. Thus, while the courts will hardly move to try to curb even intemperate press criticism of trial conduct, and whereas there will not be a great deal they will be able to do to stop the press from conducting *ex parte* trials in their media, they will continue to get at the media tangentially by setting aside convictions because of press-induced publicity, especially when that publicity is carried on television. I doubt that the year 2000 will see any clear-cut resolution of the alleged reportorial prerogative of refusing to respond to judicial inquiry on grounds of the confidentiality of sources; the votes on the issue so far, while they have begun to go rather consistently against that refusal in both the civil and criminal realm, have been too close to predict a trend—although I personally frankly see no reason why a reporter's probative, relevant, and material data should be privileged any more than that of the ordinary mortal. There appears to be a good chance that, within reason, the courts will come to feel likewise. Where I do, with some confidence, expect a change *cum* improvement is in a judge's power to control his or her courtroom. I have but little doubt that appellate courts, while insisting upon adherence to the procedural guarantees of the Bill of Rights, will nonetheless strongly support judges who will, either publicly or—as is becoming increasingly the case—by virtue of behind-the-scene understandings and negotiations between themselves, media representatives, and involved members of the bar, succeed in extracting agreements not only to abide by but to support judicially-imposed rules of conduct during the various stages of the trial. Such a course will presumably ascertain a fair trial, a reasonable measure of publicity based on the people's right-to-know, and thus realize the goal of seeing to it that justice is done to society as well as the accused—without moving to the rather tough stance of press contempt citations that are prevalent in English tribunals.[84]

On the freedom of speech front I see no major changes in store for the year 2000 with the exception of three currently particularly troublesome areas: public demonstrations, public "foul-mouthing," and obscenity. In all the other realms of that fundamental First Amendment right the basic, generally broadly libertarian commitment to free expression will undoubtedly continue. Indeed, given the rather astounding expansion of it by the Supreme Court in recognizing its presence even in such theretofore unrecognized areas as political spending and political jobs, retrenchments are not in the wind. There may be some changes, however, in one or more, and perhaps, each of those three free speech sectors just suggested. The public's fear of mass demonstrations and mass picketing, coupled with the not-infrequent reluctance on the part of the police to deal with them decisively and effectively, may well see increasing legislative and executive attempts to harness and curb them, although they cannot of course be simply forbidden and still retain the First Amendment guarantee involved. The 1978 wrench surrounding the propounded march in Skokie, Illinois, by American Nazis and the several responses thereto is a case in point of the inherent problems. If attempted curbing of demonstrations does become a phenomenon to be reckoned with, it may well follow the Supreme Court's guidelines expressed, although not entirely unambiguously, in such relatively recent decisions as *Adderley v. Florida*[85] and *Hudgens v. National Labor Relations Board*,[86] where the line drawn was not on the basis of the nebulous common law concept of "breach of the peace" but on the more specific one of "trespass." Thus, the Florida statute upheld in the *Adderley* case reads: "Every trespass on the property of another, committed with a malicious and mischievous intent . . . shall be punished." There the Supreme Court interpreted the "trespass" concept to embrace governmental property as well.

Given the present "everything goes" and "do-your-own-thing" status of society, it may be foolhardy to predict that the year 2000 will see a curbing of what would presently seem to be the protected practice of public "foul-mouthing." Moreover, it is extremely, frustratingly difficult to draw up prescriptive statutes without violating the justifiably strict constitution-judicial mandates against "overbreadth" and, especially, "vagueness" which are all but inherent linguistically. Hence any curbing of vile public epitheting that the public-at-large is increasingly beginning to regard as impermissible will in all probability not emanate from the legislative or executive branches but from the judiciary. And that may just very well occur in due course. A vehicle toward that end might become a judicial reembrace of the *Chaplinsky* "fighting words" doctrine;[87] one that could well lend itself to more generous interpretations than the Court has been willing to embrace during much of the thirty-five year period that has gone by since *Chaplinsky*'s pronouncement. It is of more than passing interest that the Court was unanimous in that 1942 decision; that it then included such champions of the Bill of Rights as Justices Stone, Black, Douglas, and Frank Murphy; and that it was the latter—who was in some ways the most advanced civil libertarian of the group—who wrote the Court's opinion upholding the New Hampshire statute involved. The years between now and 2000 give fair promise of a readoption of that line or one similar thereto—although, to repeat, it will be extremely difficult to accomplish constitutionally.

Confining oneself to fundamental considerations an obvious one is, as Chief Justice Warren so well stated it, that the obscenity problem constitutes the Court's "most difficult" area of adjudication.[88] What is "obscenity" to some is mere "realism" to others; what is "lascivious" in the eyes of one reader is merely "colorful" in those of another; what is "lewd" to one parent may be "instructive" to another. One person's smut may well be another's Chaucer! Or, as Justice Harlan I once put the matter: "One man's vulgarity is another man's lyric."[89] The tortuous line(s) the Supreme Court has drawn in this emotion-charged area of public law and community mores is as complex as it is frustrating—but as this essay was being composed four aspects of the obscenity puzzle seemed to be *res judicata*: that just about everything goes in the privacy of one's home[90] (except homosexual acts in private even if they are consensual);[91] that public hard-core pornography is not constitutionally protected;[92] that there now exists a judicially-sanctioned "double standard" vis-à-vis obscenity legislation directed at minors and adults;[93] and that while there is no judicially recognized national community standard, local (or state) standards are relevant in obscenity legislation[94]—unless federal law takes precedence.[95] Which of these four currently applicable standards or lines on the freedom of speech versus obscenity will likely be still applicable in the year 2000? It is reasonably certain that, notwithstanding its myopia about homosexual activities, the American public will not conduct a coup d'etat because the judiciary, as I fully expect it to do, will ultimately recognize and sanction fully developed free speech and privacy rights allowing consenting adults to engage in private sexual activities of whatever smorgasbord variety may appeal to them. On the other hand, there will almost certainly be no change in the, to me at least, entirely defensible prohibition against public manifestations of hard-core pornography[96]—the issue of the "avertable eye"[97] is really a non sequitur in the public forum realm. Nor, except possibly in terms of a lowering of the age limit from say, seventeen or eighteen in some states to, say, sixteen, do I expect, nor would I sanction, an eradication of what is an entirely justifiable distinction in the legislation governing obscenity as it applies to adults on the one hand and minors on the other. Granting that there are vast differences of sophistication and parental permissiveness, it seems to me that society has a right to insist on the drawing of such a legislative line, and it will assuredly continue to do so in the year 2000. Conceivably the most vexatious aspect of the quartet of obscenity problems in the light of the First Amendment freedom of speech is that of the judicially created notion or concept of "community standards." Once identified as national,[98] the Supreme Court embraced instead the local or statewide[99] one as of the early 1970s. It is a standard that the target year will almost assuredly see preserved, against the backdrop of that so tantalizingly convoluted test that asks whether the allegedly obscene work in question, taken as a whole rather than by its isolated parts, appeals to prurient interests in the eyes of the "average person" applying those local or statewide community standards—standards based on legislation that can meet the constitutional test of whether the allegedly obscene material depicts or describes, "in a patently offensive way," the sexual conduct specifically defined in the applicable law, and, furthermore, that the work "lacks serious literary, artistic, political or scientific value."[100] Whether or not this maddeningly complex test, "perfected" in 1973, remains in force by the year 2000, it is beyond doubt that the American public will insist on some kind of curbing of what is patently obscene. I doubt that the answer will be found in the results of the cascading practice of resorting to public opinion polls that characterized some parts of the United States—for example, Cleveland, Ohio—in the mid- and late-1970s, in order to identify and determine "contemporary community standards." But I would not write off the strong possibility that, within the general bounds described, lay juries might ultimately indeed have the last words on the absence or presence of, hard-core pornography. I do hope that I shall not be on one, however!

The last of the triad, freedom of association, is, I daresay, the easiest one to predict. While associational allegiances will, and to some degree must, always be a factor in the appraisal of an applicant's qualifications for a position, for example, and while one's associations are voluntary and thus material—assuming the joiner's knowledge of the association's purposes—the day of the automatic blacklist is over. It bids fair not to be revived, absent a major United States involvement in war or a domestic insurrection. Notwithstanding the tragic experiences of the two decades or so of the Cold War, the freedom of association implied in the sextet of First Amendment rights is secure—at least in the sense that the prerogative of joining associations of one's choice and of not standing convicted by mere guilt of association is fundamental. One may confidently expect its vigorous health in 2000 A.D.

Just a summary word in conclusion. As a distinguished colleague once expressed so pithily, "the philosophical test" to be applied, now as well as in those years ahead, is clear: "will the forbidding of freedom of expression further or hamper the realization of liberal democratic ideals?[101] The sole manner in which to moderate, remedy, or remove rankling discontent is to get at its cause by education, remedial laws, or other community action. Repression of expression will only serve to sharpen the sense of injustice and provide added arguments and rationalizations for desperate, perhaps reckless measures. Surely the loyalty of the mass of men to liberal democracy has been immensely strengthened by the right to free expression and the consequent feeling of a genuine stake in society, a society that allows the expression of our deepest and most rankling grievances. Hence repressive laws will fail to maintain loyalty. While they may give a false sense of security, at least for a time, since we would be excused from arguing the case for our ideals and for the carefully developed procedures for pursuing them, we must also recognize that freedom of utterance, even though it be rebellious, constitutes a safety valve that gives timely warning of dangerous pressures in our society. Committed to the principles of Western liberal democracy, we have a lasting obligation to leave open the political channels by which a governing majority can be replaced when it is no longer able to command popular support. However, to plead for a generous approach to freedom of speech, press, and assembly is not to say that it is absolute. It is not; it cannot be; nor, in the words of Justice Robert H. Jackson, are we obliged to "convert the constitutional Bill of Rights into a suicide pact."[102]

In the final analysis we must confidently look to the Court to draw a line based on constitutional common sense. No other agency of government is equally well qualified to do so now or will be in the year 2000.

NOTES

1. John W. Burgess, *Political and Comparative Law* (Boston: Gin & Co., 1890), vol. 1, pp. 225–26. (Italics added.)

2. Grand Jury Indictment; trial by jury in *civil* cases; prohibitions against excessive bail and fines; right to bear arms; proscription of involuntary quartering of troops in private homes. For a detailed analysis of these five see Henry Abraham, *Freedom and the Court: Civil Rights and Liberties in the United States* (New York: Oxford University Press, 1977), ch. 3, "The Bill of Rights and Its Applicability to the States," especially pp. 102–4.

3. See *Gitlow v. New York*, 268 U.S. 652 (1925); *Fiske v. Kansas*, 274 U.S. 380 (1927); *Stromberg v. California*, 283 U.S. 359 (1931); and *Near v. Minnesota*, 283 U.S. 697 (1931).

4. *Editor and Publisher*, 3 July 1976, pp. 1–31.

5. Ibid., p. 31.

6. *Time, Inc. v. Firestone*, 424 U.S. 448 (1976).

7. *The New York Times v. Sullivan*, 376 U.S. 254 (1964). Further expanded in *Ocala Star Banner v. Damron*, 401 U.S. 295 (1971). But apparently *narrowed* in *Time, Inc. v. Firestone*.

8. *Garrison v. Louisiana*, 379 U.S. 64 (1964).

9. For example, *Ginzburg v. Goldwater*, 396 U.S. 1049 (1970); *Indianapolis Newspapers, Inc. v. Fields*, 400 U.S. 930 (1970); *Cape Publications Co. v. Adams*, 434 U.S. 943 (1977); and *Sun Publishing Co. v. Stevens*, 436 U.S. 945 (1978).

10. See *Curtis Publishing Co. v. Butts*, 388 U.S. 130 (1967); *Matus v. Triangle Publications*, 408 U.S. 930 (1972); and *Patrick v. Field Research Corp.*, 414 U.S. 922 (1973).

11. For example, compare *Associated Press v. Walker*, 388 U.S. 130 (1967) with *Greenbelt Coop. Pub. Assn. v. Bresler*, 298 U.S. 6 (1970). Also compare both with *Time, Inc. v. Firestone*, 424 U.S. 448 (1976).

12. *Rosenbloom v. Metromedia*, 403 U.S. 29 (1971), at 44: "Voluntarily

or not, we are all public men to some degree," in Justice Brennan's words, at 48. See also *Edwards v. N.Y. Times Co.*, *certiorari* denied, 434 U.S. 1002 (1977).

13. *Gertz v. Robert Welch, Inc.*, 418 U.S. 323 (1974) at 345. That it was but a "seemingly" sharp one was demonstrated by its 5 to 3 narrowing of the "public figure" concept in 1976 when it upheld a $100,000 libel award won by a prominent Palm Beach socialite, Mary Alice Firestone, whose notorious divorce proceedings had been publicized by *Time Magazine*. (*Time, Inc. v. Firestone*). The gravamen of Justice Rehnquist's majority opinion was that Mrs. Firestone was not a "public figure" since she had not assumed "any role of especial prominence in the affairs of society, other than perhaps Palm Beach society," because she had not "thrust herself to the forefront of any particular public controversy in order to influence the resolution of the issues involved in it."

14. *Time, Inc. v. Hill*, 385 U.S. 374 (1967).

15. *Cox Broadcasting Corp. v. Cohn*, 420 U.S. 469 (1975).

16. *Paul v. Davis*, 424 U.S. 693 (1976).

17. See Justice Black's concurring opinion in *The New York Times v. Sullivan*, 376 U.S. 254 at 296 (1964).

18. Letter to Edward Carrington, in Paul L. Ford, ed., *Thomas Jefferson's Works* (New York: G. P. Putnam's Sons, 1894) vol. 4, p. 359.

19. *Zurcher v. Stanford Daily*, 436 U.S. 547.

20. *Times Mirror Co. v. Superior Court of California*, 314 U.S. 52 (1941).

21. *Bridges v. California*, 314 U.S. 52 (1941); and *Wood v. Georgia*, 370 U.S. 375 (1962).

22. *Pennekamp v. Florida*, 328 U.S. 331 (1946); and *Craig v. Harney*, 331 U.S. 367 (1947).

23. *Irwin v. Doud*, 366 U.S. 717 (1961); and *Rideau v. Louisiana*, 373 U.S. 723 (1963).

24. *Dickinson v. United States*, 414 U.S. 979 (1973); *Sigma Delta Chi v. Martin*, 431 U.S. 928 (1977); and *Leach v. Sawicki*, 431 U.S. 930 (1977).

25. For sundry tests of such proposed codes see: "Excerpts from American Bar Association's Report on a Fair Trial and Free Press," *New York Times*, 2 October 1966, p. 81; Edward Ranzal, "U.S. Judicial Conference Adopts Recommendations on the Issue of Free Press and Fair Trial," *New York Times*, 20 September 1968, p. 34; Edward Ranzal, "Cohn to be Heard by Circuit Court," *New York Times*, 11 September 1969, p. 31; "Bar Panel Opens Study on Courtroom Disorders," *New York Times*, 15 November 1969, p. 28; and *The Philadelphia Evening Bulletin*, 10 September 1969, p. 26.

26. *Nebraska Press Association v. Stuart*, 427 U.S. 539 (1976).

27. *Estes v. Texas*, 381 U.S. 532 (1965); and *Sheppard v. Maxwell*, 384 U.S. 333 (1966).

28. *Estes v. Texas*, 381 U.S. 532 (1965).

29. *Sheppard v. Maxwell*, 384 U.S. 333 at 357–62 (1966).

30. *Sheppard v. Maxwell*, 384 U.S. 333 at 363 (1966).

31. *Tribune Publishing Co. v. Caldero*, 434 U.S. 930 (1977); *certiorari* denied; *Oxberger v. Winegard*, 436 U.S. 905, *certiorari* denied; and *Hubbard Broadcasting Co. v. Ammerman*, 436 U.S. 906 (1978), *certiorari* denied.

32. *Branzburg v. Hayes*, 408 U.S. 665 (1972).

33. See the article by Deirdre Carmody, "Courts and the Process of News Gathering," *New York Times*, 28 July 1978, p. 10.

34. *Buckley v. Valeo*, 425 U.S. 946 (1976).

35. *Virginia State Board of Pharmacy v. Virginia Consumer Council*, 425 U.S. 748 (1976).

36. *Bates v. Arizona State Bar*, 433 U.S. 350 (1977).

37. *Elrod v. Burns*, 427 U.S. 347 (1976).

38. For example, see Justice Goldberg's opinion for the Court in *Cox v. Louisiana*, 379 U.S. 536 at 555 (1965).

39. Contrast *Thornhill v. Alabama*, 310 U.S. 88 (1940) with *Giboney v. Empire Storage & Ice Co.*, 336 U.S. 490 (1949), and *Amalgamated Food Employees Union v. Logan Valley, Inc.*, 391 U.S. 309 (1968) with *Lloyd Corp. Ltd. v. Tanner*, 407 U.S. 551 (1972) and *Hudgens v. N.L.R.B.*, 424 U.S. 507 (1976).

40. See *Yates v. United States*, 354 U.S. 298 (1957), particularly Justice Harlan's opinion for the 7 to 1 Court.

41. *Jenkins v. Georgia*, 418 U.S. 153 (1974).

42. *A Book Named "John Cleland's Woman of Pleasure" v. Massachusetts*, 383 U.S. 413 (1966).

43. *Chaplinsky v. New Hampshire*, 315 U.S. 568 (1942)—opinion for the unanimous Court by Justice Frank Murphy, then its leading libertarian. The statute had enacted the common-law "fighting words" doctrine: "No person shall address any offensive, derisive, or annoying word [directly] to any other person who is lawfully in any street or other public place, nor call him by any offensive or derisive name." The state court had interpreted it to ban "words likely to cause an average addressee to fight," and "face to face words likely" to produce an immediate violent breach of the peace by the addressee. Although the "fighting words" test has continued to be relied upon, it has presented major problems when applied to the "profane," the "obscene," and the "libelous," as noted below. By and large the Court's posture has been one of focusing on the specific "circumstances" in which the contested speech is uttered. See, for example, its 5 to

2 distinction of *Chaplinsky* in the 1972 Georgia "bad language" case of *Gooding v. Wilson*, 405 U.S. 418, which disallowed a Georgia statute as "on its face" unconstitutionally vague and overbroad. On the other hand, the same Court *declined* (8 to 1) to review a lower court decision that there is no "constitutional privilege to shout four-letter words on a public street" in a case in which a policeman arrested a man for disorderly conduct on the grounds that he had used obscene language. (*Von Schleichter v. United States*, 409 U.S. 1063 [1972].) For proof that the Court continues to find the *Chaplinsky* test extremely vexatious in application, see Justice Powell's diverse, pained opinions in the 1972 "foul language trilogy" cases of *Rosenfeld v. New Jersey*, *Lewis v. New Orleans*, and *Brown v. Oklahoma*, reported as 408 U.S. 901, 913, and 914, respectively—all propounding "overbreadth" and/or "vagueness" problems in the free speech realm.

44. *United States v. O'Brien*, 391 U.S. 367 (1968).

45. *U.S. v. O'Brien*, 391 U.S. at 376 (1968).

46. *Tinker v. Des Moines Independent Community School District*, 393 U.S. 503 (1969). The *Tinker* decision was confirmed in 1972 when the Court refused to review a lower tribunal's decision permitting a public school teacher of English to wear a black armband on Vietnam Moratorium Day—despite his subsequent suspension for continued political activity and educational disruption. (*Board of Education v. James*, 409 U.S. 1042 [1973].)

47. *Street v. New York*, 394 U.S. 576 (1969). "Do-Not-Dishonor-the-Flag statutes—for example, *Smith v. Goguen*, 415 U.S. 566 (1974)—came before the Court increasingly in the mid-1970s, most of them falling to challenges of "vagueness."

48. *Schacht v. United States*, 398 U.S. 58 (1970).

49. *Cohen v. California*, 403 U.S. 15 (1971). Relatedly, see *Papish v. Board of Curators of University of Missouri*, 410 U.S. 667 (1973), that 6 to 3 vote overturned a student's expulsion for circulating "offensive ideas" in print in a campus publication that used the "M—— F——" expletive with obvious relish in connection with the trial and acquittal of the member of an organization called "Up Against the Wall, Mother——." (A headline story was entitled "M—— F—— acquitted," and it printed a political cartoon depicting police raping the Statue of Liberty and the Goddess of Justice.)

50. See, for example, his dissenting opinion in *Barenblatt v. United States*, 360 U.S. 109 at 141 (1959).

51. Although the Court has been on both sides of the issue in its decisions, and may well have to come down with a definitive one ultimately, by and large it has sided with duly constituted authorities, assuming reasonable rules are at stake. See, among others, *Olff v. East Side Union High*

School District, 404 U.S. 1042 (1972); *Jackson v. New York City Transit Authority*, 419 U.S. 831 (1974); and *Kelley v. Johnson*, 425 U.S. 238 (1976).

52. *Sedition* consists of publications, utterances, or other activities, short of treason, which are deemed to encourage resistance to lawful authority. *Subversion* comprehends participation in or advocacy of any organized activity to overthrow an existing government by force.

53. *Parker v. Levy*, 417 U.S. 733 (1974).

54. For example, the "Miracle" decision (concerning Robert Rossellini's controversial movie) of *Burstyn v. Wilson*, 343 U.S. 495 (1952); that of the film "Lady Chatterley's Lover," *Kingsley Corporation v. Regents of the University of New York*, 360 U.S. 684 (1959); and that regarding the sexually suggestive "Carnal Knowledge," *Jenkins v. Georgia*, 418 U.S. 153 (1974).

55. For example, *Ullmann v. United States*, 350 U.S. 422 (1955).

56. For example, *United States v. Rumely*, 345 U.S. 41 (1953).

57. For example, *Watkins v. United States*, 354 U.S. 178 (1957).

58. For example, *Barenblatt v. United States*, 360 U.S. 109 (1959).

59. For example, *Braden v. United States*, 365 U.S. 431 (1961). Compare *DeGregory v. Attorney-General of New Hampshire*, 383 U.S. 825 (1966). Most notoriously prominent in these investigations was HUAC (the House Committee on UnAmerican Activities). Restyled the Internal Securities Committee—its constitutionality upheld in 1968 in *Stamler v. Willis*, 393 U.S. 212—it was abolished in 1975 and its functions transferred to the House Committee on the Judiciary. Its Senate counterpart, the Judiciary Committee's Internal Security Subcommittee, was abolished in 1977.

60. *Peters v. Hobby*, 349 U.S. 341 (1955); *Cole v. Young*, 351 U.S. 356 (1956); *Service v. Dulles*, 354 U.S. 363 (1957); *Vitarelli v. Seaton*, 359 U.S. (1959); and *Greene v. McElroy*, 361 U.S. 374 (1959).

61. *Stewart v. Washington*, 301 F. Supp. 610 (1969). Judge John Lewis Smith, the third member of the tribunal, agreed that the oath was invalid but did not agree that the wording of the law itself was unconstitutional.

62. Richard D. Lyons, "Loyalty Oath for U.S. Employees Abolished After Successful Suit," *New York Times*, 7 January 1970, p. 1. In late 1976 the Court ordered elimination of all political loyalty questions on federal job application forms; Peter Kihss, "U.S. Forms Drop Loyalty Queries," *New York Times*, 9 September 1976, p. 1.

63. *United Public Workers v. Mitchell*, 330 U.S. 75 (1947).

64. *United States v. Robel*, 389 U.S. 258.

65. *Schneider v. Smith*, 390 U.S. 17 (1968). In that case, however, the Court applied statutory construction to the Magnuson Act 1950 rather than hold it unconstitutional.

66. *Schneider v. Smith*, 390 U.S. 17 at 26 (1968). Congress threatened to overturn the two decisions, but never did.

67. *Garner v. Board of Public Works of Los Angeles*, 341 U.S. 716 (1951); *Gerende v. Board of Supervisors*, 341 U.S. 56 (1951); *Adler v. Board of Education of New York*, 342 U.S. 485 (1952), but overruled by *Keyishian v. Board of Regents*, 385 U.S. 589 (1967); *Knight v. Board of Regents of New York*, 390 U.S. 36 (1968); *Hosack v. Smiley*, 390 U.S. 744 (1968); and *Lisker v. Kelly*, 401 U.S. 928 (1971).

68. *Wiemann v. Updegraff*, 344 U.S. 183 (1952); *Shelton v. Tucker*, 364 U.S. 479 (1960); and *Baggett v. Bullitt*, 377 U.S. 360 (1964).

69. *Elfbrandt v. Russell*, 384 U.S. 11 (1966); *Keyishian v. Board of Regents of New York*; and *Whitehill v. Elkins*, 389 U.S. 54 (1967).

70. For example, *Rafferty v. McKay*, 400 U.S. 954 (1970), in which the Court affirmed a lower court holding striking down California's loyalty oath for teachers by relying on *Baggett v. Bullitt*, 377 U.S. 360 (1964). The oath at issue was the "mixed" type, reading: "I solemnly swear (or affirm) that I will support the Constitution of the United States of America, the Constitution of the State of California, and the laws of the United States and the State of California, and will . . . promote respect for the flag and . . . respect for law and order and . . . allegiance to the government of the United States." Had the oath stopped with "California" and before "and will" it would undoubtedly have been upheld as a simply affirmative oath. However, narrowly dividing, the Court in 1972 upheld a two-part Massachusetts loyalty oath which, in addition to the standard "uphold and defend" clause, requires public employees to pledge that they will "oppose" the overthrow of the federal and state governments by force, violence, "or by any illegal or unconstitutional methods." (*Cole v. Richardson*, 405 U.S. 676 [1972].)

71. For example, *Fields v. Askew*, 414 U.S. 1148 (1974).

72. For example, *Wieman v. Updegraff*, 344 U.S. 183 (1952), in which the Court unanimously struck down an Oklahoma loyalty oath law that made even innocent membership in a proscribed organization an offense.

73. *Pennsylvania v. Nelson*, 350 U.S. 497 (1956); *Communist Party v. Catherwood*, 367 U.S. 389 (1961); and *Mitchell v. Donovan*, 398 U.S. 427 (1970). In the 1961 case it ruled unanimously (via Harlan) that the Communist party could not be banned from state unemployment systems, and in the 1970 case it pointedly declined to rule on the Act's constitutionality.

74. *Communist Party v. Subversive Activities Control Board*, 367 U.S. 1 (1961).

75. *United States v. Communist Party*, 377 U.S. 968 (1964).

76. *Aptheker v. Secretary of State*, 378 U.S. 500 (1965).

77. *Albertson v. Subversive Activities Control Board*, 382 U.S. 70 (1965).

78. *Dennis v. United States*, 341 U.S. 494 (1951).

79. *Yates v. United States*, 354 U.S. 298 (1957).

80. *Yates v. United States*, 354 U.S. 298 at 325 (1957). The cases of five of the defendants were acquitted, nine were remanded for a new trial.

81. Abe Fortas, *Concerning Dissent and Civil Disobedience* (New York: New American Library, 1968), p. 126.

82. See J. A. Corry's Massey Lectures (CBC), *The Power of Law* (Toronto: CBC Learning Systems, 1971), p. 41.

83. In a 5 to 4 decision the Court upheld the FCC's power to prohibit the broadcasting of "patently offensive" language, *FCC v. Pacifica Foundation*, 438 U.S. 726 (1978).

84. For a description, see Henry J. Abraham, *Freedom and the Court: Civil Rights and Liberties in the United States* (New York: Oxford University Press, 1977), pp. 182.

85. *Adderley v. Florida*, 385 U.S. 39 (1966).

86. *Hudgens v. National Labor Relations Board*, 424 U.S. 507 (1976).

87. *Chaplinsky v. New Hampshire*, 315 U.S. 568 (1942). See footnote 43, above, for a discussion of the test contained therein.

88. Interview, Sacramento, California, June 26, 1969, as quoted in, "Warren Calls Vote Rulings Most Vital," *New York Times*, 27 June 1971, p. 1.

89. *Cohen v. California*, 403 U.S. 15 at 25 (1971), majority opinion.

90. *Stanley v. Georgia*, 394 U.S. 557 (1969).

91. *Doe v. Commonwealth Attorney for the City of Richmond*, 425 U.S. 901 (1976); and *Enslin v. Bean*, 436 U.S. 912 (1978).

92. *Miller v. California*, 413 U.S. 15 (1973) and *Paris Adult Theatre v. Slayton*, 413 U.S. 49 (1973).

93. *Ginsberg v. New York*, 390 U.S. 629 (1968).

94. See *Miller v. California* and *Paris Adult Theatre v. Slayton*.

95. *Smith v. United States*, 431 U.S. 291 (1977).

96. See *Miller v. California* and *Paris Adult Theatre v. Slayton*.

97. See Norman W. Provizer, "Of Lines and Men: The Supreme Court, Obscenity, and the Issue of the Avertable Eye," *Tulsa Law Journal* 13, no. 1 (1977): 52–81.

98. *Jacobellis v. Ohio*, 378 U.S. 184 (1964).

99. See the 1973 *Miller v. California* and *Paris Adult Theatre v. Slayton* cases.

100. See *Paris Adult Theatre v. Slayton* and *Miller v. California*, at 24.

101. J. A. Corry, in J. A. Corry and Henry J. Abraham, *Elements of Democratic Government* (New York: Oxford University Press, 1964), pp. 262.

102. *Terminiello v. Chicago*, 337 U.S. 1 at 37 (1949). Jackson's full warning, penned as one of the four dissenters in this well-known case in-

volving the Supreme Court's reversal of a breach-of-peace conviction of a notorious professional rabble rouser in Chicago, was: "There is danger that, if the Court does not temper its doctrinaire logic with a little practical wisdom, it will convert the constitutional bill of rights into a suicide pact."

SECTION III

The First Amendment: Religion, Religious Freedom, and the State

6

LEO PFEFFER

The Future of the Bill of Rights: Church-State Relations

The Bill of Rights—the first ten amendments to our Constitution—begins with the words "Congress shall make no law respecting an establishment of religion or prohibiting the free exercise thereof." It is perhaps symbolic that this guaranty should have been placed first among those set forth in the amendments—freedom of speech, of press, of the right of the people to assemble and petition for a redress of grievances, and the numerous procedural rights accorded to persons accused of crimes. In a sense, the priority given the Religion Clause is symbolic not only of its importance in the minds of the generation of Americans that made the Bill of Rights part of our Constitution, but also of its historical significance. It was freedom of religion that was first achieved by the English colonists who settled on these shores and established a new nation committed to constitutionally secured freedoms.[1] And out of the victorious struggle for this freedom came the achievement of the other freedoms secured by the Bill of Rights.[2]

An explanation of what the sixteen words that constitute the Religion Clause now mean, that is, how the Supreme Court has interpreted and applied them, is necessary before any prediction is made as to how the Supreme Court is likely to interpret and apply them in the year 2001, which will be two centuries and a decade since the First Amendment became part of our Constitution. It is, therefore, to the present judicial understanding of the sixteen words that we now turn.

CONFLICT BETWEEN ESTABLISHMENT AND FREE EXERCISE

There are instances where the dual First Amendment guaranties of the freedom of religious exercise and church-state separation are or appear to be in conflict with each other, apparently calling upon the courts to make a choice between them. While this conflict between two guaranties in the Bill of Rights may be real, it is by no means unique. Recently concluded litigation involving *New York Times* reporter Myron Farber, who refused to testify as a witness in a criminal case which did not involve him personally, presented a conflict between the guaranties of freedom of the press and the right of an accused to a fair trial.[3] A case that occurred in Richmond, Virginia, in 1855, indicates a conflict between the Free Exercise right and the right to a fair trial. There the judge in a murder trial refused to allow a priest who received confession from a dying woman, allegedly shot by her husband, to testify as to what she said in respect to who shot her. The records of the court were lost during the Civil War, so we do not have the ultimate outcome of the trial.[4] It is possible that the excluded testimony would have been "exculpatory of the prisoner," that is, it might have pointed to someone other than her husband as the killer. The result, therefore, is that a person might have been put to death for a crime that he never committed, an outcome that fortunately did not happen in the Myron Farber case.

Our concern here is with conflict between Establishment and Free Exercise. There have been instances in which the Supreme Court was faced with an apparent conflict between them. In *Walz v. Tax Commission*,[5] for example, exemption of churches from real estate taxes was challenged as an aid to religion and hence a violation of the Establishment Clause. The National Council of Churches and the Synagogue Council of America, on the hand, submitted friends-of-the-court briefs urging that inasmuch as the power to tax involves the power to destroy, subjecting houses of worship to real estate taxation would violate the Free Exercise guaranty. Since the Court determined that the challenged exemption did not violate the Establishment Clause, it did not find it necessary to adjudge the asserted conflict between Establishment and Free Exercise.

The same avoidance of choice has been exercised by the Supreme Court in a few other cases. Thus, on the basis of *Pierce v. Society of Sisters*,[6] it is generally understood that the right to satisfy compulsory school attendance laws by attending parochial schools is protected by the Free Exercise Clause. Advocates of aid to parochial schools have argued that in respect to parents financially unable to pay tuition, denial of governmental aid by reason of the Establishment Clause violates their Free Exercise right as well as their right to the equal protection of the laws. As of the present writing, however, the Supreme Court has not been confronted with a situation in which it has found a conflict requiring it to make a choice.[7]

The asserted conflict between the Establishment and Free Exercise Clauses may be more apparent than real. In the minds of the generation that put the First Amendment into our Constitution, no-establishment and free exercise constituted a single guaranty, two sides, as it were, of the same coin. As Justice Wiley B. Rutledge said in *Emerson v. Board of Education*:

> "Religion" appears only once in the Amendment. But the word governs two prohibitions and governs them alike. It does not have two meanings, one narrow to forbid "an establishment" and another, much broader, for securing "the free exercise thereof." "Thereof" brings down "religion" with its entire and exact content, no more and no less, from the first into the second guaranty, so that Congress and now the states are as broadly restricted concerning the one as they are regarding the other.[8]

It has often been asserted that to those who wrote the First Amendment, free exercise was the end and no-establishment the means to achieve it, and that where there is a conflict between means and ends the former must be sacrificed to secure the latter.[9] If that was what was intended by the draftsmen of the Amendment, they certainly succeeded in concealing their intention. They could easily have written: "To secure the free exercise of religion, Congress shall make no law respecting its establishment." Why they did not do so—if a means and end evaluation was intended—is not explained.

THE MEANING OF FREE EXERCISE

It is easier to guarantee free exercise than to define it, but the same is true of all the freedoms guaranteed in the Bill of Rights (try defining Freedom of Speech or Due Process of Law)—else what's a Supreme Court for? It is perhaps easier to define what free exercise is not than what it is. It is not, for example, absolute, although the Clause speaks in absolute terms: it says that Congress shall make *no* law prohibiting the free exercise of religion. "Suppose," the Court asked rhetorically in the Mormon polygamy case of *Reynolds v. United States*,[10] "one believed that human sacrifices were a necessary part of religious worship, would it be seriously contended that the civil government under which he lived could not interfere to prevent a sacrifice?" The right to believe, the Court said, was absolute, but the right to act upon belief is subject to governmental restraint.

The same thought was expressed by the Supreme Court more than a half century later in *Cantwell v. Connecticut*.[11] There the Court said:

> [T]he Amendment embraces two concepts—freedom to believe and freedom to act. The first is absolute but, in the nature of things, the second cannot be. Conduct remains subject to regulation for the protection of society.[12]

Assuming that the word "believe" means what it is generally assumed to mean, that it is a function of the mind, the definition is inadequate if not meaningless. As the common law adage put it, the devil himself knows not the thoughts of man—at least until science invents mind-reading machines. If, however, belief encompasses the expression or teaching of belief, the belief-yes-action-no formula may go too far, for it would encompass advocacy of human sacrifice and self-sacrifice, as in Jonestown, or of polygamy, as was the case in *Davis v. Beason*.[13]

In *Minersville School District v. Gobitis*, the Court, in an opinion by Justice Felix Frankfurter, suggested another test:

> The religious liberty which the Constitution protects has never excluded legislation of general scope not directed against doctrinal loyalties of particular sects. . . . Conscientious scruples have not, in the course of the long

struggle for religious toleration, relieved the individual from obedience to a general law not aimed at the promotion or restriction of religious beliefs. The mere possession of religious convictions which contradict the relevant concerns of a political society does not relieve the citizen from the discharge of political responsibilities.[14]

Under this "general law" principle, as it has been called, one cannot successfully claim exemption from a purely secular law, such as one requiring men to register for the draft or pay taxes to support the armed forces, simply because one's own religious beliefs forbid it. Applying this test, the Court in *Gobitis* rejected the Jehovah's Witnesses' assertion that the Free Exercise Clause protected their children's right not to be disciplined for refusing to salute or pledge allegiance to the flag in public school exercises.

The "general law" test never really caught on. Three years after it was tendered, it was put to rest, over the strong and somewhat bitter dissent of Justice Frankfurter, in *West Virginia State Board of Education v. Barnette.*[15] In that case, which for all practical purposes overruled the Gobitis decision and upheld the constitutional right of the children of Jehovah's Witnesses not to participate in flag salute programs, the Court treated the issue as one involving freedom of speech rather than religion. So treated, it applied the clear and present danger test,[16] although pre-Barnette decisions had already applied that test to cases determined under the Religion Clause.[17] Under the test abridgement of free exercise is constitutionally permissible only in circumstances presenting a clear and immediate danger that can be averted only by no means other than the inhibition of religious exercise.

The Supreme Court's current understanding of constitutionally permissible limitations upon the free exercise of religion is expressed in the compelling interest test, first suggested in *Sherbert v. Verner.* In that case the Court, in holding that a Sabbatarian could not constitutionally be denied unemployment compensation for refusing to accept a position requiring work on Saturday, said:

It is basic that no showing merely of a rational relationship to some colorable state interest would suffice; in this highly sensitive constitutional area . . . only the gravest abuses, endangering paramount interests, give occasion for permissible limitation."[18]

Following *Sherbert*, the Court, in *Wisconsin v. Yoder*,[19] held that "only those interests of the highest order and those not otherwise served can overbalance legitimate claims to the free exercise of religion."[20]

Thus, under the present interpretation of the Free Exercise Clause, government, state or federal, can constitutionally restrict the expression or exercise of religion only by showing that there is a countergovernmental interest of such importance as to be deemed compelling and that there is no alternative for its protection other than the limitation on the free exercise of religion.

APPLICATION OF FREE EXERCISE

Tests are made by courts to be applied by courts, and courts are made up of human beings. No matter how neutral tests may appear to be in their formulation, they are, at least to the objective observer (particularly if his training is in the social sciences rather than in law), far from neutral in their application. External factors will temper subjectivity to some extent, but on the whole there is no escape from the reality that is in each case relevant to this subject, it is the Court or a majority thereof that determines what constitutes a clear and present danger or what interest is sufficiently compelling to justify limitation on the free exercise of religion. (Basically, there is no substantial difference between the two tests.) The doctrine of *stare decisis*, without which the common law system could not survive, does of course impel the judges to justify present decisions in harmony with past rulings. Hence, to the extent possible, the Court will distinguish rather than expressly overrule prior decisions that appear inconsistent with its present ruling, even where a frank expression of overruling would appear to be more appropriate.[21]

The flag salute cases illustrate this proposition. As noted, in the *Gobitis* case the Court held that the Free Exercise Clause did not render immune from prosecution parents who forbid their children to salute the flag in school. In the *Barnette* case, on the other hand, the Court held that the First Amendment did immunize the parents from prosecution, but it was the Free Speech rather than the Free Exercise Clause on which the Court relied, thus avoiding the necessity of overriding *Gobitis*. (Neither Justice Frankfurter nor anybody else was fooled by this device.)

Another example is presented by the case of *Donner v. New York*.[22] There the Court dismissed an appeal from the decision of the New York courts that while under the Pierce decision parents could elect to send their children to religious rather than public schools, the Free Exercise Clause did not entitle them to send the children (some of whom had reached the age of fourteen) to an extreme Jewish Orthodox school wherein all the secular instruction they received was through the study of the Talmud. Implicit in the Court's per curiam affirmance was the holding that there was no interest sufficiently compelling to justify exempting the parents of these children from the specific requirements of the compulsory school attendance law. (In *Braunfeld v. Brown*,[23] the Court came to the same conclusion in respect to Sunday Closing Laws in a case involving Orthodox Jewish retail merchants who kept their stores closed on Saturdays but open on Sundays.)

Wisconsin v. Yoder,[24] involved the same type of compulsory school attendance law as did *Donner*. Yet in *Yoder* the Court held that the Free Exercise Clause did justify parents' election to terminate their children's attendance at school upon their reaching the age of 14.

It is difficult to escape the conclusion that the differing results in *Gobitis-Barnette* and in *Donner-Yoder* can best be explained in terms of the individual judgments of the members of the Court as to what interest is sufficiently compelling to require overriding a claim to free exercise in the circumstances of the particular case presented to them.

Blood transfusions and other medical procedures present another example of the Court's duty of deciding between the interests protected by the Free Exercise Clause and other societal interests sought to be protected by governmental action.

In *Jacobson v. Massachusetts*,[25] the Court held that a parent's religious objections to innoculations did not justify exemption from the state's compulsory vaccination law. In *People ex rel Wallace v. Labrenz*,[26] the Court rejected an appeal from the decision of an Illinois court that a hospital could give a blood transfusion to a child notwithstanding the objection of the parents (Jehovah's

Witnesses) that the procedure violated their religious beliefs. Where, however, an adult is involved, the state courts have reached differing results, and the Supreme Court has as of the present been able to avoid a determination of the troublesome question. In one case, a lower court, in authorizing a transfusion at a hospital, justified its decision on the fiction that the patient was temporarily insane and that the court could therefore act in his behalf.[27] Another lower court found justification in the fact that the woman had a seven-month-old child who would suffer by becoming motherless and whose welfare the State had a right to protect.[28]

One last illustrative case merits noticing. In *National Labor Relations Board v. Catholic Archbishop of Chicago*[29] the Court was called upon to decide whether the mandate of the Labor Relations Act that employers bargain collectively with unions representing their employees can be enforced against the Catholic Church, notwithstanding the Church's contention that compulsory bargaining would violate its rights under the Establishment and Free Exercise Clauses.

In justifying its assumption of jurisdiction by the National Labor Relations Board in this and other cases involving parochial schools, the NLRB relied upon the Court's holding in *Associated Press v. NLRB*[30] that application of the Labor Relations Act to the Associated Press did not violate the Amendment's guaranty of freedom of the press. The Board viewed that decision as justifying its intervention in all labor disputes involving religious organizations if they affected interstate commerce.

By a bare majority, however, the Court avoided deciding this troublesome constitutional issue. Applying a long-standing principle that a court should avoid passing upon the constitutionality of an Act of Congress if it can dispose of the case before it without doing so, it held that Congress had not clearly expressed its intent that the Labor Relations Act should cover controversies between parochial schoolteachers and management in respect to union negotiations.

The Court's decision was based upon the language of the Act as it now reads. It may be assumed that the unions will seek to persuade Congress to amend it to include church-related schools, and that the Church and its allies (including the Baptist Joint Committee on Public Affairs, which filed an *amicus curiae* brief supporting the position of the Church) will make every effort to dissuade Congress from doing so. How this conflict between two politically powerful forces in the United States will ultimately be resolved cannot safely be predicted. Should the unions succeed, it would seem that the Court would have to decide the constitutional issue. However, since the Court's decision is based exclusively on its interpretation of the National Labor Relations Act, its decision does not affect interpretation of State acts. Thus, the constitutional issue might be decided by the Court if a case arises under a State act and the State court interprets it as encompassing religious schools. For the time being, however, the constitutional issue is unresolved.

THE ESTABLISHMENT OF RELIGION—WHAT IT MEANS

In 1947, the Supreme Court, in the parochial school bus case of *Everson v. Board of Education*, sought to present a definitive interpretation of the Establishment Clause, in the following language:

> The "establishment of religion" clause of the First Amendment means at least this: Neither a state nor the Federal Government can set up a church. Neither can pass laws which aid one religion, aid all religions, or prefer one religion over another. Neither can force nor influence a person to go to or remain away from church against his will or force him to profess a belief or disbelief in any religion. No person can be punished for entertaining or professing religious beliefs or disbeliefs, for church attendance or non-attendance. No tax in any amount, large or small, can be levied to support any religious activities or institutions, whatever they may be called, or whatever form they may adopt to teach or practice religion. Neither a state nor the Federal Government can, openly or secretly, participate in the affairs of any religious organizations or groups and vice versa. In the words of Jefferson, the clause against establishment of religion by law was intended to erect "a wall of separation between Church and State."[31]

This definition was reiterated, in whole or in part, in a number of later Supreme Court decisions, including the 1963 decision of *Abington School District v. Schempp.*[32] There, however, the Court, in outlawing devotional Bible reading in the public schools, also defined the Establishment Clause in the following language:

> The test may be stated as follows: what are the purpose and primary effect of the enactment? If either is the advancement or inhibition of religion then

the enactment exceeds the scope of legislative power as circumscribed by the Constitution. That is to say that to withstand the strictures of the Establishment Clause there must be a secular legislative purpose and a primary effect that neither advances nor inhibits religion. *Everson v. Board of Education.*[33]

In *Board of Education v. Allen,*[34] involving a law providing for the loan of secular textbooks for use by pupils attending parochial schools, the Court found the challenged statute constitutional under both the *Everson* no-aid test and the *Schempp* purpose-effect test. In *Lemon v. Kurtzman,*[35] which concerned state aid to finance salaries of parochial schoolteachers, the Court added as a third element the condition that the action must also not involve excessive governmental entanglement with religion. *Lemon* and its successors indicated that the forbidden entanglement may take the form of surveillance to assure compliance with First Amendment or with statutory or administrative prohibitions against the use of governmentally financed property or services to advance religion, entanglement in the administration of the governmentally financed project, and political divisiveness on religious lines.

Thus, to be valid under the Establishment Clause, as the Court stated in *Lemon* and many later decisions up to the present writing:

> [T]he statute must have a secular legislative purpose; second, its principal or primary effect must be one that neither advances nor inhibits religion; finally, the statute must not foster an excessive entanglement with religion.[36]

As has been suggested in respect to the Free Exercise Clause,[37] there is no basic difference between the clear and present danger test applied in earlier cases and the compelling interest test applied in the later ones. Here, the same conclusion may be proposed in respect to the Establishment Clause; basically, there is no substantial difference between the *Everson* no-aid test, and the *Lemon* purpose-effect-entanglement test. Justice Byron R. White, who wrote the Court's opinion in the *Allen* case, found that the textbook aid law there challenged passed both tests and so too did practically all the later cases involving aid to parochial schools. The majority of the Court, on the other hand, reached a directly contrary decision in all the later cases concerning aid to the educational functions of church-related institutions at the elementary and secondary levels.

APPLICATION OF NO-ESTABLISHMENT

By a large majority, cases challenging governmental action as a violation of the Establishment Clause fall into two categories: cases concerning religious teachings or practices in the public schools; and cases involving governmental aid to church-related educational institutions. At the unavoidable risk of oversimplification the present status of judicially established law may be summarized as follows:

In respect to religion in public education, school-organized or school-sponsored prayer in public schools is constitutionally impermissible, and it is immaterial whether the prayer is taken from the worship of established religions or is formulated by teachers or students. Nor is it material whether the prayer is purely sectarian; that is, a prayer taken from the liturgy of one or more of the faiths and unacceptable to other faiths, or is a so-called nonsectarian prayer, which presumably can be recited by students of all faiths. School-organized silent prayer is likewise unconstitutional, and this is so even if it is called meditation. Self-initiated prayers by individual pupils, particularly before meals, are constitutionally permissible and in some cases may not constitutionally be forbidden so long as there is no school or teacher involvement.[38]

Religious teaching in the public schools is constitutionally impermissible if there is any element of indoctrination,[39] although it is constitutionally permissible to release, during public school hours, those pupils who desire to participate in religious instruction conducted off public school premises and without involvement by public school personnel.[40] Objective teaching about religion, and the study of religious art or music as integral parts of courses in art or music do not violate the Constitution. Nor, by the same token, is the study of religious writings forbidden where it is appropriate in objectively taught courses in literature, history, sociology, or other social studies.

Bible reading as a devotional act, whether it be from the Protestant, Catholic, or Jewish version of the Bible, and whether it be from the Old or New Testament, violates the First Amendment; the study of the Bible as a work of literature does not—and this notwithstanding the difficulty a devoutly religious teacher, who believes that the Bible is literally the word of God, may have in measuring the Bible by nonreligious standards of literature.[41]

A perhaps somewhat more difficult program is presented in respect to religious holiday observances in the public schools; not more difficult because the constitutional standards differ, but because of emotional conflict often engendered by demands that the school authorities adhere to these standards. Controversies revolving about Christmas or Easter celebrations in the public schools (or, to appease Jewish parents, Christmas-Hannukah or, on occasion, Easter-Passover celebrations) are often bitter and on occasion lead to litigation. Despite its bitterness, the litigation generally has salutary effects, at least if measured by First Amendment standards. In some cases the public school authorities discontinue the celebrations and leave responsibility for that aspect of the children's lives to their parents. In others, the celebrations are continued but with lesser intensity and with an effort to spare the feelings of pupils whose religious beliefs and upbringings do not encompass the religious holiday sought to be celebrated.

What has been said concerning religion in public education applies primarily to education at the elementary and secondary levels. At the college and university levels, the law allows far more leeway to the authorities, on the assumption that the students are fully able to protect their own religious integrity notwithstanding the religiosity of some of the practices.

In respect to governmental aid to religious schools, the constitutional guidelines, as fixed by Supreme Court decisions, also appear to be fairly well established, at least for the time being. At the elementary and secondary school levels, tax-raised funds may be used to finance transportation of pupils to and from home and school[42] and to provide secular textbooks for use (though not ownership) by the pupils in connection with their secular studies.[43] Other forms of financing educational material and services, such as teachers' salaries, maintenance and repairs of parochial school premises, or income tax credits for school tuition violate the Establishment Clause.[44] Nor is it constitutionally permissible to assign publicly employed teachers to religious schools to teach secular subjects, and the prohibition encompasses not only the teaching of such subjects to average pupils, but includes as well enriched teaching to gifted children or remedial teaching to below-grade pupils.[45]

The rationale that justifies, at least in part, transportation financing is a determination that its purpose is not to aid education but to protect the safety of children as they travel between home and school. Whatever benefit inures to the church that operates the school (in that if the state did not provide the necessary funds and the parents could not afford the expense the pupils might be withdrawn) is secondary or incidental. The justification of textbook financing, as the Court frankly recognizes, is that because of the importance of previous legal precedents, it is preferable to adhere to the *Allen* decision rather than overrule it, although the Court will not allow extension of the *Allen* exception to encompass, for example, instructional equipment or other educational materials.[46]

Where the beneficiaries of governmental spending are institutions of higher education, that is, colleges and universities, the Supreme Court is far more liberal in allowing financing. In *Tilton v. Richardson*,[47] it passed upon the constitutionality of including church-related colleges in funding under the Higher Education Facilities Act of 1963, which provides for governmental financing of construction and expansion of academic facilities in institutions of higher education. The Court, in *Tilton* and other cases,[48] set rather generous limits to constitutionally permissible aid. Grants to theological seminaries or divinity schools were held impermissible. So too were grants for the construction or maintenance of those facilities in church-related colleges which were used for religious teaching or practice (for example, chapels). Governmental funding of secular activities and premises (for example, gymnasiums) used exclusively for secular activities was, on the other hand, held constitutionally permissible.

The reason for the distinction is basically the same as that which justified greater tolerance in respect to the teaching of religion at public institutions of higher learning. The danger of unduly influencing students who have reached adulthood is minimal and must yield to the recognized need to make available expanded college and university facilities for the benefit not only of the students who qualify for advanced education, but no less for the nation at large.

The immediate precedent for the Higher Education Facilities Act was the National Defense Education Act of 1958, which was expressly predicated on that premise.

At all levels of educational institutions, from pre-school to university, the restrictions of the Establishment Clause do not apply to the use of tax-raised funds to finance health and welfare services as distinguished from educational services. Breakfasts, lunches, medical and dental care, and some aspects of psychological services fall within this category.[49]

THE YEAR 2000 AND PERHAPS AFTER

Prediction is a risky business, but sometimes the risk is worth taking. In the arena of the First Amendment's religion clauses as interpreted and applied by the Supreme Court, we have a century of history behind us (measured from the 1878 decision in *Reynolds v. United States*)[50] as a basis for reasonable guesses in regard to the next century, or at least to the year 2000, if not after. With this caveat, and on this basis, the following may be suggested as likely developments in the judicial interpretation of the Free Exercise and Establishment Clauses by the Supreme Court in selected areas of religious freedom and church-state relations.

Tax Exemption for Churches

The years that the churches will continue to enjoy generous exemption are limited. The financial needs of a quasi-social welfare state, which (notwithstanding temporary setbacks manifested by the California's Proposition 13 and similar events) our nation is becoming, if it has not already become so, require large sums of money. As a practical matter, taxation is about the only substantial source of these funds, and willy-nilly the financial assets and income of churches will have to be reached through taxation. The process has already begun; more and more states are taxing church-owned properties used to produce income even though the income is used exclusively for church purposes.[51] It is only a question of time until the churches will be subjected to substantial taxes based on their assets and income.

Population Control

In *Griswold v. Connecticut*[52] the Supreme Court ruled that anti-contraception laws were unconstitutional. Realistically, the decision (which had long been reached, de facto if not de jure, by all the other agencies of government, federal and state) was inevitable in the light of the universally recognized need to control population growth. Contraception having proved an inadequate means to achieve population control, particularly among the lower economic classes, the Court found it necessary, in the cases of *Roe v. Wade*[53] and *Doe v. Bolton*,[54] to legitimize abortion, at least to the extent of invalidating penal sanctions against it. As of the present writing, the Court has refused to hold that either the First or Fourteenth Amendment forbids governments, state and federal, to exclude abortion procedures in state or municipal hospitals or from coverage under Medicaid or similar state programs of health insurance.[55] Whether or not the Court will overrule or modify its decisions on this point, depends upon whether some other practicable method of controlling births, particularly among the lower economic classes, is developed. If not, then notwithstanding church opposition, governmentally financed abortion procedures will before long become the law of the land, either by legislative action or, more likely, by judicial decision.

Compulsory Sunday Observance Laws

These, for practical purposes, have pretty much expired without help from the Supreme Court.[56] Their revival to any substantial extent, is unlikely.

Homosexuality

Here too, by the year 2000 law-imposed restraints will, for all practical purposes, have disappeared, whether by legislative repeal, judicial decisions, or, as in the case of many of the Sunday laws, by nonenforcement.

Military Exemption for Conscientious Objectors

This will remain a question exclusive for legislative determination. The Supreme Court will not change its long-standing position that the Free Exercise Clause does not command such an exemption, nor does the Establishment Clause forbid it.[57]

Religion in the Public Schools

From time to time efforts are made—rarely more than half-heartedly—to nullify by constitutional amendment the Supreme Court's decisions relating to religious practices and instruction in the public schools. It is not likely that these efforts will succeed, and it is even more unlikely that in the absence of constitutional amendment the Court will overrrule its decisions in this area. Like it or not, our public schools in the year 2000 will remain substantially nonreligious, *without* religious instruction, *without* prayer, *without* devotional Bible reading, and *without* at least the most patently religious ceremonial observances of Christmas and Easter.

Aid to Parochial Schools

Here one must be somewhat less confident. The pressures for such aid are powerful and do not show signs of substantial abatement. By and large, they come from the same sources that seek governmental restraints upon abortion. Nevertheless, the probabilities are that the Supreme Court will not substantially either retreat or go forward from what must be characterized as a compromise position on the subject: financing of health and welfare services will be held permissible; financing of educational services beyond transportation and secular textbooks use, will not be allowed; greater tolerance will be exercised in respect to financing the operations of church-related institutions in the area of higher education.

WHY?

The explanation of the Supreme Court's decisions on the subject dealt with here lies principally in one sociohistoric fact: that, notwithstanding occasional visits by a charismatic Pope or periodic religious revivals by Protestants, the American people are committed to a culture that can best be described as secular humanism, at least where government is involved. Put somewhat simplistically, this means that religion is a private matter, not for government either to inhibit or advance. So long as the American people remain committed to this concept, that commitment will be reflected in Supreme Court decisions. Since there is little reason to believe that there will be any change in that commitment by the year 2000, it is a good guess that before then there will be no substantial changes in the Supreme Court decisions in respect to the principles here considered. Beyond 2000, predictions should not be made.

NOTES

1. See, Anson Stokes and Leo Pfeffer, *Church and State in the United States* (New York: Harper & Row, 1964), chs. 1–4; L. Pfeffer, *Church, State and Freedom* (Boston: Beacon Press, 1967), chs. 3–4.

2. As early as 1663 Rhode Island obtained a charter from England which provided that "no person within the said colony . . . shall be in any wise molested, punished, disquieted or called in question, for any differences in opinion in matters of religion, and do not actually disturb the civil peace of our said colony." See Pfeffer, *Church, State and Freedom*, p. 65.

3. See also, *Nebraska Press Assn. v. Stuart*, 427 U.S. 539 (1976).

4. Stokes and Pfeffer, *Church and State*, p. 356.

5. *Walz v. Tax Commission*, 397 U.S. 664 (1970).

6. *Pierce v. Society of Sisters*, 268 U.S. 510 (1925).

7. See *Committee for Public Education and Religious Liberty v. Nyquist*, 413 U.S. 756 (1973); *Sloan v. Lemon*, 413 U.S. 825 (1973).

8. *Everson v. Board of Education*, 330 U.S. 1 at 32 (1947) (dissenting opinion).

9. Pfeffer, *Church, State and Freedom*, pp. 135–36. As one commentator put it: "In determining the limits of constitutional separation, it is the concept of religious freedom which provides the criterion. The principle of church-state separation is an instrumental principle. Separation ordinarily promotes religious freedom; it is defensible as long as it does so, and only so long." Wilber Katz, "The Case of Religious Liberty" in *Religion in America*, ed. John Cogley (Cleveland: Meridian, 1958), p. 97. See also Donald Giannella, "Religious Liberty, Nonestablishment and Doctrinal Development," *Harvard Law Review* 80 (May 1967): 1381-1431, and 81 (January 1968): 513–90.

10. *Reynolds v. United States*, 98 U.S. 145 at 166 (1878). It is significant that it was in this case, involving criminal prosecution of Mormons for polygamy, an obvious Free Exercise issue, that the Court's opinion invokes not only Jefferson's Virginia Statute for Establishing Religious Freedom but also Madison's Memorial and Remonstrance Against Religious Assessments.

11. *Cantwell v. Connecticut*, 310 U.S. 296 (1940).

12. Ibid., at 303–4.

13. *Davis v. Beason*, 133 U.S. 333 (1890).

14. *Minerville School District v. Gobitis*, 310 U.S. 586, at 594–95 (1940).

15. *West Virginia State Board of Education v. Barnette*, 319 U.S. 624 (1943).

16. *Schenck v. United States*, 249 U.S. 47 at 52 (1919).

17. *Cantwell v. Connecticut*, 310 U.S. 296 at 308 (1940).

18. *Sherbert v. Verner*, 374 U.S. 398 at 406 (1963).

19. *Wisconsin v. Yoder*, 406 U.S. 205 (1972).

20. Ibid., at 215.

21. Sometimes the Court will overrule a prior contrary decision without even mentioning it. In *Sherbert* it upheld the Sabbatarian's claim without noting that it had earlier dismissed for want of a substantial federal question an appeal that raised exactly the same issue. *Heisler v. Board of Review*, 343 U.S. 939 (1952), dismissing appeal from 156 Ohio St. 395 (1951).

22. 199 Misc. 643, affirmed 278 App. Div. 705, affirmed 302 N.Y. 857, appeal dismissed, *Donner v. New York*, 342 U.S. 884 (1951).

23. *Braunfeld v. Brown*, 366 U.S. 599 (1961).

24. *Wisconsin v. Yoder*, 406 U.S. 205 (1972).

25. *Jacobson v. Massachusetts*, 197 U.S. 11 (1905).

26. *People ex rel Wallace v. Labrenz*, 344 U.S. 824 (1952), dismissing appeal from 411 Ill. 618.

27. *Application of Georgetown College*, 331 F. 2d 1000 (C.C.A., D.C.) (1966).

28. *Jones v. President of Georgetown College*, 331 F. 2d 1000, *certiorari* denied, 377 U.S. 978 (1964).

29. *National Labor Relations Board v. Catholic Archbishop of Chicago*, 440 U.S. 490 (1979).

30. *Associated Press v. NLRB*, 301 U.S. 103 (1937).

31. *Everson v. Board of Education*, 330 U.S. 1 at 15 (1947).

32. *Abington School District v. Schempp*, 374 U.S. 203 (1963).

33. Ibid., at 222.

34. *Board of Education v. Allen*, 312 U.S. 236 (1968).

35. *Lemon v. Kurtzman*, 403 U.S. 602 (1971).

36. Ibid., at 612–13.

37. Ibid.

38. *Engel v. Vitale*, 370 U.S. 421 (1962); *Abington Township School District v. Schempp*, 374 U.S. 203 (1963).

39. *McCollum v. Board of Education*, 333 U.S. 203 (1948).

40. *Zorach v. Clauson*, 343 U.S. 306 (1952).

41. *Abington Township School District v. Schempp*, 374 U.S. 203 (1963).

42. *Everson v. Board of Education*, 330 U.S. 1 (1947).

43. *Board of Education v. Allen*, 392 U.S. 236 (1968). See also *Cochran v. Louisiana State Board of Education*, 281 U.S. 370 (1930).

44. *Lemon v. Kurtzman*, 403 U.S. 602 (1971); *Earley v. DiCenso*, 403 U.S. 602 (1971); *Committee for Public Education and Religious Liberty v. Nyquist*, 413 U.S. 756 (1973); *Sloan v. Lemon*, 413 U.S. 825 (1973); *Levitt v. Committee for Public Education and Religious Liberty*, 413 U.S. 472 (1973); *Public Funds for Public Schools v. Marburger*, 417 U.S. 961 (1974) affirming 258 F. Supp. 29; *New York v. Cathedral Academy*, 434 U.S. 125 (1977); and *Byrne v. Public Funds for Public Schools*, 442 U.S. 907 (1979) affirming 590 F. Supp. 1228, 590 F. 2d 514.

45. *Meek v. Pittenger*, 421 U.S. 349 (1975).

46. *Wolman v. Walter*, 433 U.S. 229 (1977).

47. *Tilton v. Richardson*, 403 U.S. 672 (1971).

48. *Hunt v. McNair*, 413 U.S. 734 (1973); *Roemer v. Maryland Public Works Board*, 426 U.S. 736 (1976).

49. *Wolman v. Walter*, 433 U.S. 229 (1977).

50. *Reynolds v. United States*, 98 U.S. 145 (1878).

51. See *Diffenderfer v. Central Baptist Church*, 404 U.S. 412 (1972).

52. *Griswold v. Connecticut*, 381 U.S. 479 (1965).

53. *Roe v. Wade*, 410 U.S. 113 (1973).

54. *Doe v. Bolton*, 410 U.S. 179 (1973).

55. *Beal v. Doe*, 432 U.S. 438 (1977); *Maher v. Roe*, 432 U.S. 464 (1977); *Poelker v. Doe*, 432 U.S. 519 (1977).

56. See *McGowan v. Maryland*, 366 U.S. 420 (1961).

57. *Arver v. United States*, 245 U.S. 366 (1918).

7

SISTER MARIE AUGUSTA NEAL

The Future of First Amendment Provisions Regarding Church-State Relations

The First Amendment of the Constitution—"Congress shall make no law respecting an establishment of religion or prohibiting the free exercise thereof"—provides both for the free exercise of religion and for the separation of church and state. Neither can the state legislatures—since 1940, when the Fourteenth Amendment was interpreted to cover the first—make laws establishing or prohibiting religions.[1] Over the years, the First Amendment has been invoked effectively to protect conscientious objectors, opposed to participation in war; Amish believers, opposed to the public education of their children beyond the eighth grade; Christian Scientists, opposed to medical treatment for themselves and their children; and Jehovah's Witnesses, opposed to saluting the flag in the classroom.

In all these cases, the express intention of the law has been to protect the right of individuals to act according to their belief in, and religious commitment to, a law higher than patriotism. That higher law has traditionally been understood as originating in a Supreme Being, the God of world religions, however immediate or remote believers might conceive the deity to be, or else as a set of universal ethical norms rooted in a common humanity. The constitutional restriction on the establishment of religion was designed to prevent the ethical code of any particular belief system from being used to limit the freedom of those not subscribing to those specific beliefs.

A number of current developments threaten to undermine respect for the First Amendment provisions regarding the relation between church and state, as evidenced by the state's growing reluctance to grant religious exemptions from citizenship obligations. Among these developments are the erosion of belief in a deity, or the relegation of religious conscience to the private realm, which has accompanied the progressive secularization of the state. The privatization of religion has in turn spawned a variety of cults claiming exemption from taxes, military service, and the other acts of allegiance that denote a readiness to share the burdens and responsibilities of society.

The privatization of religion presses on the courts the questions of how to reconcile freedom of religion with the needs of the state, of determining which beliefs and practices defined as religious are worthy of protection under the Constitution. The courts are being forced to draw distinctions. At the same time, the secularization of the state presses on believers the question of whether a law designed to protect individuals from state-imposed religion should not also protect them from state-imposed secularism.

At the heart of both issues is the question of whether God is a public figure. The sociological evidence points to an affirmative answer. Religion is not a private matter; it is a social phenomenon. Religion is associated not with the individual but with society.

A number of broad social trends are apparent in the changing social context in which court decisions affecting church-state relations will be made. The most important are in the areas of human rights, civil religion, and altruism.[2]

HUMAN RIGHTS

Allegiances on the church-state issue are shifting as a result of basic shifts among Protestants, Catholics, and Jews on the question of public order. People no longer divide on the issue along the lines of denomination or ethnic identification. The critical division is now within each church and ethnic group, cutting across older alignments and making allies of strangers. The concrete issues include opposition to war, arms production, uses of nuclear energy, and mistreatment of political prisoners, and the affirmation of minority-group rights to employment, good education, health care, and choice of residence area. The fundamental issue, across many religious persuasions, is whether one's religious commitment demands simply the alleviation of the results of poverty or the elimination of its causes.

All three religious traditions have biblical roots that call for the alleviation of human suffering, and all have historically been involved in delivering health, educational, and welfare services. But the three also share a tradition of social justice; one which goes well beyond the requirements of a distributive justice honoring rights of property acquired by fair exchange of the stipulated collateral.[3] The deeper definition of justice calls for the elimination of the causes of poverty. At issue, behind these definitions of justice and therefore of the religious commitment, is the definition of human rights.

How human rights are to be defined is the subject of two United Nations' Covenants on Human Rights, which won the thirty-five votes needed to become official U.N. policy in 1976. The United States was not among the affirming voters. Not until October of 1977 did the Covenants receive the signature of the U.S. President, and they do not yet enjoy the necessary treaty ratification of the U.S. Senate.

Many of the rights described in the Covenant entitled "Civil and Political Rights" are familiar to us, but the Covenant entitled "Economic, Social and Cultural Rights" contains many we still consider privileges rather than rights, such as the rights to free medical care, access to free education through the college years, care in retirement regardless of amount of work done, access to the benefits of employment, full employment, the right to form labor unions, and the rights of peoples to self-determination and to the free use and enjoyment of their natural wealth and resources.[4] To the poorer nations, the latter category of rights is of principal concern at present. For some 20 million of our own fellow citizens also, these rights are not available in our economic program, itself the mainstay of our political system.

Yet our traditional religious systems are affirming these rights,[5] and in so doing they are reactivating a membership alienated in recent decades by the churches' conventional insensitivities to human oppression and poverty. True, such insensitivities still characterize affluent, mainline, local churches in America, which are still more interested in issues such as personal tax exemption than in sharing the common wealth with the unemployed, for whom the national economy can provide no jobs. But when the churches and synagogues do hear a religious call to action for justice, they bring to public consciousness critical questions of domestic and foreign policy—questions about the denial of human rights to health, education, and welfare services in this, the world's most affluent, nation; questions about the dispossession of the unemployed and under-employed for whom the national economy cannot provide needed jobs; questions about our support of apartheid in South Africa;[6] about the free press needed to provide an accurate understanding of what is happening in South Africa, the Middle East, Northern Ireland, Latin America, and Cambodia; about who has the power to shape public conscience and to what purpose; questions about the structure of world capitalism;[7] about the implementation of the United Nations' Covenants on Human Rights; questions about the survival of peoples.

As the churches raise public issues as matters of religious concern, issues in which we as a nation play a predominant role, they experience new pressures from the state. The pursuit by the FBI of religiously-motivated protestors against the Vietnam War was a case in point. So is the threat of denying to the churches their tax-exempt status on the argument that they are moving outside the area of legitimate religious discourse.

In the past, the churches themselves have sometimes—for example, in distinguishing "faith and order" concerns from "life and work"—separated the spiritual agenda from the social. And, even today, some inside and outside the churches criticize theologies that incorporate the social agenda as merely political ideologies in religious guise. But increasingly the churches are defining the economic, political, and social concerns as religious concerns. Such religious convocations as the Second Vatican Council, the international conferences of the World Council of Churches, and the Detroit "Call to Action" Conference of 1976 call their members to active participation in bringing about social justice as a religious responsibility. Moreover, while the themes of liberation theology are political, economic, and social, I submit that they are also eminently religious and rooted in Scripture.[8]

As the churches pick up this social justice agenda as their common cause, the emphasis is frequently missed by the media, which concentrate instead on narcissistic themes in the religious and other areas of popular culture.[9] But the new focus of the churches is not on narcissistic but on public concerns.

The First Amendment should protect the resulting dialectical tension between church and state. In fact, the religion that has come to enjoy the protection of the law is the private worship of an esoteric

God. This trend is furthered to the extent that, despite the growing religious affirmation to the contrary, political, social, and economic issues are defined by the state as nonreligious.

The relegation of religion to the private sphere should itself be recognized as a political strategy, growing out of a specific ideology of containment and facilitating the development of a specific type of secular society, one that attempts to render ineffective the social justice component of the Judeo-Christian tradition. That social justice tradition is more concerned with shaping the future than it is with sustaining the past. It calls for a review in the public forum of what are defined as properly religious concerns.

CIVIL RELIGION

Civil religion is a relatively new concept, a term coined in the 1960s with a content different from its earlier meaning and itself a contribution to the shaping of the national culture.[10] The insight it highlights is this: we have little need to fear church establishment at the present time; what we need to fear more is the loss of a focus for shaping an altruistic public conscience, a conscience that can generate and preserve public concern for the survival of the poor when their labor is no longer needed in an automated and computerized production system.

Civil religion in America refers to a national faith that has a creed and moves the people of the nation on occasion to stand in judgment on the laws of their own state when they perceive that those laws violate what the creed affirms. It also moves people to rejoice in their nation-state when they experience it as realizing the values of the creed.

Robert N. Bellah extracted the term "civil religion" from Jean-Jacques Rousseau's *Social Contract*,[11] where it was used with a narrower meaning to refer only to a set of beliefs that support the political authority of the state. In Rousseau's analysis, these included beliefs in the existence of God, in a life to come, and in the reward of virtue and the punishment of vice, with an added dictum regarding the "exclusion of religious intolerance." Rousseau, as social philosopher, was recommending a way to civic harmony through support for civic authority, a development of the ancient *pietas*.[12]

Bellah adds new meaning to the term. He is shaping it to refer to something more specifically religious in the sense of transcending the law of the land yet capable of passing judgment on it. He introduced the term in 1967 as a concept for sociological analysis of a phenomenon he thought could be distinguished from several others. At that time he wrote, "While some have argued that Christianity is the national faith and others, that church and synagogue celebrate only the generalized religion of the 'American Way of Life,' few have realized that there actually exists alongside of and rather clearly differentiated from the churches, an elaborate and well-institutionalized civil religion in America."[13] The main tenets of this faith, which he extracts from the Declaration of Independence and the Constitution, are the beliefs that God created all people equal and endowed them with certain inalienable rights.[14] The critical quality of this religion, he claims, is that people who believe in it can call upon it as a framework from which to judge the nation when that nation violates the rights of people or fails to protect them in time of unrest. Thus, the test of the depth of the institutionalization of America's civil religion in the mid-sixties was to be its response to the civil rights and antiwar movements.

Bellah wrote again about civil religion in 1974.[15] "Civil religion at its best," he explained, "is a genuine apprehension of universal and transcendent religious reality as seen in or, one could almost say, as revealed through the experience of the American people." Political theorists and activists who have taken a position on separation of church and state are disturbed by Bellah's passion and, for this reason, question his objectivity as a sociologist, claiming that the intent of his analysis is to bring about a condition of critical self-examination from the perspective of religious symbol and fervor, while they believe that the failures of states are better addressed from the perspective of cool reason and secular values.

In Bellah's analysis, civil religion is a normative reality. It is essentially prophetic and stands in contrast and opposition to the folkways of the people. It judges idolatrous tendencies of particular forms of Christianity and Judaism. As he puts it, "It is of the essence of the American civil religion that it 'challenges institutional authority.' "[16] He locates in civil religion the prophetic function of calling the nation, including its civil leaders, to account whenever they fail to provide the members their rights as people "created equal." Among the martyrs of the republic he includes Abraham Lincoln and Martin Luther King.

When Bellah's writings turned more prophetic than analytic, though his social science colleagues chided him for his lack of objectivity,[17] religionists espoused his cause and made him the central figure of major bicentennial celebrations.[18] The debate continued, therefore, pursuing two main questions: whether the covenant is in fact broken,[19] and whether the focus of civil religion has moved from the nation to the world society.[20]

The intellectual and religious interest in the idea of civil religion is directly associated with a new political consciousness in modern theological speculation. The attention of theologians has been drawn to the growing problems of a world economy that outstrips the power of the state and the corresponding need for some type of association capable of addressing in a serious way the ethical and social problems generated by new international centers of power.[21] The survival of the poor requires a public religion with an informed conscience. This need is hardly served by the churches simply affirming their diversity or by social commentators allocating religion to the private sphere.

Legislation guaranteeing the "free exercise of religion" often assumes, understandably, that religion will attract small, eccentric groups. Legislation erecting a "wall of separation" between church and state, however, is rooted in the perceived need to restrain certain effective moral bodies (often the Catholic Church) from disrupting the public conscience. This assumes that the envisaged church intervention does not enjoy popular support: a dislodging of the American democratic process, for example, by the Catholic Church's hierarchical structure. Suppose, however, that there should develop among Catholics and others a new shared religious commitment and the moral strength that this implies, around a high valuing of genuine participatory democracy with a special concern for the participation of the poor as equals. Suppose that such a moral force called to account the laws of the land, insisting on due process whenever the poor, the ill, and the old were excluded from decisions affecting the uses of the common wealth. There is a growing sense among the religiously committed that this is no idle dream but rather the wave of the future. Moreover, the focus of their religious concern is not simply the nation-state but world society.

From this point of view, privatized religion, though seemingly congenial to the libertarian conviction, is recognized as the ideology of a secularized state comprised of atomized human units.[22] What Bellah began analyzing as civil religion may be emerging as a religious consensus protesting the plight of the poor and resisting decision makers who would dispose of them according to the ethics of the lifeboat or of triage.[23] Such a concern for the survival of peoples other than one's own interest group would be rooted in a "genuine apprehension of universal and transcendent religious reality;" and it would characteristically "challenge institutional authority," standing in judgment on those laws of the nations that permit the destruction of peoples.

Such religion will need vigorous protection by the courts under the "free exercise" clause. It will require different arguments than those used to protect the rights of exotic cults and creeds. It will be less easily ignored if it is rooted in a recognizable belief in "a universal and transcendent religious reality," shared by many denominations and affirmed in local worship services.

ALTRUISM

This new religious consciousness owes nothing to the narcissism of much of the current religious feeling. Rather, it exalts altruism, the giving up of one's life for the stranger, the so-called folly of the Judeo-Christian doctrine of the love of one's neighbor.[24] Though it is the central value of all world religions, altruism—the disinterested love of the other—is today the object of a radical, politically-motivated, scientific challenge.

The notion of altruism assumes special importance in a world characterized by a growing population with markedly uneven access to material resources and decision-making power. One's chances of surviving the first year of life, or of living to be forty or eighty, differ dramatically depending on where one is born. There are religious and secular strategies for dealing with these inequities. Today, despite our advances in recognition of human rights, some scientists advocate a policy of triage and the lifeboat ethic receives legitimation.[25]

A recent academic focus providing a rationale for the selective development of peoples is sociobiology, a synthesis of biology, ethnology, sociology, and psychology. It claims as its central thesis that altruism, like all behavior, is basically motivated by selfishness through the gene-programmed determination to preserve the tribe, a programming to which even the richest religious and humanitarian efforts are necessarily subservient.[26] According to the theory of Edward O. Wilson, what he calls "hard-core" altruism—giving one's life that others may continue to live—extends only to one's family, tribe and, in a mild way, to one's nation. The motive of self-sacrifice is always the extension of one's own gene pool. All other kindness to others, "soft-core" altruism, is extended only on a quid pro quo basis: one gives in proportion to an expected return, where the expected return is the advancement of one's own kin's interest even at the expense of that of all others. He testifies that religion is intentionally a part of this soft core altruism.[27]

Sociobiology is a new form of Social Darwinism. It provides no rationale beyond self-interest for our helping the poorest nations to survive; and at the same time rationalizes aggression against strangers by reason of which the populations of poor nations die. Religious love of neighbor is redefined as selective of one's kin. The object of religious love is narrowed to ethnic survival;[28] the otherness of God is denied.[29] In sum, it aggressively denies the possibility of an ethic of love that is world population inclusive.

Just at the time when there begins to be a wider recognition of people's rights to human services on the basis of their human nature, as evidenced by the United Nations Covenants mentioned earlier and by recent church documents,[30] there arises this scientific argument against the very existence of real altruism as a human possibility building on human nature. This argument has clear implications for public policy, namely, that to plan solutions for the problems of need on the basis of an utopian dream of universal love would be not only impractical but a threat to the survival of the species.

Why is the sociobiology debate raised now as a church/state issue? Sociobiology's redefinition of altruism raises new questions about the exclusion from public education of the study of religion and the resistance of private religious schools to public support. An earlier secularism, in rejecting the reality of God, nevertheless recognized a natural law of love of neighbor, a natural responsibility for the poor even when the poor are not kin. This is denied by the new biology, according to which selfishness is not only natural but altruism is an unattainable ideal and a distraction from necessary decisions. The meaning of altruism undergoes a profound transformation in the new theory. It includes only the drive to kin selection and the guide of reciprocal services.[31] All other meanings are excluded, and this by a discipline that presumes to unite biology, psychology, sociology, and eventually all of the humanities, including religion. In this way the stage is set for a basic secularism to be taught in the schools with no provision for reflection on its consequences within the same environment. In this subject matter area, talk about God and the distinction between God and religion are part of the scientific agenda.[32]

What is taught from the perspective of sociobiology directly influences human consciousness and behavior and particularly public policy with respect to the survival of marginal peoples. If religious altruism is not taught in the public universities and lower schools alongside "scientific" altruism, then a bias is introduced in the shaping of the public conscience, a bias that can further legitimate the extinction of peoples. The present stance of the courts, excluding religious moral teaching from the schools and privatizing religious reflection from the learning experience, reduces the capacity of students to reflect critically on "scientific" altruism from the standpoint of the religious traditions and the survival of peoples.

Does not this exclusion from public support of the serious study of religion as a guide to conscience mean that public education is freed for an uncritical legitimation of triage as public policy for dealing with the world's poor? May not this in fact be its intent?

NOTES

1. C. Herman Pritchett, *The American Constitution* (New York: McGraw-Hill, 1977), p. 329.

2. The author has pursued these trends at greater length elsewhere. See "A Turning Point of Religious Ethics," *The Ecumenist* 46 (November–December 1977); "Sociobiology," book review in *Sociological Analysis* 39, no. 2 (Summer 1978); "Civil Religion," *New Catholic Encyclopedia* 17 (1979); "Civil Religion and the Development of People," *Religious Education Review* 22 (May–June 1976).

3. As an example of the more limited concept of justice, see Robert Nozick, *Anarchy, State and Utopia* (New York: Basic Books, 1975).

4. *The United Nations' Covenants on Human Rights* (New York: United Nations Information Center, 1976).

5. See *The Church and Human Rights* (Vatican City: Pontifical Commission on Justice and Peace, 1975); and *Church Alert*, nos. 16–18 (Geneva: Sodepax, World Council of Churches, 1977–1978).

6. "Southern Africa Perspectives" (New York: The Africa Fund , 1977).

7. See William Ryan, "Multinational Corporations and the New International Economic Order," *Church Alert* 16 (1977); "Evangelization—A Political Problem?" *Pro Mundi Vita* 38 (1975).

8. For a discussion and bibliography on liberation theology, see Gustavo Gutierrez, *Theology of Liberation* (Maryknoll, N.Y.: Orbis Books, 1971); Robert McAfee Brown, *Theology in a New Key* (Philadelphia: Westminster Press, 1978); Dorothee Soelle, *Political Theology* (Philadelphia: Fortress Press, 1974). See also the recent general listings of Orbis Books, Maryknoll, N.Y., 1979.

9. This was particularly evident in the reporting of the 1976 "Call to Action" conference, a national convocation of the Catholic Church in Detroit. One hundred and sixty decisions were taken, dealing mainly with action for the renewal of life for people in exploitative situations, including the cities, Appalachia and among farm workers. The media, however, focused on concern for a married clergy, divorced Catholics, and women priests—all important issues, but not the conference's main agenda.

10. This section is taken, with minor changes, from my article, "Civil Religion," *New Catholic Encyclopedia* 17 (1979).

11. Jean Jacques Rousseau, *The Social Contract and Discourses*, trans. G. Cole (New York: Dutton, 1950), pp. 129–41.

12. Martin Marty, "Two Kinds of Civil Religion," in *American Civil Religion*, ed. Russell E. Richey and Donald G. Jones (New York: Harper and Row, 1974), pp. 139–57.

13. Robert N. Bellah, "Civil Religion in American," *Daedalus* 96 (1973): 1–21.

14. Robert N. Bellah, "Comment on 'Bellah and the New Orthodoxy' ", *Sociological Analysis* 37 (Summer 1976): 167–68.

15. Robert N. Bellah, *The Broken Covenant* (New York: Seabury Press, 1975).

16. Ibid., p. 167.

17. See Phillip O. Hammond, "The Sociology of American Civil Religion," *Sociological Analysis* 37 (Summer 1976): 127–39; and Richard Fenn, "Bellah and The New Orthodoxy," *Sociological Analysis* 37: 160–67.

18. See *Religious Education* (May–June 1976).

19. Michael Novak, *Choosing Our King: Powerful Symbols in Presidential Politics* (New York: Macmillan, 1974).

20. Sr. Marie Augusta Neal, "Civil Religion and The Development of Peoples," *Religious Education* (May–June 1976): 244–60.

21. See Gregory Baum, *Religion and Alienation* (New York: Paulist Press, 1975); Sr. Marie Augusta Neal, *A Socio-Theology of Letting-Go* (New York: Paulist Press, 1977); Jose Comblin, *The Church and The National Security State* (New York: Orbis Books, 1979).

22. See Peter L. Berger, *The Sacred Canopy* (Garden City, N.Y.: Doubleday, 1967).

23. Garrett Hardin, "Living on a Life Boat," *Bioscience* 24 (October 1974): 561–68.

24. See Alessandro Cussianovich, *Religious Life and the Poor: A Liberation Theology Perspective* (New York: Paulist Press, 1979). Contrast Robert N. Bellah and Charles Glock, eds., *New Religious Consciousness* (Berkeley, Calif.: University of California, 1977).

25. See the writings of Garrett Hardin, including "The Tragedy of the Commons," *Science* 162 (December 1968); "Living on a Life Boat," *Bioscience* 24, no. 10 (October 1974): 561–68; and "Where the Thinking Heart Beats the Bleeding Heart," *Boston Globe*, July 14, 1979, p. 11. Contrast Geoffrey Barraclough, "Wealth and Power: The Politics of Food and Oil," *New York Review of Books*, August 7, 1975; Frances M. Lappe and Joseph Collins, *Food First: Beyond the Myth of Scarcity Global Reach: The Power of the Multinational Corporations* (New York: Simon and Schuster, 1973).

26. The sociobiology debate has centered on Edward O. Wilson's *Sociobiology: A New Synthesis* (Cambridge, Mass.: Harvard University, 1975), and his recent *On Human Nature* (Cambridge, Mass.: Harvard University Press, 1978). For the debate, see Arthur L. Caplan, *The Sociobiology Debate: Readings in Ethical and Scientific Issues* (New York: Harper and Row, 1978). See the new journal devoted to the field, *The Journal of Social and Biological Structure: Studies in Human Sociobiology*, ed. Harry Wheeler and James P. Danielli (New York: Academic Press, 1976). Psychology and sociology textbooks in paperback and hardcover are already on the market. See David P. Barash, *Sociobiology and Behavior* (New York: Elsevier, 1977); my review of this book in *Sociological Analysis* 39 (Summer 1978) pp. 185–87; and Pierre L. Van der Berghe, *Man and Society*, (New York: Elsevier, 1978). The latter book is an introductory sociology text; these three authors recognize one another's contributions. See also, Michael S. Gregory, Anita Silvers and Diane Sutch, eds., *Sociobiology and Human Nature: An Interdisciplinary Critique and Defense*

(San Francisco: Jossey-Bass, 1978). *Time* magazine recognized the field with its cover story on August 1, 1977, and the 1978 annual meeting of the American Association for the Advancement of Science devoted two days of its program to the topic. Wilson and Hardin have received the National Medal of Science from the President of the United States and acclaim from AAAS. To hear Wilson speaking across the disciplines, see his "Biology and the Social Sciences," *Daedalus* 2 (Fall 1977): 127–39. See also the entire issue of *Society* 15, no. 6 (September–October 1978).

27. Wilson, *On Human Nature*, pp. 165, 193.

28. Edward O. Wilson, "Altruism," *Harvard Magazine* (November–December 1978): 23–78; Wilson, *Sociobiology*, chs. 1, 5, and 27. Wilson, *On Human Nature*, chs. 7, 8, and 9, especially pp. 199, 189.

29. Edward O. Wilson, *Sociobiology*, p. 120; Wilson, *On Human Nature*, chs. 1, 8, and 9, pp. 177–92, 205–7. See also Stuart Hampshire's review, "The Illusion of Sociobiology," *New York Review of Books*, October 12, 1978.

30. For a review and summary of these Church documents see "Rocca di Papa Colloquium on the Social Thinking of the Churches," *Church Alert* pts. 1, 2, 3, 4, nos. 17–20.

31. Edward O. Wilson, "Altruism," p. 25; *Sociobiology*, pp. 561, 120.

32. See Wilson, *On Human Nature*, p. 192 and Van der Berghe, *Man and Society*, pp. 60, 170, 99–100 in that order. *Man and Society* (second edition) should be read *in toto* to see this problem manifest. The critical factor has to do with the evidence. Wilson and Baruch admit there is none. Van der Berghe claims the other two have provided it. All admit that systematic observation of primate behavior is less than two decades old (Van der Berghe, p. 27). Yet given that fragile basis of plausibility the discipline has invaded the classrooms of human psychology, sociology, and anthropology at every grade level. Why this popularity for a thesis so in keeping with a public policy regarding outsiders and the uses of aggression?

SECTION IV

Mental Illness and State Power

8

DAVID ROTHMAN

Government Power and the Right to be Different

The issue of "government power and the right to be different" presents some very unusual considerations. There is something odd about the very formulation of the subject. The Bill of Rights contains no right to be different and, in fact, the notion that there may be such a right is unique to our own times. It is difficult to imagine any prior generation framing the problem in this manner or even expressing a special concern about it. Often, an historian who addresses a present concern is in the position of reminding his audience that their worries are not nearly as novel as they believe. In the study of the family, for example, it is generally appropriate to note that a concern about its breakup goes back at least to the 1660s, and one can easily compile a long list of dire predictions in which each generation laments imminent disappearance of the family. The assignment here, however, is quite different—to explain just how unusual it is to pose questions about the right to be different and to trace how it came to assume such importance.

If the right to be different had any meaning at all to the Founding Fathers, they would have translated the point into a matter of religious tolerance. Their concern was to assure a right to practice one's religion and to allow for a diversity of religious practices. But clearly, tolerance is not the problem at hand. What, then, is? It is no simple matter to define it, for we are terribly conscious of the import of a label. This conference used the word "different" as an effort at neutrality, but as we shall see, it is not a neutral term at all. What one person calls "different" another may call "sick"; what one person thinks of as a "life-style" another may consider an "illness." And the terminology applied is critical, since it carries the most fundamental implications for state policy and individual rights. Label a behavior sick, and one series of responses seems appropriate; label it different, and altogether different responses seem appropriate. Indeed, the very formulation of the subject here as a "right to be different" prejudges the matter in a way that may be far more appropriate to a civil libertarian than to a psychiatrist.

For most of the nineteenth century and well into the twentieth, the inquiry would have been framed in a very different way. The opposition would not have been between government power and the right to be different, but rather, the government's obligation to help those in need. The eighteenth-century colonists recognized the presence of disordered minds, but they defined the problem in terms of the poverty that would then ensue; the insane were treated as the poor, and thus the law looked to protect their property if they had any or to insure them of a degree of comfort and support in one or another community household.

A major transformation in perspective occurred during the opening decades of the nineteenth century, when for the first time the insane were understood to be in need of treatment. They were no longer the poor, but the sick, and policy looked to cure them. To this end, Jacksonian Americans created public mental hospitals—asylums, as they were called. Well-ordered and disciplined settings would rehabilitate the insane, and the psychiatrists of the day, the medical superintendents, were remarkably confident that they would deliver on this promise. By the 1840s, insane asylums reported 80, 90, even 100 percent cures. Accordingly, the first superintendents and the legislators who followed their lead were very intent on minimizing the legal barriers to treatment. Why allow the insane to languish on a courtroom bench if they could be getting help within an institution? Thus, they enacted commitment laws to bring the mentally ill quickly to an institution. It was the needs of the insane, not their rights, that guided public policy.

It did not take very long for the promise of the insane asylums to fade. By the 1860s, even more clearly by the 1870s and 1880s, the failure of the institutions to cure was readily apparent. In these decades evidence of the custodial and oftentimes inhumane treatment within institutions became incontrovertible and, as would be expected, a reaction against liberal commitment laws set in. States did attempt to tighten their procedures in order to give the mentally ill greater protection against simple commitment. Now one begins to hear a language of power and rights competing with treatment. But the change was relatively short-lived and left little mark on legislation. By 1900 a dedication to treatment of "needs" once again became the hallmark of the programs.

This second stage of enthusiasm for treatment emerged in the Progressive era and established the tradition in this field that we are now debating. The principles of the Progressives' ethos can be summarized quickly: they were confident that they understood the roots of deviant behavior; they believed that they had at hand effective means for treating deviant behavior; and they were altogether confident that the state could be trusted to carry out the program. In essence, to be different meant to be deviant, and the state had the obligation to intervene in order to eradicate such kinds of behavior.

This formulation cut across many fields. It dominated the thinking about adult offenders and juvenile delinquents, as well as the mentally ill. To choose examples from the field of mental health, the Progressive era witnessed the rise of a new kind of psychiatry; the work essentially of men like William Healy and Adolf Meyer. The psychiatrists believed that if one compiled the facts of an individual case history and plunged into the details of biography, then common sense together with some medical knowledge would clarify the causes of the disease as well as suggest the appropriate mode of treatment. Once the dossier was complete, treatment could take place. The new psychiatrists looked to create psychopathic hospitals and outpatient clinics, two facilities that would effectively treat the patient. Once again, the promise of a cure was great; the mentally ill who came to the psychiatrist in the earliest stages of illness and cooperated with him would readily improve. Accordingly, the vast discretionary authority of a physician was appropriate and legitimate; he had to be allowed to gather types of information and even treat the patient against his will. Any legal requirements that hampered him in his work were inappropriate.

Progressives were prepared to pursue the implications of this program with a marked degree of confidence, not only because they believed in the efficacy of treatment but because they were confident that the state could act in the best interest of the deviant. To them, the state was the protector of the weak, the friend of equality, altogether suited to follow paternalistic styles of behavior.

The Progressives' concern was not with liberty, not with the right to be different, but with using the power of the state to assist those in need. In almost every area that affected the deviant, they demonstrated little patience for "legal niceties"—whether the issue at hand was the rights of the juvenile offender before the juvenile court, or the parolee before the parole board, or the mentally ill with their doctors. Hence, in the field of mental health, the Progressives enacted temporary commitment laws and emergency commitment laws all for the purpose of bringing the patient more rapidly into professional hands.

Perhaps the most significant element defining the Progressive attitude toward the state was a fundamental and shared sense of the promise of American life. Progressives perceived no crisis of values, and no difficulty in defining what ought to be the goal of state action. To the contrary, they were certain that native-born, middle-class values were appropriate for all citizens. In a very real way, the melting pot metaphor was not simply to make all immigrants over into Americans, but to make all lower-class Americans into middle-class Americans. This goal seemed eminently realizable, because the wealth available to Americans appeared to be almost unlimited. There was no need for trade-offs, no need to balance one group's interests against another's. The pie was large enough for everyone to have a fair share. In other words, personal and social considerations both pointed in the same direction: in terms of values and material comforts, the state could promote everyone's best interests.

This ideology persisted right down to the mid-1960s. No matter how great the gap might be between rhetoric and reality, observers were convinced that the dream could be fulfilled. If one or another institution was not living up to the mandate, then the problems rested with the failure of this administrator or that legislator. The design was right, the imperfections were minor, the fault was with one or another actor in the system, not in the program itself. Then, beginning in the mid-1960s, for a host of reasons, these postulates came under attack. There was much less confidence about anyone's ability to understand the roots of deviant behavior, and there was even less confidence about the ability of anyone to cure deviant behavior. This was markedly apparent in the field of criminal justice, where a host of nitty-gritty sociological research all indicated that programs were not effective in reducing recidivism. In mental illness, outcome measurements were more complicated, at least in part because psychiatrists were not trained to cure or comfortable about a measure of cure. Nevertheless, it was apparent that the state institutions were doing very little to improve the functioning of their patients.

Perhaps even more important than the disappointing performance of the institutions or the conceptual difficulty of dealing with the deviant was a loss of faith in the Progressives' sense of shared and unitary values and, thus, in the character of state intervention. Where Progressives saw a harmony of interests, reformers in the post-1960 period, the post-Progressives, perceived a conflict of interest. From a shared sense of values, Americans moved to a conflict over whose values would dominate. The point became not to satisfy needs, but to promote liberty; not to emphasize treatment, but to maximize rights. Perhaps it was the civil rights movement that sparked this reorientation, or perhaps economic stagnation and the Vietnam War debacle contributed most. Whatever the cause, the result was clear: the new goal was liberation, as in mental patients' liberation movement, women's liberation movement, and gays' liberation movement.

The most notable manifestation of this perspective came in the rise of the lawyer as reformer and the new popularity of litigation strategies. In no other period of our history have lawyers played such a dominant role as in the social reform movement. Indeed, in no other period has the court become such a critical mechanism in promoting social change. Obviously, this shift has sparked a good deal of controversy, particularly from the professionals whose domain the lawyers have intruded upon. The notion that a patient would need a lawyer to protect his rights strikes those in the mental health field as grossly inappropriate or even perverse. Legal efforts to alter commitment laws have been especially controversial. The lawyer-reformer's wish to abolish involuntary commitment is consistent with their perspective that patients are persons whose rights must be defended. For their part, many psychiatrists believe that the abolition of involuntary commitment would be disastrous, trapping the sick in their illness and preventing them from getting the help that they need. Some meeting points between the two groups can be found but, finally, a major difference of perspective and in policy does separate them.

In the best of all possible worlds, some kind of balance would exist; a way of bringing psychiatrists to cooperate with lawyers. It is possible that a focus on rights will promote neglect; on the other hand, a traditional commitment to treatment has certainly created nightmares of its own—one need only cite the perpetuation of the sixteen-thousand-bed hospitals, which were no more than warehouses. But rather than pursue what such a balance would look like, it is more important to understand the significance of the role of the litigators. In the end, after all the compromising is done, the role of the litigators will remain of critical importance. Hence, let us pursue this side of the argument most diligently.

The current movement for deinstitutionalization, to move persons from state hospitals into the community, is an excellent case in point. What have been the respective roles of the lawyers and the professionals? What can we anticipate in the future?

If a reform is going to be translated into practice and have a policy impact, it must gather for itself a constituency. As one examines the history of American reform, one discovers inevitably a marriage between high-minded idealism and a day-to-day operational input. For example, the origins of the mental hospital in the Jacksonian period reflected a commitment to cure; it also coincided with a widespread sentiment that communities would be better off (safer, more sanitized) if the insane were removed. To choose an example from the world of criminal justice, probation seemed to make a good deal of sense to social workers who looked to adjust the deviant to his society; it also had an appeal to district attorneys who were eager to clear their crowded court calendars through plea bargaining. To be sure, this kind of coalition often had the effect of undercutting the reform program. The new procedures turned out to be not as beneficial to the clients as they were convenient to administrators. In all events, without something of a constituency for reform, it is very doubtful whether any measure can be implemented.

When one turns with this perspective to the deinstitutionalization movement, it becomes readily apparent how little of a constituency exists for the process. The roster of opponents is very lengthy. The unions, which have a deep financial stake in their jobs in the institutions, are one of the most active groups combatting the deinstitutionalization movement. Community opposition has also been strong. Lower-class neighborhoods, in which most of the first group-homes have been placed, are already saturated, and their residents do not want any more exinmates in their midst. Middle-class communities are afraid that the mere presence of a facility will lower their property values; and many upper-class neighborhoods have sufficient political influence to make certain that no state-operated group home enters their midst. By the same token, the construction industry is eager to build more institutions rather than seeing them close down. Private physicians are in no rush to fill their offices with exinmates, and private voluntary associations have not been eager to extend their services to difficult clients.

The forces lined up on the other side seem quite limited in power. The ideology favoring deinstitutionalization is very strong, but the rhetoric does not find a solid base of support among constituents. At times it almost appears that the only groups that want a group-home are neighborhood churches, whose basements are vacant Monday through Friday.

Thus, it appears that given this imbalance of forces, the only possible mechanism for change may well be the court. Or put in other terms, if lawyers do not actively press for the rights of their clients, very little will happen. Further, a combative quality is almost inevitable. Antagonisms are strong, and it is only through a clear-cut assertion of individual rights that progress in this movement appears to be possible.

Take, for example, the matter of locating a group-home in a community. Reason and persuasion will go just so far, and many a community will continue to protest. The only point at which the deadlock can be broken is when a lawyer announces to the community that, like it or not, for better or for worse, the court is behind the effort, and the community will simply have to adjust itself to it. In other words, however much one may bemoan an adversarial stance, however much one might not wish to see lawyers dominate, it is clear that conflict is endemic, and without the lawyers on the side of their clients, the line-up of forces is such as to stalemate any change.

I believe that this kind of analysis has relevance to other areas concerning the mentally ill in particular and the question of the right to be different in general. Psychiatrists may now complain that the procedural barriers around commitment are so great that people in need of help are denied it. On the other hand, speaking as an historian, it is apparent that the professionals themselves did terribly little to improve the all too often wretched conditions of their institutions. They may criticize the lawyers for focusing so narrowly on the rights of the patients, but the professionals themselves were incapable of monitoring, let alone improving, their practices and institutions. By the same token, professionals may say that a right to refuse treatment makes little sense—why so narrowly circumscribe their ability to deliver helpful remedies? But again, looking at the historical record, one sees that many abuses persisted for such long periods of time when the power of professionals was not counterbalanced by a sense of the rights due their clients.

In sum, it is appropriate to note that just as this book framed the inquiry in terms of a right to be different, thereby suggesting that a label of "sick" or "in need," was inappropriate, so our society as a whole has shifted its perspective in this arena and is more prepared than ever before to tolerate what it now considers differences in styles. The Progressive perspective no longer holds sway, and it is very doubtful that efforts to resurrect it will be successful. I would anticipate that for some period to come, the balance of social policy will tilt from an emphasis on the right of government intervention to the right of an individual to be different.

9

ALAN A. STONE

Psychiatry and the Bill of Rights

During the last decade, the Bill of Rights has been constantly invoked by lawyers in litigation at the juncture between law and psychiatry.[1] A pattern of significant constitutional precedents has emerged from that decade of litigation, and it is that pattern which I shall address in this chapter, since it seems to portend the future of what has been called "government power" and "the right to be different."[2]

At the outset, I should make it clear that I believe the pattern that has developed is ill-advised and unworkable. In brief, the pattern is toward a rejection of every single legal intervention that is predicated on psychiatric expertise. That means the abolition of all involuntary confinement and treatment based on psychiatric and medical grounds. It means there will be further movement toward the abolition of the insanity defense in criminal trials. It means a repudiation of all of those special state laws that treat psychopaths or sexually dangerous persons differently from other criminals. It means, in short, that the government will be totally without power or authority to intervene in the lives of those who are different. The right to be different, you should realize, will mean the right to be psychotic or, if you prefer, the right to be stark, raving mad without anyone having the right or responsibility to see that you get proper professional help. Because involuntary civil commitment potentially affects the most people, I shall limit my discussion to that aspect.

To understand the ways in which the Bill of Rights has been invoked to abolish civil commitment and to make your own judgment about the value of invoking these rights, it is first, necessary to place these developments in some historical context. My colleague at Harvard Law School, the famous constitutional law professor Paul Freund, has used a penetrating aphorism in his approach to this subject: "It has been said that sociology is history with the history left out, and the same can be said of law." It may be irreverent to say so, but in my experience the historical perspective sometimes provides a better framework for understanding the Supreme Court's decisions than does the Justices' legal reasoning. Therefore, I shall give you a brief summary of my version of the recent history.

The Supreme Court, under Chief Justice Earl Warren, was perhaps the most powerful liberal-progressive force in America during the decade of the 1950s and early 1960s. The Court fashioned a variety of new constitutional rights whose impact is still being felt to this day. Many of these new constitutional rights were intended to protect the citizen against his or her state and local government, against police brutality, against racism, and against discrimination. For example, alleged criminals who were indigent were given lawyers at government expense, and new constitutional due-process safeguards were set up to protect alleged criminals against "stop and frisk," coerced confessions, and other potentially brutal intrusions by law enforcement officers.[3]

The Bill of Rights was the mainstay of legal reform in this area. But transcending the various narrow constitutional arguments in each instance was the basic principle that loss of liberty is the most grievous penalty in a democratic society. It is historically important to recognize that much of the new criminal law handed down by the Warren Court in fact had racial significance. A disproportionate percentage of those charged with crimes were members of America's racial minority groups. Thus, more procedural safeguards for alleged criminals meant more protection for minorities against racially biased law enforcement.

Running parallel to these reforms in criminal law were many important explicit civil rights cases based on the Bill of Rights' guarantee of equal protection of law, holding that no citizen should be treated differently because of membership in a group whose members were determined on some suspect discriminatory basis.[4] Most of these important constitutional decisions were in place by the middle of the sixties. The Bill of Rights had been the vehicle for restructuring our socially segregated society under law.

At about that time, a small group of lawyers began to examine the domain of psychiatry. They argued that it was the last battleground of the great civil liberties/civil rights struggle, and they proceeded to convince groups like the American Civil Liberties Union to take the lead and press the same due process and equal protection arguments that had carried the day in the area of criminal law and civil rights. Essentially, their claim was that the involuntary hospitalization of alleged mental patients involved deprivation of liberty without due process of law. Furthermore, they argued that psychiatric diagnoses like schizophrenia were essentially suspect classifications. A psychiatric diagnosis was like a racial epithet; calling someone paranoid was equivalent to calling someone a "Negro."[5]

Using these arguments, the constitutional litigation on behalf of the mentally ill was packaged as part of the civil rights movement. But the question is whether the problems of the mentally ill really fit within that package and whether the procedural safeguards developed for the alleged criminal work when they are applied to the alleged patient.

Before I begin that discussion, let me note another historical development. During the period that the constitutional litigation which interests us got under way, the Supreme Court was being transformed by the presidential power of appointment. What emerged was the Warren Burger Court with its Nixon and Ford appointees, which seems to have shifted the progressive engines of justice into reverse. In the old days, activist lawyers were eager to bring cases to the Supreme Court when the more conservative lower federal courts ruled against them. But now the lower federal courts are apt to be more liberal than the Supreme Court, and the prudent legal activist may choose to get his or her reform accomplished at that level, avoiding the Supreme Court whenever possible.

That is just what has happened in the litigation seeking to abolish civil commitment. The lower federal courts have announced sweeping new precedents, while the Supreme Court has denied *certiorari* and remanded or trivialized every issue presented to it. Indeed, they have sidestepped all the crucial issues. Can patients who are not dangerous be involuntarily confined? Sidestepped. Do involuntarily confined mental patients have a right to treatment? Sidestepped. Do they have a right to refuse treatment? Sidestepped. What procedural safeguards do mental patients have in involuntary confinement? Sidestepped.[6] The Supreme Court has avoided all of these questions, while various lower federal courts have given explicit answers to all of them. The general pattern in the litigation on civil commitment is for the lower courts to impose all of the procedural safeguards that the Warren Supreme Court imposed in criminal cases.[7]

But before considering these specifics, it is important to consider another historical development. That is the growth of what can be called the anti-psychiatry movement. The anti-psychiatry movement is part of a much larger development in which Americans are increasingly dissatisfied with all of their major institutions. The government is incapable of governing, the schools and colleges do not teach, the penitentiaries do not make anyone penitent, the reformatories do not reform, the civil service is incompetent to serve, hospitals make people sick, and psychiatrists make them crazy, and so forth.

But the anti-psychiatry movement has special nuances of its own. In the intellectual climate of the late sixties, there was a tendency to see the insane person as an heroic victim. Dr. Ronald Laing, for example, portrayed the schizophrenic as the only sane member of an insane society.[8] Dr. Thomas Szasz declared that mental illness was a myth, and the people called mental patients were merely the scapegoats of society—victims of the psychiatric inquisition.[9] Other social scientists, including sociologists and historians, adduced evidence to suggest that for two centuries psychiatric diagnoses have been totally illusory and unreliable.[10] Psychiatry was portrayed as transforming class, ethnic, and religious biases into the Greek and Latin mumbo-jumbo of psychiatric diagnosis, and thus obscuring and contributing to social oppression. The liberal of the fifties had looked to psychiatry as a fount of wisdom and an ally in the liberal cause, but the new liberals of the seventies—often the same people—twenty years later had come to see psychiatry as an enemy of the liberal cause.

Ironically, the radical criticism of psychiatry began during a decade when the scientific foundations of psychiatry had been convincingly demonstrated and when new biological and psychological treatment methods were revolutionizing the treatment of the seriously mentally ill: the population in our state mental hospitals had been cut in half. But the scientific progress of psychiatry seemed to pose an even greater threat. During the American Psychiatric Association Convention in Miami in 1969, a small plane flew back and forth over the hotels. Behind the plane a sign fluttered. Its legend read, "Psychiatry Kills." That message reflects this greater threat of a therapeutic state—a clockwork orange vision of citizens drugged and bugged by the psychiatric establishment with its science fiction powerful and arcane methods.

Antagonism to psychiatry, feeding on those fears, has, in states like California, become a political force uniting the radical left and radical right in a shared nightmare in which they see political dissenters transmogrified into madmen and drugged into insensibility by conspiratorial psychiatrists. I refrain from exercising psychiatric license to interpret the nightmare, but perhaps two comments about it should be emphasized.

First, its most extravagant premise is to reject the fundamental intuition of every known society and to claim that madness does not exist and that insanity is always a political invention. A second point follows from the first. If madness does not exist, then psychiatric treatment is always either brainwashing or brain-damaging. These, then, are the two historical trends I want to emphasize. It was the union of the radical anti-psychiatry movement with the civil rights movement that spawned the litigation we shall now consider.

In discussing the law, it is good to have a case and facts in mind, so let us assume the following. Mr. Jones has, for the past month, been increasingly agitated. He had for some time been convinced that people at work were conspiring against him. Last week he decided people were reading his mind, and he began to hear voices accusing him of sexual perversity. Since then he has been unable to sleep and has stopped going to work. He now refuses to communicate with his wife and children. He paces up and down with a pained expression on his face; he is obviously suffering. He is now either crazy or, if you prefer, exercising his right to be different. Mrs. Jones begs and cajoles her husband to come with her to the emergency room of the nearby community hospital. He reluctantly agrees. There he sees a psychiatrist who, after interviewing Mr. Jones and getting a history from Mrs. Jones, makes a diagnosis of acute paranoid schizophrenia and recommends hospitalization. Mr. Jones adamantly refuses any treatment at all. Mrs. Jones begs the doctor to do something. She is afraid her husband will lose his job and she worries about the effect of his strange behavior on the children.

The question is, what should happen now. In states where the

Bill of Rights has been successfully invoked, the psychiatrist would have to say, "I am sorry, Mrs. Jones, the law allows me to do nothing unless we can prove that Mr. Jones is dangerous." But Mr. Jones, like the vast majority of psychotic patients, is not dangerous. If the psychiatrist did believe Mr. Jones was dangerous and did want to confine him, this is what one of the federal courts has ruled are the steps that must be followed in order to confine and treat him.[11]

First, Mr. Jones must be provided with a lawyer whose duty it is to advocate Mr. Jones's freedom. Second, he must have a hearing before a judge within 48 hours and, no matter how disturbed he may get, the doctors are not to begin treatment until that hearing. Third, the psychiatrist must inform Mr. Jones of his right to remain silent and his Fifth Amendment privilege against self-incrimination. Fourth, Mr. Jones must be given timely notice of the charges justifying his confinement. Fifth, he must have notice of the right to a jury trial. Sixth, he is entitled to a full hearing and a trial with the right to cross-examine Mrs. Jones and his doctors, who must testify about the details of his illness and his dangerous behavior. Seventh, it must be proved beyond a reasonable doubt that Mr. Jones is mentally ill and dangerous. And, finally, there must be inquiry into whether some less restrictive alternative can be found for Mr. Jones before inpatient involuntary care is ordered.

In the space allotted, I cannot discuss the implications of all of these procedural safeguards as they apply to civil commitment. I shall touch on only a few of the most problematic. But first, consider the cost of these legal procedures mandated by the federal court. If these procedures were properly carried out, the cost would amount to hundreds of dollars and, if Mr. Jones opted for a jury trial, the costs would amount to thousands. But, given the cost in time and money, why should anyone want to go to all that trouble? The state is being asked to justify putting Mr. Jones in a hospital that will cost still more. What is in it for the state? Prosecutors have all sorts of incentives for putting away criminals, but what is their incentive for putting away Mr. Jones? And what about the psychiatrist? Experience demonstrates that psychiatrists have always disliked being involved in civil commitment; with these new procedures, that dislike has become abhorrence. In sum, procedures have been developed to protect patients against a powerful adversary, but it turns out that no one but Mrs. Jones really has an incentive to confine Mr. Jones. The powerful adversary of the mental patient turns out to be a paper tiger. But if Mrs. Jones is able to cajole the doctor and the prosecutor, there remain insuperable problems.

One such problem is that there is no rational basis on which courts can use the criterion of dangerousness beyond a reasonable doubt. No matter how attractive it may be in legal theory, it simply will not work in practice. Elsewhere I have reviewed the intractable statistical problems that preclude any valid prediction of dangerousness.[12] Let me only summarize what people on both sides of this argument agree on, namely, that predictions of future dangerous conduct are impossible in light of current knowledge. Not a psychiatrist, not a psychologist, not a sociologist, not a computer can tell the courts beyond a reasonable doubt that a certain patient is dangerous. A system of law that relies on something which is impossible, that is, predictions of dangerousness, cannot function; it can only lead to chaos.

But, as one reviews the status of the constitutional law as it affects the mentally ill, one finds that both the law and attempts to reform it are caught up with this shibboleth of dangerousness. Mentally ill persons can no longer be confined unless found dangerous, and yet no one knows who is dangerous.

The civil libertarians who recognize the problems of predicting dangerousness have argued that a solution is to be found in looking instead to past acts. Thus, they would allow a mentally ill person like Mr. Jones to be confined if he had already done something that could be proved beyond a reasonable doubt to be dangerous, like attacking his colleagues at work. But that approach, recommended by civil libertarians, does not really solve the practical problems inherent in the concept of dangerousness. Imagine someone like Son of Sam, who has committed a series of very dangerous acts such as killing people. Assume further that he is found not guilty by reason of insanity at a criminal trial and is now in one of those jurisdictions where, if he is to be confined, he must be civilly committed.[13] Now, obviously, he fulfills the civil libertarians' criteria: he has committed very dangerous past acts. However, his lawyer argues at his civil commitment trial that all of his killings took place one or two years ago, and he is no longer dangerous. At that point, although it may sound incredible, I am prepared to argue that there will be no valid basis for psychiatrists or anyone else to say that Son of Sam is still dangerous. If the burden is on the state to prove that possibility beyond a reasonable doubt—that Son of Sam is still dangerous—it will have no basis for doing so. Thus, the new pattern of law not only prevents people who need treatment from getting it but also fails to protect society from dangerous people.

Obviously, most of the people who are candidates for civil commitment will not have committed such heinous crimes as did Son of Sam. But, for the less violent, the problems of predicting continued dangerousness are even more difficult. Within a few days after such a person is confined, the question must arise of the legal justification for continuing confinement. The repudiation of the medical model, justified by invoking the Bill of Rights, has created a system that cannot work and, where it is employed, causes serious hardship to the mentally ill and their families.

The truth is that the vast majority of patients with severe forms of treatable mental illness are, like Mr. Jones, not dangerous.[14] This is the group of patients who have psychotic illnesses, who have delusions, who have hallucinations, who have terrifying anxiety, and who can be treated, but who, like Mr. Jones, do not realize that they are ill and therefore can exercise their right to be different and no longer are subjected to psychiatric care. On the other hand, the population of dangerous persons who, under the reformed civil commitment statutes, are being sent to mental hospitals are, in the main, either difficult to treat or untreatable. Thus, the legal standard erected by invoking the Bill of Rights selects an untreatable patient population who require more security than is available at most mental hospitals. A large concentration of this kind of patient in any hospital will create havoc. They make treatment impossible for other patients, and they destroy any notion of an open hospital concept. If the trend is allowed to continue and develop, the public mental hospital will become a jail, and the psychiatrists and nurses—if they remain—will become the wardens. That scenario is already apparent in some hospitals operating under these kinds of law.[15]

Ironically, the movement towards reform in the law will itself be constitutionally suspect, as well as destructive to important social resources. If commitment is not based on treatability, but on dangerousness, then involuntary confinement becomes almost nothing but preventive detention, which has been anathema to civil libertarians on a variety of constitutional grounds. Thus, the reformers' rush to invoke the Bill of Rights to declare that dangerousness is the only justification for involuntary civil commitment results in a legal system that cannot honestly function, which ends up—if it confines anyone—confining people who tend to be untreatable. Further, it will destroy the public mental hospital and may after all be itself unconstitutional. Hopefully, psychiatrists will recognize their inability to predict dangerousness and will refuse to participate in this bizarre creation of legal progress.

The starkest picture has been painted here because it is important to confront people with the implications of the current wave of legal reform in terms of its impact on future mental health care in the United States. One of my colleagues, with whom I am often involved in arguments over these issues, likes to say, "The law is a rough and heavy instrument. It can come smashing down on a problem; it cannot fashion subtle and precise solutions." The Bill of Rights has, I believe, been invoked in just this harsh and heavy-handed way in an area that can only respond to subtle and precise solutions. The mental health care system and the rules that govern it have been totally disrupted.

The future offers no prospect that subtle and precise solutions will be found in law. Indeed, what is now happening at the intersection of the law and the mental health system provides a mirror in which the observer can see the ills of the entire society. There is the pseudo-technical solution of human problems, as if that could replace personal care and involvement. There is increasing concern about autonomy and the fear of governmental intrusion, symbolized by involuntary civil commitment. There are the growing and unresponsive bureaucracies, which seem to defeat their own goals. There are uncertainties about common values undermining all sense of united enterprise. There is neglect of the young, which diminishes hope, and abandonment of the aged, which erodes dignity. There is the demand for law, but there is the degeneration of law into legalism, as rules replace responsibility. And, of course, there is racism and the uneasiness of the relationship between the caretakers and the subjects.

These are the problems that will challenge us all for the next quarter of a century. The status of the law and the pattern which has emerged suggest that people will have the right to be different during the years ahead. The question that now confronts us is whether, by invoking the Bill of Rights, government will abandon its responsibility to take care of those who are suffering.

NOTES

1. See, for example, *Lake v. Cameron*, 364 F.2d 657 (D. C. Cir. 1967); *Jackson v. Indiana*, 406 U.S. 715 (1972); *Lessard v. Schmidt*, 349 F. Supp. 1078 (E. D. Wis. 1972), vacated and remanded, 94 S.Ct. 713 (1964); *Wyatt v. Stickney*, 325 F. Supp. 781 (M.D. Ala. 1971), enforced 344 F. Supp. 373 and 344 F. Supp. 387 (M.D. Ala. 1971), *aff'd sub nom. Wyatt v. Aderholt*, 503 F.2d 1305 (5th Cir. 1974).

2. See Alan Stone, *Mental Health and Law: A System in Transition* (Washington, D.C.: U.S. Government Printing Office, 1975).

3. See, for example, *Argersinger v. Hamlin*, 407 U.S. 25 (1972) (right to counsel whenever imprisonment is imposed); *Gideon v. Wainwright*, 372 U.S. 335 (1963) (right to counsel in felony cases); *Miranda v. Arizona*, 384 U.S. 436 (1966) (rights of suspects); *Mapp v. Ohio*, 367 U.S. 643 (1961) (rights against unreasonable searches and seizures).

4. *Cf.* "Developments in the Law—Equal Protection," *Harvard Law Review* 82, no. 5 (March 1969), pp. 1065–1192.

5. See, for example, Thomas Szasz, *Law, Liberty and Psychiatry* (New York: Macmillan, 1963).

6. See *O'Connor v. Donaldson*, 422 U.S. 563 (1975); *Lessard v. Schmidt*, 349 F. Supp. 1078 (E. D. Wis. 1972); *Bartley v. Kremens*, 431 U.S. 119 (1977).

7. See *Lessard v. Schmidt*.

8. *The Politics of the Family* (New York: Vintage Books, 1972).

9. *The Myth of Mental Illness* (New York: Dell, 1961); *The Manufacture of Madness* (New York: Harper & Row, 1970).

10. David Rothman, *The Discovery of the Asylum* (Boston: Little, Brown, 1971); Michel Foucault, *Madness and Civilization* (New York: Pantheon, 1965).

11. *Lessard v. Schmidt*.

12. See Stone, *Mental Health and Law*, ch. 2.

13. *Bolton v. Harris*, 395 F.2d 642 (D.C. Cir. 1968).

14. See Stone, *Mental Health and Law*, ch. 2.

15. See Alan Stone, "Recent Mental Health Litigation: A Critical Perspective," *American Journal of Psychiatry* 143, no. 3 (March 1977), pp. 273–79.

SECTION V
Economic Liberty

10

HERMAN E. DALY

Economic Growth, Nongrowth, and Freedom

Just at this moment Alice felt a very curious sensation . . . she was beginning to grow larger again, and she thought at first she would get up and leave the court; but on second thought she decided to remain where she was as long as there was room for her.

"I wish you wouldn't squeeze so," said the Dormouse, who was sitting next to her. "I can hardly breathe."

"I can't help it," said Alice very meekly: "I'm growing."

"You've no right to grow *here*," said the Dormouse.

"Don't talk nonsense," said Alice more boldly: "You know you're growing too."

"Yes, but *I* grow at a reasonable pace," said the Dormouse: "not in that ridiculous fashion." And he got up very sulkily and crossed over to the other side of the court."

—Lewis Carroll, *Alice's Adventures in Wonderland*

Clearly this little story illustrates a conflict. Some will take Alice's part. Poor thing, she can't help growing. Besides growth is healthy. The dormouse was also growing, so he had no right to condemn Alice for just doing a bit more of the same thing he was doing. Rodents are all lazy hypocrites anyway. Others will defend the dormouse. He kept his growth within limits; he was not squeezing Alice; Alice was squeezing him. Poor fellow could hardly breathe. Alice's first inclination, to leave the finite court if she could not limit her growth, was the correct one, and her contrary decision to remain in the court as long as there was room *for her*, showed insufficient respect for the rights of the dormouse. Besides, everyone knows that bratty little girls get fat from ravenous overconsumption of candy.

Expert witnesses could be called in by both sides. Mad Hatter economists would explain that growth is necessary for full employment, that if Alice stopped growing, millions of dormice would be unemployed (better squeezed than unemployed!), that it is a grave error, often committed by laymen, to think the court is finite. Economists know that as scarcity increases, prices will rise and induce substitution and resource-saving technical changes. Besides, there are surely other courts in other solar systems waiting for us. In opposition, Humpty-Dumpty ecologists would testify that converting one more pound of the flora and fauna of the court into a pound (or rather a tenth of a pound) of Alice, could well unbalance things, causing us to fall from our ecological niche in the wall, and all the king's men would not be able to restore the life-support systems that we ignorantly sacrificed in exchange for just a few more ounces of Alice, which will do no one any good, not even fat Alice.

I won't try to play Solomon and resolve the difficult case of dormouse vs. Alice, which was wisely left unresolved by Lewis Carroll. However, as you might expect, and in any case will soon see, my instinctive sympathies are with the dormouse and Humpty-Dumpty.

One of the particular issues in the general debate over economic growth versus nongrowth has to do with this same conflict of rights or freedoms. Growth partisans accuse the steady-state advocates of favoring policies that must be imposed by force and that will constitute a Draconian intervention in personal affairs, such as telling citizens how many children they can have and how much electricity they can consume. Furthermore, without growth poverty can be attacked only by redistribution, which means that the government must take from someone (big Alice) and give to someone else (little dormouse) and thus interfere in the lives of both parties to a greater extent than before. It is usually considered axiomatic that a general context of growth provides a more healthy environment for civil liberties than does a stable economy.

Some advocates of a stable economy have responded by arguing that some things are more important than civil liberties, namely survival, and if we must pay a price in terms of the former to accomplish the latter, then so be it. That seems to me a reasonable enough position if one is forced to it, but for the present I think it concedes too much to the critics of a stable economy. In any case I want to consider a different response here.

The relevant issue is not whether the steady-state economy of the future will permit less civil liberties than did the growth economy of the past, but whether it will permit more or less civil liberties than the growth economy of the future. To give an analogy, if one wants to compare the cost of solar or nuclear energy with the cost of fossil fuel energy, the relevant comparison is at the margin of additional supply for the future. One does not compare the cost of new solar with the cost of old east Texas oil that some rancher accidentally found fifty years ago while digging for water with a shovel. Rather one compares the cost of solar energy with the cost of finding and extracting new offshore Alaskan oil from below deep, icy, remote waters with the aid of highly capital-intensive technology. In like manner, we must compare the implications for civil liberties of a future steady state with those of a future growth economy, not with the civil liberties prevailing in the familiar growth economy of the past when growth was as easy as pumping oil out of east Texas. It will be difficult to institute a steady state, but it may be more difficult to continue growing in the face of increasing environmental resistances to extraction and waste disposal.

The great enemy of civil liberties is crisis. In the face of imminent disaster or war, we willingly put drastic curbs on individual freedom. Is growth or nongrowth more likely to provoke the kinds of crises that require a degree of social discipline inconsistent with civil liberties? Judgments differ. My own judgment is that a future steady state offers much better prospects for individual freedom than does a future growth economy striving to climb ever steeper mountains of natural and social resistance. The growth economy of the future will not be a world of free enterprise and atomistic or even workable competition, but rather a world of subsidies, $100 billion bail-outs, public regulation of privately-owned oligopolies, and government guarantees that throw the real cost of risk-bearing on to the public. The role of government in forcing growth to continue will be greater than the role of government in helping us accommodate to nongrowth.

Here are a couple of specific examples to support this general judgment.

Most advocates of growth are also defenders of fission energy and the "plutonium economy." A few years ago I attended a lecture by Dr. Edward Teller, who extolled the virtues of the atom to a group of utility executives and businessmen. Someone raised the issue of plutonium safeguards and the dangers of diversion and asked Dr. Teller what he thought about those issues. His reply was,

"I don't want to talk about it." Why not? Because there were reporters in the room, and whatever he said would have appeared in the newspaper the next day. "Why give people ideas?" Dr. Teller asked.

Academically this presents an interesting dilemma. How can decisions about a technology be made democratically when the very act of public discussion entails risks that make the technology unacceptable? I say academically because people are not dependent on Dr. Teller or even the newspapers for all of their ideas. Furthermore, the sabotage cat had long been out of the nuclear bag, and Dr. Teller knew it.

The point is, however, that a plutonium-based energy technology does not mesh well with the cogs of democratic institutions. Yet many people feel that we must replace a "few" democratic cogs to allow plutonium to fit, so as to keep growing, because if we do not grow the whole system will collapse and much more freedom will be lost. This proposition is more often supported by vigorous reassertion than by reasoned argument.

There is a serious question whether any technology that requires billions in investment, ten years to bring on line, and thirty years of operation beyond that to pay back the initial costs and yield a profit, even if it does not involve dangerous materials, is compatible with democratic decision making. The difficulty is that the fundamental rules on the basis of which the decision is made initially are subject to the risk of being changed every four years or so. Continued growth will require more and more of these large-scale, long-term investments in novel technologies. Such investments will probably not be attractive to private entrepreneurs unless the freedom of Congress and the public to change its mind is somehow restricted. The government will either guarantee the private firm against such reverses or take over the investment itself. As the scale and technical novelty of our already pharoanic projects increase, measurable risk is replaced by unmeasurable uncertainty. We no longer have a history of the relative frequency of malfunction of a technology, nor any sound estimate of the consequence in damages. Insurance becomes actuarially unsound; it becomes a shot in the dark. Government tries to fill the void, as with the Price-Anderson Act, and simply ends by throwing most of the undetermined but real cost of uncertainty on to the general public.

Technical failure is no longer a cost to be rationally weighed against benefits, but is rebaptized as "an act of God" for which liability cannot be assessed.

If growth requires fission power or similarly demanding technologies, then the implications of growth for civil liberties are bleak indeed. To argue in reply that the military has been handling plutonium for years merely illustrates the point that military forms of management, with limited civil liberties, are required. Since the case of the plutonium economy has been widely discussed, I will turn to my second example, which is the rather far out but highly instructive case of space colonization—or what might be called "economic growth of the third kind."

To the immense credit of those seeking to colonize space, unlike most economists, they admit that the earth is finite and cannot be the stage on which the comedy of infinite growth is enacted. (They agree with Alice's first inclination, to leave the finite court in order to have room to grow.) They say we must colonize space (especially such nice gravity-free places as L-5), since the alternative of a steady-state on earth is impossible in the absence of an iron-fisted dictatorship. Their reasoning, in the form of a syllogism, is: continuing growth is necessary for freedom; space colonization is necessary for continuing growth; ergo, space colonization is necessary for freedom. The framers of the first ten amendments might find that surprising, but I think we at least must give the spacemen an "A" in logic, although they deserve an "F" in dialectics and in common sense. Many people would like to grant the first premise (growth is necessary for freedom) but escape the conclusion (space colonization is necessary for freedom) by denying the second premise (space colonization is necessary for continuing growth). I regard the second premise as sound because physical growth cannot continue indefinitely on a finite planet. But I would completely reject the first; while insisting that whoever accepts the first must live with the conclusion.

Garrett Hardin has shown that the whole idea of space-colonizing expansion is vulnerable to a political *reductio ad paradoxum*.[1] A rotating torus in L-5 containing an artificial ecosystem capable of sustaining human life is a very complex and precise technology, infinitely more fragile and vulnerable to sabotage than the massive spaceship earth. Who will be the 50,000 or so peopl chosen to inhabit one of these marvels? It makes no difference whether we consider then lucky or unlucky, since in either case they have to be chosen. How do we choose? Perhaps by some Health, Education and Welfare (HEW) guidelines, which require a fair share of blacks, whites, Chicanos, Indians, Protestants, Catholics, Jews—not to mention Cajuns, Creoles, Mormons, and Unitarians? Or if that seems like a recipe for tribal warfare, should we strive for "ethnic purity" and religious homogeneity? What then happens to religious freedom, right to dissent, and ethnic pluralism?

But there is still a more basic *reductio ad absurdum*, because even if the number of habitats can increase indefinitely, *each* habitat must be managed in a steady-state mode. Births plus in-migration must equal deaths plus out-migration, with analogous material and energy-balance equations for import and export of artifacts and raw materials. The aggregate of all habitats may grow, but each habitat must be managed as a steady state. The very discipline that the spacemen were trying to escape from on earth is encountered once again on each and every space colony. If a steady state is by hypothesis socially impossible on spaceship earth, then why isn't it also socially impossible on spaceship L-5 × 351? True enough, we would have added migration to the steady-state balance equation, which was not previously possible for the earth as a whole, although it has always been a fact of life at the international level on earth. But that additional variable is not very significant. In as much as each space habitat must be run as a steady state, does it not make sense first to learn to live in the steady-state mode on the large, resilient, forgiving, and relatively self-operating spaceship earth before attempting the same difficult feat on a fragile and unforgiving tiny rotating inner tube protected from the cold vacuum of space by a thin layer of aluminum and plastic, and perhaps assembled by union labor on a Friday afternoon while the managerial executives are out playing golf? This question must be asked even by those who feel that eventually space colonies are desirable.

The discipline that the complex and precise technology of a space colony would impose on its citizens would be much greater than that of a plutonium economy on earth, which would be bad enough. It would be like a world in which nearly anyone could wreak destruction equivalent to a nuclear attack. No doubt the required military style of discipline would be referred to as "rationality." Whatever is not instrumental to and supportive of the unified technology upon which all life would immediately depend would be declared irrational and dangerous—and indeed it would be! Potentially irrational people, who might endanger the community, must be identified before the fact and treated to an ounce of prevention. Enter behavior control and genetic engineering, exit any remaining civil liberties. Space colonists would be totally dependent on the technologists for their existence, even in the immediate short run. It would be as if everyone's breathing or heartbeat depended on a technical apparatus under the control of someone other than himself.

These may be extreme examples, but they show very clearly that it is nonsense to accept as axiomatic that more growth is better for civil liberties than no growth. Growth could and in my judgment is likely to have implications for civil liberties that are more negative than the implications of a steady-state economy, to which we now turn.

What price, in terms of individual freedom, must be paid in order to achieve a steady-state economy and escape the even greater costs implied by growth? Clearly, we must accept some aggregate limits on procreation and production. The goal should be to impose ecologically and ethically determined macro limits on aggregate production and population, with a minimum sacrifice of individual freedom and micro-level variability. A general strategy embodying this principle is to set physical quotas (in conveniently divisible units) on the total amount of the basic resource inputs to be controlled, but allow exchanges of the limited quota rights among individuals. In this way macro stability is attained, but micro variability is preserved.

But why do we need any ecologically and ethically determined limits on the total flow of resources? The central fact that we must face is that the number of people or, more precisely, the number of person-years of industrially developed high-consumption living are limited. They are limited by the finitude of the earth, but more immediately by the laws of thermodynamics, the fixed solar flux, the complexly co-evolved interdependencies of the ecosystem, and the pattern of geological concentrations in the earth's crust. Take it as a brute fact that economic development, as it is understood in the U.S. today, cannot be generalized to the other 94 percent of the earth's four billion people and much less to all future generations. Pointing to the virtues of the price system is completely unavailing in this regard. Market prices are relevant only to temporally and ecologically parochial decisions; that is, decisions whose major consequences lie wholly within the human economy of commodity exchange and within the present generation. Market prices should *not* be used to decide the rates of flow of matter-energy across the economy-ecosystem boundaries (in either direction; that is, depletion or pollution), or to decide the distribution of resources across generational boundaries. The first must be an ecological decision, the second, an ethical decision. These decisions will, of course, influence market prices, but the point is that these ecological and ethical decisions are *price-determining*, not *price-determined*. Most economists simply fail to grasp this point.

As soon as we admit the fact that the total person-years of developed living is limited, a number of very difficult ethical questions arise. How should the limited total of person-years of developed living to be apportioned: among nations? among social classes? among generations? among individuals? To what extent should subhuman life be sacrificed in exchange for more person-years of developed living? Not all subhuman life is supportive of man—some is competitive. Are we justified in exterminating sparrows if that adds a few more years developed living? A man is worth many sparrows, but a sparrow's intrinsic worth is not zero. How many sparrow-years are worth one person-year? How many sparrow-years are worth the difference between one person-year of luxurious living and one person-year of frugal living? What is the cost of present luxury in terms of future lives forgone?

We are not prepared seriously to ask such questions, much less answer them. But they are not entirely new questions either. Thoreau, with much insight, wrote that, "the cost of a thing is the amount of what I will call life which is required to be exchanged for it immediately or in the long run."[2]

Modern economists have assumed that "cost" in Thoreau's sense is zero. We prefer to believe in infinite growth—that there is no limit to the total number of person-years of industrially developed living. But Walt Disney's First Law, that wishing makes it so, is of less than universal validity. The market certainly cannot deal with such questions. As previously argued the ethical and ecological questions must be treated as price-determining, not price-determined.

But I have strayed a bit from the question of freedom without yet having mentioned the most critical issue concerning that subject. Edmund Burke put it as follows:

> Men are qualified for civil liberty in exact proportion to their disposition to put moral chains on their own appetites. . . . Society cannot exist unless a controlling power upon will and appetite be placed somewhere, and the less of it there is within, the more there must be without. It is ordained in the eternal constitution of things, that men of intemperate minds cannot be free. Their passions forge their fetters.[3]

Moral chains on appetites must arise from a shared sense of value. As C. S. Lewis put it, "A dogmatic belief in objective value is necessary to the very idea of a rule which is not tyranny or an obedience which is not slavery."[4] The biggest cause for pessimism about the future of civil liberties is that the very term "dogmatic belief in objective value" triggers a conditioned reflex that automatically shuts the minds of most modern intellectuals. We must overcome that positivistic prejudice and reason together in search of objective value.

A further reason for pessimism about civil liberties in a growth economy is that growth depends on more science and technology, which endeavor rests, in R. L. Sinsheimer's words, "upon the faith that our scientific probing and our technological ventures will not displace some key element in our protective environment and collapse our ecological niche."[5] In a growth economy that faces ever greater environmental resistances and consequently has to perform ever more impressive technological encores to elicit an ever greater volume of applause from the market, it is just a matter of time until an ecological crisis is provoked. And crisis is the enemy of civil liberties.

I submit that a steady-state economy offers a more propitious context for freedom in the future than does a growth economy. But no future economy is going to be as free from governmental regulations and harsh choices as was the growth economy of the past, which enjoyed the double bonanza of unused available natural resources and of underused environmental capacities for waste absorption. The freedom inherent in such frontier conditions is a thing of the past and a nostalgic commitment to the growth economy won't bring back the unique conditions that made it feasible. It will just make the remaining freedoms harder to preserve.

NOTES

1. Garrett Hardin, *Exploring New Ethics for Survival* (New York: Viking, 1968).
2. Henry David Thoreau, *Walden* (New York: Harper and Brothers, 1950), p. 39.
3. *The Writings and Speeches of Edmund Burke*, 4 (Boston: Little, Brown, 1901), pp. 51–52.
4. Clive Staples Lewis, *The Abolition of Man* (London: Oxford University, 1944), p. 36.
5. Robert L. Sinsheimer, "The Presumptions of Science," *Daedalus* 107 (Spring 1978): 24.

11

GERALD SIRKIN

The Future of Government Regulation and Freedom

The most remarkable thing about freedom may be how little we know about it. It is one of those mysterious creations, like truffles, which we greatly value but whose origin we do not understand and which we do not know how to produce.

If anyone doubts our ignorance, he need only consider our innocent hopes for the implantation of free institutions throughout the world. The world is littered with the wrecks of these efforts. Of those wrecks that are still afloat, some are listing badly. A number have been refloated several times, only to sink again. Yet, where are the analyses that will explain what the conditions necessary to sustain freedom are and why free institutions survive in some societies and die in others?

Even the meaning of freedom has become less rather than better understood. When freedom in Western countries was in its infancy, its meaning was clear enough: government coercion limited to what was strictly essential; government made accountable and responsive through elections; and government arbitrariness prevented by a system of impartial laws.

But societies that have lived for a time on a high plateau of freedom from government coercion and abuse find substitute concepts of freedom cropping up. Freedom is said to mean freedom from risks; freedom from worry; freedom from hardships, illness, responsibility, and all the other unpleasant facts of human life. Freedom is confused with utopia. And the more our freedom from government coercion and abuse is infringed upon, the more vociferously we are promised these utopian "freedom" lollipops as a consolation.

We have a historical perspective of eight hundred years of the growth of freedom in some countries, of the aborted efforts at imitation in other countries, and of the beginnings of the decay of freedom in countries where it has achieved its highest development. From that history, we ought to be able to derive some understanding of the conditions necessary to sustain freedom.

I intend to put the narrow subject of government regulation into that long perspective. Otherwise, the discussion will be condemned to superficiality.

Government regulation comes in different shapes and sizes. Government regulation is not new in this country; we have a history of government regulation going back to our beginnings as a nation. What is new is the size and shape that government regulation is now assuming.

This "new" regulation emanates from a change in our fundamental ideas and attitudes about society—the *ethos* of our society. That changing ethos must be understood before we can grasp the implications of the current trend of government regulation, which is only one of many symptoms of the changing ethos. We must go back into the history of the rise of freedom to understand where we are now and where we are going.

FROM AUTHORITARIANISM TO INDIVIDUALISM

Throughout most of history, the prevailing view of how society should be managed has been authoritarian. Political authority, religious authority, the authority of custom—all these, generally working together—ruled the society and even the details of individual behavior.

Not only was it accepted that the means of rule should be authoritarian; more important, it was accepted that the ends of rule should be authoritarian. That individual objectives should take precedence over collective objectives (as determined by the authorities) could scarcely be conceived. Ask not what your society can do for you; ask what you can do for your society.

From that traditional idea of rule-by-authority for the purposes of authority, it was a long road to the modern idea of a society managed by individuals for the purposes of individuals.

The concept of an individualistic society is not easy to grasp or to have faith in. To people who have known only an authoritarian society, the dangers of individualism must seem immense. How can people pursuing individual ends achieve the coordination and cooperation necessary to make a society work? Without an authority to control and direct individual behavior, will the society not be subject to perpetual disruption, conflict, and chaos?

Even among people born, raised, and prospering in an individualistic society, the understanding of how it works is limited, and confidence in it is infirm. At the hint of an emergency, the ranks of the unbelievers swell, and thoughts turn toward authoritarian control.

An individualistic society, therefore, could only have emerged with great difficulty and under unusual circumstances. The rise of individualism in Western Europe is a complex history of interacting forces. But underlying all of it appears to be one fundamental explanation—the weakness of authority because of the political fragmentation of society.

From the disorder left by the disintegration of the Roman Empire, there arose the system of division of power among kings, princes, and lords known as "feudalism." The constant struggles among these contenders for power forced openings for ability and imagination. In politics, as in economics, competition creates opportunities and inducements for the individualistic behavior which is unwanted and suppressed under monopoly. These competitors for power tolerated a degree of independence and initiative among the commercial classes, innovators, and thinkers because their help was needed. Talented men, restrained or oppressed by one ruler, could find refuge and encouragement under another.

The rising individualistic mentality next produced cracks in the unified religious authority, and the dispersion of political power permitted those cracks to widen, until in many countries, religious authority was as fragmented as political authority.

In its early phase during the Renaissance, this novel individualistic outlook was known as "humanism." The origins of the new individualism or humanism can be traced back to medieval times, for the Renaissance was an outgrowth from—and not a clean break with—medieval life. But the Renaissance was a period when individualism developed rapidly from its hesitant beginnings and brought with it the exuberant burst of creativity that is the essence of the Renaissance.

Individualism in the Renaissance was not a mass phenomenon in the modern sense. It was perceived as a privilege of an elite. But it spread gradually; and though there were setbacks from attempted reassertions of centralized political and religious authority, the movement persisted.

With individualism came economic development and scientific development. The development of property rights and the freedom to initiate change stimulated production and technological innovation.

These events, here so sweepingly summarized, stretched out over more than five centuries. The extreme slowness of this movement toward an individualistic society is readily understood when we consider the difficulty of conceiving a workable society in which individuals are free to pursue their own goals in their own way, uncontrolled and uncoordinated by a central authority. The risks to order and security must have been frightening. As late as 1831, Alexis Charles de Tocqueville came to America to study whether individualism, carried as far as it was in the United States, could work; and, if so, what made it work.

But by that time the inconceivable had become conceivable. Those societies which crept gradually toward individualism found that the anticipated disasters did not occur. Production increased, living conditions improved, population grew. By the eighteenth century, the groundwork had been laid in several countries for the economic outburst called the Industrial Revolution. Success overcame fears. In the nineteenth century, change accelerated and spread by imitation in varying degrees to countries that had lagged in the drift toward individualism.

Today it is obvious that the high tide of individualism is behind us, and the reverse drift toward authoritarianism is well under way. I refer not only to the measurable evidence—the rise of government expenditure from 10 percent of gross national product to over 35 percent in the past fifty years and the massive increase in the number of regulations and regulatory agencies—but also to the even more significant change in the underlying ethos.

The idea of individual responsibility is on the decline, and the idea of reliance on government is on the rise. The prevailing orthodoxy is no longer that the individual is accountable for his behavior; blame has been shifted from him to "society" or "the system." Crime, misbehavior, or shiftlessness are becoming collective responsibilities, not to be restrained by penalties upon the individual culprit, but to be ameliorated by some governmental reform of a guilty society.

Responsibility for the most basic decisions of life is increasingly being shifted to government. Provision for the individual's future, job-training, and job-performance, the risks of economic decisions, and the teaching of morality to children are burdens to be transferred to the shoulders of government.

This transfer of responsibility has already gone beyond basics into comparatively trivial facts of life. Shoppers need no longer calculate the price per ounce of cornflakes. Laws require that this calculation be done for them. Baby-sitting services are a government function. Amusements for the young, the elderly, and the intermediates have become a government responsibility, irrespective of the poverty or the affluence of the beneficiaries. One has only to listen to the stream of broadcast messages, urging the public to claim the benefits of government's proliferating paternalistic programs to realize that we are in the midst of an active campaign to hasten the drift from the self-reliance of individualism to the dependency of authoritarianism.

FROM INDIVIDUALISM TO AUTHORITARIANISM

That the free world is in the throes of a profound change is widely recognized. Conflict and disorder are increasing, economic difficulties are intensifying, and our traditional optimism about the future has turned to pessimism. But the explanations for the change, though numerous, remain superficial or nebulous. One hears the apparent social decay attributed to a "loss of nerve," to the influence of television and corrupt journalism, to permissive child-rearing, to the pernicious influence of intellectuals, to population-growth, to an energy crisis, and to an environmental crisis.

The analysts of social change have not yet seen our current malaise as part of the long wave, which, having taken us from authoritarianism to individualism, is now returning us to authoritarianism. When recent history is looked at in that perspective, the host of popular explanations will fall into place as components or symptoms of the general movement.

The intriguing question is, Why the reversal? If the rise of individualism was fed by its success—success in the forms of rising standards of living, astounding technological achievements, and freedom without disorder—why should the decline of individualism have begun while the successes were flowing faster than ever? The beginnings of the reversal can be discerned in the nineteenth century in Great Britain and in the twentieth century in the United States, even while those countries were still faintly astonished at what they had accomplished and what they expected to accomplish.

Evidently, we are dealing with a common phenomenon, like eating, or watering crops, in which the gains from increasing an input eventually turn into losses. Folk wisdom, which warns that one can have too much of a good thing, is soundly grounded in experience.

The links between the success of individualism and its decline must, at this time, be a matter of conjectures—of which I offer several.

First, the working of an individualistic society depends heavily on self-discipline, on self-restraint, and on self-reliance. When the controls of authority are removed, they must be replaced by the self-controls of the individual. The individual must accept the disciplines of saving to provide for the future, of making intelligent choices, and of responsibility for his own errors or shortcomings. Individuals must exercise restraint in what they expect from the economy and the government and in the use of the power that the democratic process gives to the majority. Individuals must have the firmness and the foresight to prefer to rely upon themselves rather than to turn readily to the help and the favors of authority.

The requirements for an individualistic society are severely demanding. Self-discipline, self-restraint, and self-reliance are developed under conditions of hardship, provided the possession of those qualities offers a promise of improvement. The maintenance of those qualities and their inculcation in the young is hard work.

As a society progresses from hardship to affluence, changes occur in the relative valuation that people put upon the gains and costs of self-discipline, self-restraint, and self-reliance. First, the gains from those attributes, in the form of higher incomes, decline in value to the recipients. That is, the effort or sacrifice that individuals are willing to make for more income, decreases as their incomes increase. This proposition, known to economists as "diminishing marginal utility" of income, cannot be rigorously tested, since utility is not measurable. But it is a plausible proposition and one which is consistent with much observable human behavior.

Secondly, the costs of maintaining the individualistic attributes rises as income rises. Higher income widens the opportunities for amusements and diversions. The cost of the time and effort in preparing oneself to handle one's own affairs; in gathering information for personal decisions; in bearing personal responsibilities; and, above all, in teaching discipline, restraint, and reliance to the young are measured by the value of what could be done with alternative uses of that time and effort. When the alternative uses of time and effort are highly enjoyable—sports, travel, hobbies—the cost of individualism seems high. How much more preferable it now seems to turn unpleasant or tedious tasks over to government than it did when the alternative activity was equally unpleasant or tedious.

My hypothesis, in brief, is that the decline of individualism and the return to dependence on authority, which we see occurring, can be explained by the declining marginal utility of the gains from individualism and the rising cost of maintaining individualism.

It will be instructive to compare this hypothesis with an earlier, justly-admired, analysis of the same question. Joseph Schumpeter, in his classic *Capitalism, Socialism and Democracy*, first published in 1942, pondered "the nature of the process that is killing capitalism" and concluded that "capitalism is being killed by its achievements."[1]

Schumpeter saw capitalism being killed by two processes, both of them generated by the economic success of capitalism. The first is the crumbling of the front-line defenders of capitalism—the entrepreneurs and the bourgeoisie. The entrepreneurs decline in numbers and influence as the growth in the size of business widens the separation between ownership and management. The owners become increasingly a widely scattered group of stockholders with only limited knowledge of and stake in the business. The managers are no longer owners and entrepreneurs; they are essentially bureaucrats. As bureaucrats, their concern is not with the long-run future of the firm, and therefore not with the long-run future of the free enterprise system.

The bureaucrat-manager's concern is with the immediate outlook, on which his position, promotion, and income, depend. If compliance and cooperation with authorities and with the propagators of authoritarianism can secure current gains or alleviate current conflicts, the bureaucrat-manager is satisfied. It is not in his interest to bear the penalties and risks of defending the principles of free enterprise.

Schumpeter attributes the bourgeoisie's loss of will to defend the bourgeois order to the decay of the bourgeois family. The family, he says, was the mainspring of the typically bourgeois kind of profit motive. The bourgeois worked primarily to invest, and he invested for a future beyond his own lifetime, that is, for his family. With the breakdown of the family, the rationale for bourgeois behavior disappeared. The breakdown of the family, Schumpeter attributed to the success of the economic system, which opens up such attractive and enjoyable opportunities that time devoted to rearing children seems increasingly an unwarranted sacrifice.

While the defenses of capitalism weaken, its enemies grow stronger. Schumpeter saw a growing hostility to capitalism, led by the intellectuals. He defined intellectuals in a broad sense as people who wield the power of the spoken and written word without having direct responsibility for practical affairs.

In a striking section on "The Sociology of the Intellectual," Schumpeter argues that the intellectual, having neither responsibility for nor direct knowledge of practical affairs, gains notoriety and advancement by criticising the existing system.[2] In precapitalist societies, the intellectual did not have the freedom to criticize nor the means to disseminate his criticism. But capitalism gave him both. Moreover, the affluence of capitalism has vastly multiplied the number of intellectuals. The crowding in the intellectual ranks makes them more discontented and more critical. The nature of the intellectual's work gives him access to the means of communication and indoctrination, as well as the time—"the leisure of the theory class," as a wag has called it—to carry on his hostile criticism. On the other hand, those who still labor and produce, but not in the vineyard of verbiage, lack the competence, the means, and the time to counter the intellectual's assault.

Schumpeter's analysis, though remarkably far-sighted, seems to me now to be somewhat incomplete. We are in the midst not merely of the movement from capitalism to socialism, as forecast by Schumpeter, but of something more fundamental: the decline of the individualistic ethos, which underlies capitalism, and the rise of the authoritarian ethos, which underlies socialism.

While large business may be chiefly in the hands of bureaucrat-managers rather than entrepreneurs, there are over twelve million unincorporated businesses and two million corporations in the United States. Most of these businesses are owner-operated, so that in terms of sheer numbers, there is no shortage of people to hold the viewpoint of owners of enterprises. But business owners have never had the ability, the courage, nor the will to lead the defense of the free-enterprise system. I find it improbable that the decline of individualism can be attributed to any significant extent to a decline of entrepreneurship.

The belief in individualism was not confined to entrepreneurs or the bourgeoisie. It pervaded the society. To explain the decay of the individualistic ethos by the breakdown of the family, does not go deep enough. The breakdown of the family is only one aspect of the changes wrought when the growth of affluence reduces the marginal utility of the gains from individualism and raises the cost of sustaining individualism.

The other side of Schumpeter's analysis—the growing power of the hostile intellectuals—also needs closer examination. When individualism was on the rise, the main body of the intellectual community was among its strongest supporters. That support was only natural, for intellectuals are among the chief beneficiaries of individualism. Their swing to an anti-individualist position is a suicidal movement as puzzling as the rush of the lemmings to the sea. Intellectuals do not flourish in an authoritarian world.

But intellectuals, like others, follow the rewards. When the tide of authoritarianism is rising, the rewards for authoritarian intellectuals—jobs, fellowships, publications, and status—also rise. Intellectuals must dance to society's tune, and the tune is changing. Powerful as intellectuals are in speeding the process of change, they are still a product of the change.

THE PATHS OF CHANGE

The paths away from individualism are many, though they all lead to the same destination. We cannot follow all the paths, which would take us into an examination of every facet of social organization and individual behavior. But we can look at the main ones, starting with the economic path.

The Economic Path

The drift from individualism to authoritarianism is characterized in the economic sphere by the growth of government regulations and controls, more income redistribution, growth of the government sector relative to the private sector, and deterioration in the management of government monetary and fiscal policies.

In an individualistic society, government regulation of the economy is viewed as a last resort for dealing with serious and irremediable defects in the market system. Individualists, fearful of government power and well acquainted with government incompetence, only call upon government to interfere in markets where the market failure is clear and the probability is high that government will improve rather than worsen the situation. As individualism wanes and the propensity to rely on government increases, the tests of the acceptability of regulation weaken. An indication that the market is seriously defective or even only moderately defective is no longer required. Whether the government is capable of improving on the market is no longer questioned but presumed.

What distinguishes the new spirit of regulation from the old is that regulation is inspired not by failures or supposed failures of the market mechanism, but by the desire to escape from the market mechanism and the individualistic responsibilities that it imposes. Some of the regulations are frankly paternalistic, seeking to relieve individuals of their own responsibility for gathering information and exercising due care in investing, consuming, and making other personal decisions.

A major part of the new regulation is aimed at eliminating risk. Regulation of new products; limitations on technological change; controls on oil drilling, pipelines, or other investments that may entail a risk for someone, somewhere; the massive and picayune safety regulations of the Occupational Safety and Health Administration—these are all part of the effort to create a risk-free society. Regulations for job security and income security are antirisk devices, far advanced in some countries and moderately advanced in this country.

A risk-free society would be a pleasant and worthy objective, were it not for four problems. The goal is unattainable. The pursuit is pushed to the point where the costs exceed the benefits. Risklessness is incompatible with an efficient and progressive economy. Individualism demands the acceptance of risks; the relentless pursuit of risklessness must end in authoritarianism.

Another objective of regulation is the redistribution of income, particularly through price controls and the regulation of labor markets. The chief instrument of redistribution, however, is public finance—taxation, government spending, and government transfer payments.

How income should be distributed is a question that has no answer. It has no answer, that is, if the question is one of distributive fairness or justice, and the answer sought is an empirical revelation of the "best" distribution of income. If the question were one of maximizing productive efficiency, a scientific principle of distribution would be conceivable, since productive efficiency is conceivably measurable. But fairness and justice are not measurable or even definable. Recent efforts by philosophers to find a solution have brought forth the suggestion that a principle of distributive justice could be discovered by asking what distributive principle everyone could agree upon if everyone were completely ignorant of his own income prospects. But there is no reason to suppose that ignorance of individuals' personal positions would be sufficient to produce general agreement. And, in any event, we do not live behind a veil of ignorance; the principle philosophers arrive at by imagining such a veil is not the principle men will live by.

The distribution of income remains, therefore, a question not to be decided but to be fought over. A society which can reach a moderate compromise, can avoid a destructive battle. Modern individualistic societies, for a time, maintained such a compromise. Income distribution was basically to be determined by individual ability, effort, and property. But victims of bad fortune ("the deserving poor") were to be assisted by private or public philanthropy. The role of government, aside from modest aid to the deserving poor, was to be that of a referee, keeping order, maintaining competition, and promoting equality of opportunity. Deviations from these principles were naturally to be expected, but as a compromise generally accepted by society, they were broadly adhered to.

This individualistic approach to distribution was highly stimulating to production. It was the engine of economic expansion. Economic expansion, in turn, helped to make the compromise acceptable. Attention and energy were concentrated on enlarging the pie, rather than on struggling over how to divide it. But the success of the system, having undermined individualism, has produced the paradoxical result that the attention and energy of the country are redirected from production to conflict over distribution.

A third economic consequence of the decline of individualism is the relative growth of the burden of the government sector. The rising tax on productive effort and the burgeoning benefits obtainable without productive effort, erode the incentive to make productive effort. The rising tax burden also distorts economic activity as people seek employment or investments in which tax evasion will be easier. The growth of the government sector retards economic growth in another way; it increases the relative portion of the economy in which productivity probably does not increase and may decrease as government grows. We cannot be sure, because of the deficiency of measurements of government productivity, a deficiency that reflects both the difficulties of measuring the productivity of government workers and the fact that productivity is not of much concern in government. The difficulties of measurement and the absence of motivation to increase productivity practically guarantee that there will be no increase of productivity in government.

A final economic consequence is the deterioration of the management of monetary and fiscal policies. The control of the government's power to create money and to spend by borrowing rests ultimately in a free society, on the self-discipline of a people who are determined to prevent inflation, to bear any temporary hardships arising from anti-inflationary policy, and to forego the temporary pleasures of loose monetary and fiscal policies. As individualism evaporates, these restraints on the inflationary government policies also evaporate.

In the transitional phase when individualism is deteriorating and before strong authoritarian rule is imposed, a country will experience more or less continuous and accelerating inflation.

The Political Path

The decline of individualism and the growth of government will produce political changes that will move a democratic system along the path toward an authoritarian system.

As the scale of government activity increases, the work load outruns the capacity of elected officials to oversee it, and the making of policy is turned over more and more to the bureaucracy. These nonelected managers, being neither directly accountable to the public nor much supervised by the public's representatives, who lack the time and the information for adequate supervision, acquire powers that, in a democratic system, they were never intended to exercise.

The diversion of power from elected representatives to bureaucrats is augmented by the nature of economic regulation. The complexities of these regulations preclude the writing of laws that will be uniformly applicable to all cases. The regulations must be written by an administrative body and must be carried out by the administrative body, which thereby acquires substantial power to make policy.

The growth of the bureaucracy also acts to increase the voting bloc, which has a strong interest in enlarging government. More bureaucrat-voters voting for more bureaucrats becomes a self-feeding process.

The enlarged government requires more centralization of government. The allocation of powers to state and local governments, which was adopted in order to limit government power, is obviously incompatible with the movement toward expanding government power. Means are found for states to increase their control of local affairs and for the Federal Government to increasingly control state affairs.

A conspicuous political symptom of the movement toward authoritarianism in this country and perhaps in others is the propensity of the courts to take on some of the functions of legislatures. Our constitutional system impedes the expansion of government power, as it was intended to do. The political process moves slowly when interests conflict and compromises must be reached. This system works well when most social problems are handled through the voluntary action of individuals and groups. But, when the government's role is enlarged and impatience with the democratic political process develops, the society turns toward some authority outside the political process.

The courts in the United States are such an authority. They have responded boldly to the invitation to make laws, to decide social policies, and even to determine certain budgetary expenditures.

Legislatures, which in an earlier era might have been expected to resist this encroachment on legislative territory, now seem to welcome the opportunity to have the courts bear the responsibility for controversial decisions.

Still another change in the political process occurs because of changes in voter thinking and strategy. As government expands its activities, new vistas open up to voters. Demands for government interventions or special benefits, which were unthinkable under the rules of the individualistic game, now become thinkable. Each new government action whets the appetite for more. Those who bear the cost of government think less about ways to restrain government spending and more about ways to achieve partial recompense through some special benefits for themselves. The competition for a share of the loot speeds up the growth of government and weakens confidence in democracy as a workable method of government.

Under the strain of the expanding role of government, the democratic method will eventually break down. The transfer of power from politicians to the bureaucracy and the scramble for government benefits will contribute to the breakdown. If democracy should survive those stresses, it will eventually face a more severe test. In countries where government dominates the economy and is the principal source of privileges, rewards, and even livelihood, control of government is not something to be lightly risked. Free elections are not a menace to those in power when government is unimportant and not much is at stake. But when government becomes a vital concern of those in power, we can expect to see, as we have seen in so many failed democracies, a military takeover or a declaration of "emergency" with suspension of elections or the establishment of a one-party system by the suppression of opposition.

The Sociological Path

The decline of individualism produces certain sociological phenomena, which add to the forces pushing the society toward authoritarianism by the anxiety or distress they create.

The weakening of family ties can be expected, as duties that were once the responsibility of the individual (especially the care of children) become the responsibility of government.

In multiethnic societies ethnic hostility tends to increase as power, which is widely dispersed in an individualistic market system, becomes concentrated in the hands of government. Market relations make it worthwhile to ignore ethnic differences and engage in mutually beneficial exchanges. Government power, on the other hand, is sought through the formation of cohesive special interest groups. Such groups will naturally follow ethnic lines, where ethnic divisions exist. The contest between ethnic groups for political power, where political power is recognized as being of supreme importance, becomes fierce and brutal.

Another sociological phenomenon that we observe during the transition from individualism to authoritarianism is the growth of crime. Crime is an economic activity, and it can be analyzed in terms of costs and gains like any other economic activity.

The chief cost of crime to a criminal is punishment. When individualism decays, the probability of a criminal's being caught, convicted, and effectively punished decreases. When individuals are no longer to be regarded as responsible for their actions and when in some mysterious way guilt becomes the fault of the society ("we are all guilty"), the will to enforce the law weakens. Moreover, the elaborate machinery of justice becomes overloaded as the laws and regulations to be enforced proliferate. To handle the overload, prosecutions are dropped or settled by easy bargains.

While the punishment-cost of crime is falling, the expected income from crime is rising relative to lawful incomes. Lawful incomes are taxed; illegal incomes are not. The higher the tax rate, the more attractive crime becomes.

THE DOWNHILL RUN

It should be self-evident that the paths that I have described lead to an authoritarian society.

Economically, the system of rewards is being turned wholly away from the individualistic system that underlay the great economic development of the past two centuries. Productivity, initiative, technological improvement, and risk-taking are now being penalized. Nonproductive activity and even antiproductive activity are being rewarded. The growth of production will decelerate, the prevailing expectation of rising incomes will be disappointed, conflict over the distribution of income will sharpen, and demands that the government "do something" will increase. More government regulations, controls, subsidies, income redistribution, and inflationary creation of money will follow. The efficiency and productivity of the economy will be further damaged, followed by demands for more government intervention, and so on to the eventual authoritarian destination.

Politically, government's deteriorating performance will destroy confidence in the democratic process and breed belief in the need for authoritarian rule.

Sociologically, the instability arising from the decay of individual discipline and responsibility, the increase of crime, ethnic conflict, and similar disruptions will create such discontent and anxiety as to make authoritarian rule welcome.

In short, when the individualistic foundations of our free societies disintegrate, a vacuum is left that can only be filled by authority.

IS AUTHORITARIANISM INEVITABLE?

The process we have been considering is essentially a struggle of ideas. Ideas do not have the same inevitability that phenomena of nature have, like the coming of the next Ice Age or the destruction of the solar system. But I can see no automatic self-reversing mechanism in the drift from individualism to authoritarianism. The successes of individualism have eroded individualism; but it does not follow that the consequent social failures of collectivism will restore individualism. The reaction of nonindividualists to the failures of authority is to demand more and stronger authority.

A positive and conscious effort to understand the present course and to reverse the trend of ideas will be required to preserve freedom. What the chances are of deflecting a tidal movement of history by the powers of knowledge and persuasion, I will not attempt to estimate.

NOTES

1. Joseph Schumpeter, *Capitalism, Socialism and Democracy* (New York: Harper and Row, 1950), p. 134.
2. Schumpeter, *Capitalism, Socialism and Democracy*, pp. 145–55.

SECTION VI
Beneficent Social Control

12

CHRISTOPHER LASCH

The Bill of Rights and the Therapeutic State

The men who drew up the Bill of Rights and insisted on its incorporation in the Constitution believed that governments always tend to aggrandize their own power at the expense of the rights of citizens—even governments ostensibly resting on the consent of the governed. Some of the proponents of the Bill of Rights feared a movement to restore monarchy, others believed that an oligarchy might attempt to use government to promote its own interests at the expense of the majority, still others feared the majority itself; but all agreed on the inevitability of an adversary relation between the people and the state. They could not have foreseen the rise of a new kind of state that claims to understand the citizens' needs better than the citizens themselves understand them and that justifies its increasingly intrusive intervention in their lives in the name of medical authority. Not content with equal and impartial enforcement of the law, administrators now model government on public health, seeking not merely to treat the symptoms of public disorder and maladjustment but to remove their causes. Modern administrators conceive of themselves as experts in social pathology, specialists in the art of social healing or crisis management, and doctors to a sick society. Safeguards designed to protect the citizen against arbitrary authority have proved ineffective in the face of therapeutic authority, which dissolves the conflict of interests between the people and the state and enlists the citizen in his own control. The Bill of Rights offers little protection against the benevolent despotism of the welfare state and the helping professions through which it administers its discretionary powers.

Modern humanitarianism has redefined crime as sickness and replaced criminal sanctions with a more subtle system of social controls. It substitutes treatment for punishment, pleading for understanding of and tolerance for the criminal or deviant on the grounds that he bears no responsibility for his actions. Hugo Black felt that retribution was no longer the dominant objective of criminal law and that reformation and rehabilitation of offenders had become the important goals of criminal jurisprudence. The liberalism of the eighteenth and nineteenth centuries assumed that the pursuit of self-interest is the principal determinant of human conduct; hence the need for laws to protect the weak against the strong. Twentieth-century progressivism, having assimilated the wisdom of the social sciences, believes on the other hand that men act from irrational motives and cannot always be held responsible for what they do. Formerly the courts regarded the actions of adults as deliberate and calculating, but as Judge David L. Bazelon pointed out in 1954, modern psychiatry "now recognizes that a man is an integrated personality and that reason, which is only one element in that personality, is not the sole determinant of his conduct."[1] On these grounds, Bazelon overturned an old rule under which the courts allowed a plea of insanity only if the defendant showed no ability to distinguish right from wrong. Relying heavily on a brief submitted by Abe Fortas, he ruled that "an accused is not criminally responsible if his unlawful act was the product of mental disease or mental defect."[2] Other progressive lawyers feel that the concept of "treatment" has replaced the concept of "punishment."

The psychiatric critique of the law makes a virtue of substituting personal treatment for the impersonal, arbitrary authority of the courts. Instead of fitting the punishment to the crime, it fits the punishment to the criminal, or in its own language, fits the treatment to the need of the individual to whom it is administered. Thus a federal court in 1962 broadened the definition of cruel and unnatural punishment to include not only punishment in excess of the crime but the use of criminal sanctions in cases such as drug addiction, where medical measures were allegedly more appropriate. Specialists in the sociology of law, acknowledging their intention to substitute scientific therapies for legal sanctions—for "justice"—have deplored the irrationality of legal procedures. They maintain that there is in the concept of justice an element of "fate," which is absent in the concept of scientific treatment. The offender simply gets what he himself initiated and society as a whole is blameless. The criminal himself was the one who chose. The lawyer's approach to a human problem is viewed as nonscientific; therapy, by contrast, treats the criminal or patient as a victim and thus puts matters in their proper light. The shift from "sin" to "sickness," is represented as the first step in introducing science into human conflicts, and in recognizing social problems as medical problems, in which cooperation with the therapist becomes perhaps the central problem for the deviant.

Therapeutic modes of thought and practice by their very nature except their object, the patient, from critical judgment and relieve him of moral responsibility. Sickness by definition represents an invasion of the patient by forces outside his conscious control, and the patient's realistic recognition of the limits of his own responsibility—his acceptance of his diseased and helpless condition—constitutes the first step toward recovery (or permanent invalidism, as the case may be). Therapy labels as sickness what might otherwise be judged as weak or willful actions; it thus equips the patient to fight (or resign himself to) the disease, instead of irrationally finding fault with himself. Inappropriately extended beyond the consulting room, however, therapeutic morality encourages a permanent suspension of the moral sense. There is a close connection, in turn, between the erosion of moral responsibility and the waning of the capacity for self-help—in the categories used by John R. Seeley, between the elimination of culpability and the elimination of competence. "What says 'you are not guilty' says also 'you cannot help yourself.' "[3] Therapy legitimates deviance as sickness, but it simultaneously pronounces the patient unfit to manage his own life and delivers him into the hands of a specialist. As therapeutic points of view and practice gain general acceptance, more and more people find themselves disqualified, in effect, from the performance of adult responsibilities and become dependent on some form of medical authority. Nicholas N. Kittrie, noting in 1971 that juvenile delinquents, the mentally ill, alcoholics, drug addicts, and many of the economically disadvantaged had all been transferred from the penal to the medical realm, estimated that less than one half of the American population may now be subject to the sanctions of criminal law. "Ours is increasingly becoming a society that views punishment as a primitive and vindictive tool and is therefore loath to punish."[4]

What the expansion of therapeutic jurisdiction does to the Bill of Rights appears most clearly in cases where the "patient" refuses to cooperate with medical authority. The concept of "incompetence to stand trial," originally designed to help the accused, has undergone an alarming psychiatric expansion, which makes it possible for ostensibly well-meaning courts to send people to mental asylums against their will on the grounds that they are mentally incompetent to defend their own rights. Sometimes the indictment itself creates a suspicion of the defendant's mental incompetence; otherwise what is he doing in court in the first place? As Thomas S. Szasz has shown, in such cases the pre-trial hearing on the issues of mental incompetence becomes in itself a trial, as a result of which the defendant may in effect be sentenced without a real trial or a chance to prove his innocence to incarceration in a mental hospital. The possibility that he can be repeatedly tried and convicted for the same offense (refusal to cooperate with the court-appointed psychiatrists) violates another provision of the Bill of Rights, protection against double jeopardy. Finally, the judge sentences him to a sentence of indefinite duration, whereas in a real trial he would be more likely—or once would have been more likely—to receive a definite sentence. As a federal court ruled in the landmark case of *Overholser v. Lynch*, in which a man accused of passing bad checks was held not guilty by reason of insanity and confined to a mental asylum, "By its very nature, a jail sentence is for a specified period of time, while by its very nature hospitalization, to be effective, must be initially for an indeterminate period."[5] Lynch shortly proved just how badly he needed medical attention by committing suicide.

The appearance of permissiveness in our society often conceals a stringent system of controls, all the more effective because it avoids direct confrontations between authorities and the people on whom they seek to impose their will. Because confrontations provoke arguments about principles, the authorities whenever possible delegate discipline to someone else so that they themselves can pose as advisers, "resource persons," and friendly helpers. Parents rely on doctors, psychiatrists, and the child's own peers to impose rules on the child and to see that he conforms to them. Teachers, although they "know what goes on and who the offensive kids are" (in words of one high school student), "don't want to stir up any trouble so they keep quiet." School administrators try to keep order by surrounding themselves with the aura of scientific detachment. If one of the students gets "out of line," they send him to a counselor for "guidance." The students themselves, according to Edgar Friedenberg's study of the American high school, reject both authoritarian and libertarian measures and regard social control as a technical problem to be referred to the right expert for solution.[6] Thus, if a teacher finds an unruly student smoking in the washroom, he should neither "beat him calmly and coolly and with emotional restraint" nor publicly humiliate him, on the one hand, nor ignore the offense, on the other hand, as a minor infraction that should not contribute to the student's reputation as a troublemaker. The teacher should refer him instead to the school psychiatrist. Beating him would make him more unmanageable than ever, in the students' view, whereas the psychiatric solution, in effect, enlists his own cooperation in the school's attempt to control him.

The movement to bring youthful offenders under special jurisdiction illustrates in their clearest form the connections between organized altruism, the new therapeutic conception of the state, and the appropriation of familial functions by outside agencies. When penal reformers and humanitarians established a new system of juvenile justice at the end of the nineteenth century, they made it possible for the courts to treat youthful offenders as victims of a bad environment rather than as criminals. They eliminated the adversary relationship between the child and the state and made the prevention of crime, not punishment, the chief object of the law—in reformers' eyes, a great advance toward a more humane, more scientific system of justice.

As so often happens in modern history, reforms that presented themselves as the height of ethical enlightenment eroded the rights of the ordinary citizen. Conceiving of the problem of social control on the model of public health, the "helping professions" claimed to attack the causes of crime instead of merely treating the consequences. By converting the courts into agents of moral instruction and psychic "help," however, they abrogated the usual safeguards against arbitrary arrest and detention. Their reforms empowered the courts to pry into family affairs; to remove children from "unsuitable homes"; to sentence them to indeterminate periods of incarceration without proving their guilt; and to invade the delinquent's home in order to supervise the terms of probation. The probation system, according to one reformer, created "a new kind of reformatory, without walls and without much coercion"; but in fact the establishment of this reformatory without walls extended the coercive powers of the state, now disguised as a wish "to befriend and help," into every corner of society.

The state could now segregate deviants for no other reason than that they or their parents had refused to cooperate with the courts, especially when refusal to cooperate appeared as *prima facie* evidence of a bad home environment. Judges, who considered themselves specialists in the art of human relations, sought to get the whole truth about a child, wrote Miriam Van Waters, in the same way that a physician searches for every detail that bears on the condition of a patient.[7] The judge did not punish the boy, but rather he sought his confidence so that he could help him. In effect, the court now certified the "patient" into what Talcott Parsons has called the sick rule. Consequently, once a delinquent juvenile admitted his need of help—the real meaning, in this essentially therapeutic setting, of giving the judge his "confidence"—he exchanged his legal rights for the protective custody of the state, which in practice often proved to be as harsh and unrelenting as the punishment from which the new system of judicial therapy had delivered him in the first place.

In the progressive period, when the foundations of the therapeutic state were laid in place, few people pointed out that the applied science of social pathology was undermining traditional safeguards against central authority. The passion for social engineering continued uncriticized through the New Deal, the Fair Deal, the New Frontier, and the Great Society. Only in the seventies did a full-scale revulsion against organized benevolence set in. A growing distrust of philanthropy has been nourished in part by scholars such as David Rothman, who showed, in his *The Discovery of the Asylum*, that nineteenth-century reformers did more to control deviance than to help criminals, madmen, paupers, and the other victims of their attempts (sometimes well-intended, sometimes not so well-intended) at "rehabilitation."[8]

Erving Goffman in his critique of total institutions, Thomas Szasz in his attacks on psychiatry and the "myth of mental illness," Ivan Illich, and other critics of professional dominance have also contributed to the current revulsion against the welfare state.[9] Those who believe that even a benevolent paternalism degrades those it seeks to help can now cite a large body of revisionist scholarship, which often calls into question the disinterested motives of professional do-gooders and condemns their intervention in our lives as a flagrant invasion of privacy.

The revulsion against philanthropic paternalism, although it derives in part from a reinterpretation of professionalism, the welfare state, and the history of earlier reform movements, springs more immediately from recent political events. Gross abuses of power, culminating in Vietnam and Watergate, have aroused in ordinary citizens a profound suspicion of the state and of the sweeping schemes for social betterment that have played such an important part in its growth. The most important question for American politics in the immediate future is whether this well-founded public skepticism will continue to express itself in policies of drift and inaction, in "taxpayers' revolts" and other petulant gestures that curtail needed services without making any real inroads on bureaucracy, or whether a disenchantment with official pretensions will give rise to serious attempts to limit the power not only of the state but of the business corporations that ultimately control it.

Recent criticism of the welfare state too often ignores the corporate contribution to the growth of paternalism. Ever since the progressive period, liberal industrialists have attempted—increasingly in close conjunction with the social sciences, the helping professions, and the state—to discipline the work force, allay labor unrest, and socialize the working class into the pleasures of consumption in the hope that they could thereby substitute cooperation for competition and corporate planning for class conflict. The new corporate paternalism, instead of trying to destroy labor unions, has promoted the idea that labor and capital share a common stake in the health of American capitalism, has admitted labor leaders into a qualified partnership in its operation, and has even succeeded in delegating to unions much of the daily discipline of the worker.

One of the hallmarks of neopaternalism, as we have seen, is the replacement of adversarial relations by therapeutic relations. But this has long been one of the goals not only of government bureaucrats but of personnel managers in industry, who have stressed the harmony of interests between capital and labor, tried to implant in workers a sense of personal loyalty to the organization, and dealt with grievances not by denying their importance but by translating them from generalized complaints about exploitation into specific complaints about particular conditions of work. Industrial sociology, industrial psychology, and other professions less directly involved in the management of labor unrest (such as social work) have modeled themselves on public health and medicine and have based their activities on the assumption that social conflict represents a disease amenable to therapeutic intervention.

Like the other social institutions of caring, these agencies of control depend on various forms of public (as well as corporate) subsidy and must be seen, therefore, as extensions of the state. What has been said of the liberals who manage the welfare apparatus applies equally to those who manage labor relations.

Unless we grasp the interconnections between the corporations, the helping professions, and the state, we shall make the mistake of thinking that the new paternalism emanates from government alone. We shall confuse the defense of privacy with the defense of private enterprise, the struggle for liberty with the struggle against equality. Recent criticisms of the therapeutic state can easily be appropriated by conservatives who wish to scale down welfare payments, cut taxes, and curtail government regulation of business without mounting any comparable attack on the military-industrial complex or the multinational corporation. Liberal critics of the welfare state invite a conservative misapplication of their work not only by ignoring corporate paternalism but by arguing that we must choose between a "liberty model" of social action and an "equality model," in David Rothman's terms—between policies designed to protect individual rights and policies based on the illusory promise of social justice. A much-needed criticism of the helping professions and the therapeutic state thus appears to signal an abandonment of the struggle to close the gap between wealth and poverty.

A purely libertarian strategy, however, will defeat the very purposes it seeks to advance. One of the points on which most of the framers of the Bill of Rights agreed was that republican institutions rested on a broad distribution of property. Thus Jefferson retained a property qualification for the suffrage in his 1776 draft of a constitution for Virginia but proposed, in effect, to universalize the suffrage by granting fifty acres of land to every adult male holding a lesser amount. Madison feared that in the future a great majority of the people would not only be without land but any other sort of property as well and that the masses would either rise up against the propertied class or, more probably, become the tools of opulence and ambition. These apprehensions have become more and more pertinent as the propertied class—those deriving their incomes from property and controlling a major share of corporate stock—shrinks to a tiny minority, leaving the rest of the population helpless in dealing with the huge corporations that wield most of the power in our society.

It is the growing disparity between the rich and the rest of society that provides the social basis of neopaternalism. A political strategy that seeks merely to limit the powers of the state and the welfare agencies, without perceiving the connection between the welfare state and corporate capitalism, will merely substitute "private" for public paternalism. A strategy that proposes to preserve liberty by giving up the fight against inequality will leave citizens without the indispensable economic resources with which to defend their freedoms.

NOTES

1. *Durham v. United States*, 214 F.2d 862, at 871 (1954).
2. 214 F.2d 862, at 874–875.
3. John R. Seeley, *The Americanization of the Unconscious* (New York: International Science Press, 1967).
4. Nicholas N. Kittrie, *The Right to be Different* (Baltimore: Johns Hopkins University, 1971), p. 5.
5. *Overholser v. Lynch*, 288 F.2d 388, at 393 (1961).
6. Carl Nordstrom, Edgar Friedenberg, and Hilary Gold, *Society's Children: A Study of Ressentiment in Secondary Schools* (New York: Random House, 1967).
7. Miriam Van Waters, *Youth in Conflict* (New York: Republic, 1925); *Parents on Probation* (New York: New Republic, 1927).
8. David Rothman, *The Discovery of the Asylum* (Boston: Little, Brown, 1971).
9. Erving Goffman, *Asylums: Essays on the Social Situation of Mental Patients and Other Inmates* (Chicago: Aldine, 1961); Thomas Szasz, *The Myth of Mental Illness* (New York: Harper & Row, 1974); Ivan Illich, *Medical Nemesis: The Expropriation of Health* (New York: Pantheon Books, 1976).

13

FRANCES FOX PIVEN

Public Education and Political Democracy

As civil libertarians we worry about the undermining of our constitutionally guaranteed rights by government. Typically we focus our concern on the intelligence and police agencies of the state, and rightly so. Here, however, I want to propose for your consideration that apparently beneficent activities of the state can also undermine constitutional rights in a deep and pervasive way. In particular, I will argue that the institution of public education has intruded upon and weakened the capacity of ordinary people to recognize and act on their political interests. Such an argument has about it the aura of a crackpot's assault on big government. But be patient, and wonder with me, for my attack is not on big government, which I consider to be an inevitable feature of an industrial society. Rather, my attack is on particular uses of government and particular uses of beneficence to further the interests of the few by weakening the political capacities of the many.

Implicit in my argument is a conception of the Bill of Rights as not merely a legal document, but a political document. I consider that the rights codified in 1791 were not rights in and of themselves sufficient for all time. Rather each such right was intended as a means to guarantee a measure of political democracy. The particular rights fastened upon reflected the particular experiences of people who had fought for a measure of political democracy in a particular historical context. Thus the right to free speech and assembly, the guarantee against arbitrary searches, and the right to bear arms each represented a distillation of the lessons learned in specific historical struggles. Moreover, these struggles were not merely struggles against arbitrary state power but were struggles against the uses of state power in the interests of landowning and merchant classes. Both in England and the colonies, working people had learned through actual and bitter experience that the suppression of free speech and assembly, for example, were crucial instruments in the suppression of their political mobilization. But underlying each such formulation of a right was a larger intent, a larger vision, for each right was perceived as a condition necessary to protect the capacity of ordinary people to interpret their situation and to act on that interpretation in political society. Moreover, even in 1791 the encroachments against their political capacity which the artisans, farmers, and other working people of the revolutionary period were trying to prevent were not simply encroachments of an abstracted governmental power but encroachments of the landed and merchant elites who had already, with the formulation of the Articles of the Constitution, begun to fashion a government in their own interests.

My critique of public education is therefore a critique in terms of the ideal of political democracy underlying the Bill of Rights rather than in terms of the specific rights it codified. If the experience of the eighteenth century led to the conclusion that free speech and assembly were essential to political democracy, it was because unhampered political discussion was perceived as the means by which people could recognize and formulate their political interests. Surely this was a profound insight, an insight which argued that the conditions which make it possible for people to recognize and formulate their own interests are fundamental to any other political right. I will argue that the institution of public education encroached upon political democracy because it encroached upon these conditions. The public schools strangled the ability of people to recognize and interpret their situation and in this way eroded all other rights.

In 1791 the people who had fought a revolution against state oppression asserted that Congress shall make no law respecting the establishment of religion. The experience of the eighteeenth century argued that the state and dominant classes acting through the state had used control of the church to control the minds and therefore the politics of men and women. Congress made no law respecting the establishment of religion. But there were many laws made, by all levels of government and by dominant classes acting through all levels of government, respecting the establishment of public schools. The schools were to become the modern church, controlling the minds and therefore the politics of Americans.

THE RISE OF PUBLIC EDUCATION

In 1840 less than 38 percent of children in the United States between the ages of five and nineteen attended school.[1] By 1860, 59 percent attended school; by 1898, 71 percent did so. Expenditures climbed from $63 million in 1870 to $190 million in 1898. By the end of the century a public, compulsory, and universal school system had been established, and except in the still feudal agricultural states of the south,[2] it embraced virtually all of the children of the laboring classes. And the system continued to expand. In 1870 those enrolled in school attended for an average of seventy-eight days; today children attend school for half the days in a year.[3] In 1898 children attended school an average of five years; but as the percentage of children enrolled in high schools increased from 11 percent in 1900 to 51 percent in 1930,[4] the average years of schooling increased to thirteen in the 1970s. In short, the public education system spread laterally so as to include more and more children and vertically so as to subject children to longer and longer periods of schooling.

None of this was accomplished smoothly; the school system did not grow gradually out of a broad social consensus. Rather, it was business elites who were active at crucial historical junctures in the emergence and expansion of the schools. Thus it was the wealthiest merchants of the colonial and post-Revolutionary cities who sponsored the early charity schools.[5] In the course of the nineteenth century, industrialists became active as educational reformers, and by the end of the century the Carnegie and Rockefeller corporations were playing a large role in educational expansion and reform.

Moreover, the institution forged by elites had to be imposed on the working class,[6] partly by means of legal compulsion. The first compulsory school attendance law was passed in Massachusetts in 1852; by 1900, thirty-one states had passed some form of compulsory attendance law, and by 1918 all the states had passed such laws.[7] The laws were enforced by means of enlarging battalions of truant officers, of school censuses to determine how many children were attending, and funding formulas that rewarded school districts on the basis of attendance.

The imposition of a specific system of schooling was pursued not only by compulsion, but through a century-long effort by elites to centralize control of the proliferating schools, placing them under the control of small, elite boards and committees, the better to ensure that all schools conformed with the new educational procedures they were developing. It was through centralization that compulsory attendance;[8] a standardized curriculum; and the new procedures for grading, tracking, and testing could be imposed on all schools everywhere. Inevitably, in the absence of either the tradition or structure of a strong central state, and given the American ideological emphasis on local self-government, the village, district, and ward schools that had been established had come to be influenced by local communities. It was this influence that the centralization movement sought to eliminate.[9] It did so through a series of drawn-out campaigns to consolidate school districts and enlarge the role of state boards of education; to eliminate working-class members from school boards under the guise of seeking to remove education from the tainted influence of politics;[10] and to professionalize the administration of the schools and standardize school organization and curriculum.

CLASS CONFLICT AND SCHOOL REFORM

Why, then, did American business elites undertake to initiate, enlarge, and assert control over a public school system? And why was that process often resisted by the people who were the presumed beneficiaries?

One theme in the statements of school reformers was that schools were needed to train working-class children, partly because traditional training institutions like the family had weakened, and partly because the specific behaviors required by an industrial and urban society were different, and perhaps more stringent than those necessary in pre-industrial contexts. If we take such statements at face value, they seem to imply that elites were prompted to take major action by a process of abstract analysis of "social problems" through which they concluded, for example, that families and communities were decaying, and that something ought to be done about it. It seems more reasonable to us to think that elites were prompted to act not by analysis alone, but by their experience of actual and serious disturbances. And if the action taken by elites was designed to train working-class children, then it seems reasonable to think that the disturbances that stimulated elite action were the result of working-class defiance.

Thus if elites were worried about the "decay" of family and community it was because of the socially disruptive behavior that such "decay" signified. In fact, the argument that education would eliminate disruptive behavior runs through the statements of school reformers.[11] The mayors of New York complained during the commercial instabilities of the post-Revolutionary period that "an idle and profligate Banditti disturbed the peace,"[12] and New York philanthropists advanced programs for the education of poor children, particularly the children of such troublesome groups as blacks, Indians, and paupers. These charity schools were the experiments that came to inform the expansion of the public school system, and the argument for the one was the argument for the other. The schools, said New York Secretary of State Van Ness Yates in 1824, were "so many moral engines at work for the extirpation of crime and pauperism."[13] By mid-nineteenth century, when the Massachusetts school system was already quite highly developed, the superintendent of the Lawrence schools still complained of the many children who continued to learn from the streets instead of the schools, spending their "time in prowling about shops, alleys and backyards, pilfering swill [and] old iron."[14] In the large cities, lawlessness assumed more threatening proportions as the nineteenth century wore on and even took collective form in the immigrant slum street gangs, which came to control large areas of the industrial cities, stimulating the familiar elite preoccupation with "the dangerous classes" for whom education was a solution.[15]

Education would not only prevent the more commonplace disturbances of vagrancy and crime, but it would eliminate the threat of revolt as well. Raymond Mohl's comments about the views of early New York reformers on the beneficial effects of religious education are illustrative: "It made the working class and the poor 'peaceable' and docile. It forced them to recognize," one tract asserted in an obvious reference to bread riots in England, "that *destroying* provisions is not the way to *lower* their prices."[16] Of course, bread riots were indeed a way to lower the price of provisions, at least temporarily, as Edward Thompson and others have argued.[17] For most ordinary people, they were the only way to inhibit the encroachments of the market system. If education could indeed prevent bread riots, then it could prevent affective resistance.

As industrialization advanced, the dangers of revolt increased. Working people reacted against their degradation into the status of wage laborers, against the erosion of traditional worker rights, against declining wages, against periodic mass unemployment, and they reacted with mass riots and strikes. One remedy was public education. Thus the secretary of the Massachusetts Board of Education pointed out in 1859 that it was factory owners who were concerned with the "intelligence" of their laborers, for "when the latter are well-educated . . . controversies and strikes can never occur, nor can the minds of the masses be prejudiced by demagogues and controlled by temporary and factious considerations."[18] After the great and violent railroad strikes of 1877, the U.S. Commissioner of Education proposed that "Capital . . . should weigh the cost of the mob and the tramp against the cost of universal and sufficient education," and the president of the National Education Association reported a citizen's comment that "it was the good sense of an immense majority of working people, created, fostered, and developed by public education, that saved us from the terrors of the French Commune." The public school, an educator declared in 1892, was "an instrument for disintegrating mobs," and the Governor of Massachusetts proposed that the militia, which had proved so unreliable in dealing with the railway strikers, would become more dependable with proper schooling. In 1894, as industrial conflict mounted, the National Education Association resolved that "we deem it our highest duty to pronounce enthusiastically, and with unanimous voice, for the supremacy of law and the maintenance of social and political order."[19] And in the aftermath of the populist movement that spread through the West and South, major corporations moved to promote agricultural educational reform in the states that had been the centers of populist agitation.[20]

If the elaboration of the school system were prompted by crime, vagrancy, fighting gangs, mass protests, and strikes—by working-class defiance—then it makes sense to suppose that the schools were designed to subdue this working class, to enforce their subservience to the requirements of the new industrial order. And this is surely the purpose for which public school practices seemed to have been intended. The evolving public schools of the nineteenth century were preoccupied with inculcating the habits of obedience, imparted at first in the form of religious training in Christian docility. Later, as the United States industrialized, urbanized, and became more secular, obedience training became more complex and even more mindless, for deference to bureaucratic rules and authorities replaced deference to certain Christian precepts as the guiding principle of school training.[21]

The schools did not, however, succeed in enforcing docility, at least not entirely. Not only is it transparently not the case that American children grew up to conduct themselves as they were taught in classroom rituals, but it is not the case that American working people were simply forced into the mold that the schools decreed. They continued to react against the conditions that shaped their lives, but under the influence of the public schools, these reactions were subtly redirected and transformed.

EDUCATION AND THE TRANSFORMATION OF WORKING CLASS POLITICS

All people train their young. In this sense, education is a natural activity in any society. And in any society the pattern of this training will reflect larger patterns of social differentiation and hierarchy, as well as patterns of social conflict within a differentiated and hierarchical society. But not only will the pattern of training reflect larger social patterns of hierarchy and conflict, it will also react upon them, for training will affect the capacity of people not only to conform to patterns of subordination, but to resist them.

One feature of the school system that has provoked much speculation is that modern schools provide little in the way of training in specific occupational skills.[22] In this respect, schools are different from other systems for training the young and different also from the systems of family and apprenticeship training that were supplanted by the schools. Nor does it seem reasonable to think that an emerging industrial order required literate workers. The functional illiteracy of immigrant workers did not seem an obstacle to the industrialists, who lobbied for unlimited immigration and then readily hired immigrants in preference to literate native workers.[23]

If the schools provided little in the way of skills training, they did provide other kinds of training and that training helps to account not only for the subordination of the mass of the working population to the requirements of industrial capitalism, but to the alterations in the capacity of that population to resist the incursions of industrial capitalism. It did so by transforming the social context, particularly the ideological context, that informed popular resistance.

The Extirpation of Traditional Beliefs

Schooling did not emerge in the context of an egalitarian or libertarian society. It emerged in the context of an hierarchical society and a society in which popular beliefs and behaviors ensured deference to those in the upper reaches of hierarchy. But, in the context of an industrializing society, the persistence of those popular beliefs had mixed effects. If, as school reformers argued, traditional patterns of belief and deference were weakening because the social arrangements in which they were embedded were collapsing, it was also true that traditional beliefs did not simply disappear. They persisted, and their persistence was a source of strength to people confronting the incursions of the new order.

Pre-existing beliefs as to how social and economic life should be organized, as to the rights and obligations of different classes, as to what was right and what was wrong in social life constituted a shared framework through which people could evaluate the hardships and disruptions imposed upon them by the encroaching industrial order. Moreover, successive waves of immigrants each brought with them their own beliefs and the patterns of deference and sense of rights lodged in these beliefs. These sets of meanings and rules of behavior arose from a different social order and therefore constituted an alternative framework for interpreting the experiences of American society. For both natives and immigrants, traditional beliefs and traditional rules of behavior provided a coherent perspective through which people could evaluate and react to the experience of industrial capitalism. Tradition could inform resistance and lend it moral strength.

The intense preoccupation of the schools with inculcating obedience can be viewed, therefore, not only as an effort to compensate for the weakening of older socializing institutions or as a way to impose new patterns of docility consistent with industrial capitalism, but as an effort to destroy earlier sets of meanings and rules of behavior.[24] By destroying those beliefs, the cultural bases for many forms of resistance to the new industrial order were extirpated.

Literacy Training and the Erosion of Class Autonomy

The majority of Americans were literate before the systematic expansion of compulsory education in the nineteenth century, but although the campaign to achieve literacy preceded the campaign to establish a universal compulsory school system—Massachusetts required that all children learn to read along with its first public school legislation in the mid-seventeenth century—it is surely not incidental that no matter what else was taught in the public schools, and no matter what else was taught in the Sunday schools into which English working-class children were inducted in the absence of public schools, working-class and poor children were taught to read and to write.

Indeed, no matter what organizational form it has taken, the training of the young in Western societies has been dominated by training in literacy skills, and it is worth contemplating the implications of this virtually universal feature of education as we know it. The emphasis on literacy in the West clearly has some connection with Protestantism, with the Protestant emphasis on the Bible as the source of wisdom and goodness, and on the individual's responsibility for learning and abiding by the Word. (It is the religious zealotry of Puritan New England to which Diane Ravitch attributes the early literacy laws of Massachusetts.) In its secular application, the emphasis on literacy training that pervades Western education also implies the existence of a fount of wisdom, in the form of educated authorities and written works that originate outside the community, and of the individual's responsibility to absorb and conform to that wisdom. Literacy training, therefore, no matter what its content, no matter whether the source of literate wisdom is the Bible or *Das Kapital*, implies a hierarchy of wisdom, making those who learn vulnerable to the definitions of those who teach, write, and print. Eric Hobshawn, despite his decidedly ambivalent attitudes toward political struggles among preliterate peoples, has recently made a similar argument:

More generally the popular classes fall under the influence of hegemonic culture because it is in a sense the only culture that operates as such through literacy—the very construction of a standard national language belongs to

> the literate elite. The very process of reading and schooling diffuses it, even unintentionally. The most traditional repertoire of popular literature inevitably contains thick deposits of upper-class origin, as in the *Bibliotheque Bleue* of the seventeenth and eighteenth centuries. . . . [T]he most important popular function of books was not . . . to fertilize a few lone and original autodidacts, who are impressive but rarely influential. Most popular readers, like most readers of any class, are followers.[25]

Not only does literacy breed deference, but widespread literacy obviously expands the range of influence of those who control literate sources. Masses of people can be reached through the printed word. Literacy is thus not only inherently hierarchical, but it enlarges the scope of hierarchical influences, which now penetrate every village and working-class quarter.

And now a crucial point: mass literacy inhibits the capacity of people to develop relatively autonomous interpretations of their particular social reality, for ordinary people do not produce their truths in literate form. It is for this reason that preliterate people appear to have a greater capacity to resist interpretations that come from outside their community and from beyond their experience, a point that Thompson makes in accounting for the vigor of the "moral economy" that guided the actions of the preliterate English food rioters.[26] Literacy training thus not only expands the range of influence of class-based literate sources but intensifies that hierarchical influence. And this is true whether literacy training is imposed by a nineteenth-century bourgeoisie, or by a twentieth-century socialist regime.

There are, of course, numerous historical instances where literacy training has seemed to stimulate revolt by exposing people to critical perspectives on their society that they might otherwise never have imagined. Nevertheless, those who control literate sources are not *usually* revolutionaries. Moreover, even when they are, they are revolutionary elites. Thus there is no gainsaying that when the self-taught nineteenth-century English working class gained access to the dissenting essays of Thomas Paine, William Cobbett, Thomas Carlisle, Wilfred Owen, and so forth, literary dissent lent legitimacy to deep working-class grievances and in that sense helped to stir revolt, just as exposure to Marxist writings has helped to stir revolt among colonial peoples in our time. But that these writings were dissenting did not make them the product of English working-class experience. They were rather the product of dissenting bourgeoisie and tended therefore to direct the energies released by working-class grievances toward solutions that suited this rising class. The costly participation of English workers in the agitation leading to enfranchisement of the bourgeoisie in the Reform Law of 1832 is only one example.

Finally, literacy training is also necessarily training in ideological individualism. Preliterate peoples distill their shared experience into wisdom through a process of communication within the group; there is no other way to "know." But literacy training implies that the individual is the sole agent of learning, via the printed word. In this sense, as in the Protestant emphasis on the individual's responsibility for reading and abiding by the Bible, the individual becomes the agent of his or her own subordination to literate wisdom, and the group becomes irrelevant.

The belief that the source of wisdom is external to the community and the belief that the individual is the agent responsible for acquiring this wisdom may also tend—no matter what the content of literate wisdom—to encourage a search for solutions to problems by individual self-improvement through the deferential process called education, rather than through collective struggle. Indeed, the belief in the redemptive power of literate knowledge that prevailed among the nineteenth-century English working class led some among them even to believe that organization and struggle were not necessary; that individual enlightenment would of itself produce the transformations that would ease the plight of the working class.[27]

In other words, perhaps the ubiquitous emphasis on literacy training in Western capitalist societies is not incidental. Perhaps it is one of the central mechanisms of domination by national elites. Literacy training eroded the communal traditions through which people interpreted their life situation, and it weakened the capacity of ordinary people to develop new collective interpretations of their changing situation. It dissipated their older world views, and it hierarchized and individualized the process through which people come to understand their changing conditions. In these ways, it weakened the capacity of people to act and react collectively in defiance of their betters.

Literacy training itself, however, goes only a part of the way toward accounting for the transforming effects of education on the political capacity of working people. Moreover, literacy training did not spread through the agency of autodidacts. It was implemented through specific structures called schools, and features of school structure also help to illuminate the role of public education in the transformation of popular resistance.

Structured Arrangements and Education in Self-Blame

Certain features of the structure of schooling that emerged from the nineteenth-century period of institution building are, when considered together, striking for their doctrinal implications. First, the American school system was a universal and common system, open to all children presumably without distinction. Indeed, educators themselves considered this feature of great import:

> The children of the rich and the poor, of the honored and the unknown, meet together on common ground. Their pursuits, their aims and aspirations are one. No distinctions find place, but such as talent and industry and good conduct create. In the competitions, the defeats, and the successes of the schoolroom, they meet each other as they are to meet in the broader fields of life before them. . . . No foundation will be laid in our social life for the brazen walls of caste.[28]

But even as the structure of the universal common school system was being forged, so were the internal structural arrangements of the schools that were to mark the distinctions "such as talent and industry and good conduct create." The introduction of age-grading in the mid-nineteenth century was the first phase. The result of grading was that "over-age" children accumulated in lower grades in a pattern that closely matched the socio-economic origins of these children.[29] The elaboration of stratification schemes later in the century took the form of the development of "ability groups," presumably introduced to enable the more efficient instruction of children with different capacities. The problem of instructing children with inferior capacities was particularly pertinent:

> A very large proportion of the pupils in our cities and populous towns come from homes utterly destitute of culture, and of the means and spirit of culture. . . . There are schools in which four-fifths or more of the chil-

dren are of this class. I at one time had under my supervision a school in which ninety-nine percent of the children were of foreign parentage. . . . In such minds a sunken foundation must be laid by months or years of uncompromising toil.[30]

As such comments by the intensely class- and race-conscious educators of the nineteenth century make evident, schooling was not expected to overcome innate differences, but rather to reveal them. Like Calvinism, school ideology argued that election was preordained; striving and success within the school system could only reveal what had already been fixed by racial origins or nature.

As with grading, it was, of course, children from lower socio-economic groups that found themselves in the low-ability tracks, a pattern which acquired the patina of scientific objectivity when I.Q. testing spread through the school system in the twentieth century.[31] Testing resulted, not surprisingly, in the labeling of as many as 60 to 70 percent of the children from some low status ethnic groups as "retarded." Special training for special groups, particularly industrial or vocational training for children presumably suited for the manual trades, produced a similar pattern, reifying in levels of school achievement and failure the socio-economic origins of particular groups of children. And, as the number of years of schooling was expanded, rates of failure were simply pushed upward to higher levels of the school system.[32]

The point, however, is not simply that the schools stratified children in a pattern that matched the larger socio-economic order. Rather the point is that the conjunction of a universal common school system that advertised "no distinction of rich and poor" with highly systematized arrangements to impose just such distinctions was a structural arrangement that had the effect of legitimating differential socio-economic status by attributing it to qualities of the individual. If all children were given an opportunity for achievement and needed only to demonstrate "talent and industry and good conduct," it followed that those who failed, even when large proportions of the children from particular groups failed, had only themselves to blame. One system had embraced all and embraced all equally. Some succeeded, others did not, and not because of the economic and political realities of a class society, but because some possessed personal qualities of talent and industry that others lacked. The structural arrangements of the schools implied a doctrine, in other words, about the causes of the economic hardships that people suffered and what could be done about them. The causes were in individual characteristics, and the solution was in individual striving to demonstrate talent and good conduct. And if such strivings failed, why then there was no one to blame but oneself.

Indeed, the specific designations and treatments designed by the schools for those it considered its worst failures, for those who were at the bottom of its hierarchy of merit, are particularly illuminating of the ideological doctrines of the schools. These were the truants or the "retarded" or more recently the "minimally brain damaged" or the "hyperactive." In dealing with the worst failures, the schools invented categories whose meaning was that the individual was defective, and they proceeded to treat them in ways that reflected this diagnosis, from reform schools for truants,[33] to special classes for the "retarded," to rehabilitation programs for the "brain-damaged," to the drugging of "hyperactive" children. All of this confirmed both for those who had failed so drastically as to slip into the deviance nets at the bottom of the school hierarchy and for those who merely watched and learned, that failure was the result of individual defects. And, to the extent that this individualizing indoctrination succeeded, it not only helped secure the acquiescence of many people to a highly stratified society, but also shaped the forms of resistance that remained possible within that society.

STRUCTURAL ARRANGEMENTS AND THE EDUCATION OF POPULAR POLITICS

Structural arrangements are one large determinant of the patterns of political activity that emerge in any political system. Structural arrangements encourage or block the articulation of political groupings and help to direct those groupings to focus on some issues and not on others. In the United States, the structures of school governance have had a large impact on the pattern of popular politics.

I have already referred to the centralizing reforms imposed upon the schools during the course of the nineteenth century. But the structural arrangements that resulted from those campaigns are complex. To all appearances, the schools in the United States are not centrally administered, as the term centralization is usually understood. The national government plays a far smaller role in education, for example, than it does in most other state policies; federal funding for the public schools is minimal, and federal education law and administration scarcely exist. To the contrary, the public schools are administered under state and local law by state and local agencies and paid for by state and local taxes. Indeed, few state policies are structured so as to be administered in so visibly a decentralized fashion. Every locality has its school board, and the activities of the school board usually excite local interest and participation. Indeed, in many communities school budgets are even subject to local referenda. In these respects, the structure of the school system epitomizes the values of local democracy.

But the centralization campaigns did occur, and they did succeed. School districts were consolidated, the role of state boards of education enlarged, at-large election districts were created or school board officerships were made appointive, all of which had the effect of eliminating much working-class influence. But those centralizing reforms were never pushed too far, in part because they continued to be resisted by people who understood that the schools would absorb and shape their children. Moreover, there was not much need to push centralization in these overt forms too far for, as the nineteenth century drew to a close, national standard-setting organizations were acquiring the ability to shape school administration everywhere, no matter what the local administrative structures. These standard setting organizations included the National Education Association, and the foundations, together with the institutions of higher education that were themselves much influenced by foundation campaigns to establish standardized structures, procedures, and curricula in the schools. The pervasive use of uniform I.Q. and achievement tests greatly facilitated these methods of centralization.

In other words, a decentralized apparatus of local school administration persists side by side with centralizing and hierarchical structural arrangements. One might speculate that this dual system serves to lend democratic legitimation to centralized and hierarchical imposition. But it does more. The features of school structure that lend the appearance of local accessibility and local control not only generate ideas about politics, they generate politics as well.

There is a school politics in local communities, and it is relatively vigorous. Most of the time, this politics follows conventionalized patterns, dictated by the rules and traditions of school structures. Some of the time, however, people are driven by hardship and indignation to act outside these rules and traditions. Even then, however, the very existence of a structure and tradition of local participation acts to channel indignation into educational protest.

EDUCATION AND SUPERCESSION OF POLITICS

The distinctive system of training called education was institutionalized in a system called the public schools, and imposed at first upon some young children of the working class and slowly expanded until it reached all children. That system emerged and was expanded and elaborated at least partly in response to popular resistance, and as it spread, its effects were to limit and shape subsequent efforts at working-class resistance.

One such long-term change was the channeling of popular protest into educational protest. On those occasions when people were prodded to defiance by new economic and social hardships and when circumstances enabled them to act collectively, they came increasingly to express their discontent in the form of demands for different or better public education.

This transformation is all the more remarkable because the public schools were initiated and imposed by elites, often over the resistance of the people who were the presumed beneficiaries. In New York City, for example, the philanthropists of the Free School Society (renamed the Public School Society in 1826 to justify the receipt of public monies) found they were least successful in drawing the children of the poor into their classes. To overcome this resistance, the Society recommended to the Common Council in 1832 that poor relief be denied to parents who failed to send their children to school. The council did not act on the request, and the society had to be content with hiring visitors to go through the slums to persuade parents of the advantages of education.[34] Similarly, Samuel Bowles and Herbert Gintis report that the Lovell School Board found that the Irish boycotted their schools, and several attempts were made to burn down the school in the Irish part of town.[35]

It was to overcome this resistance that legal compulsion spread. But resistance continued, with the result that the machinery of compulsion became more and more elaborate. The first truant officer in Lawrence, Massachusetts handled over 500 cases in his first year on the job;[36] as late as 1910 New York City truant officers investigated over 130,000 cases; between 1911 and 1920, 30,000 to 50,000 truancy cases were investigated each year in Pittsburgh.[37] Moreover, the reasons for resistance were often articulated, as in the drawn-out struggle by the Irish in New York City to keep their children out of what they considered the Protestant schools of the Public School Society.[38] David Tyack reports on the findings of an inspector who interviewed 500 factory children to find why they were not in school. Almost all the children said they preferred the factory. A thirteen-year-old explained why: "they hits ye if yer don't learn, and they hits ye if ye have string in yer pocket, they hits ye if ye whisper, and they hits ye if yer seat squeaks, and they hits ye if ye don't stan' up in time, and they hits ye if ye ferget the page."[39]

Centralization and the uniform school methods of compulsion, grading, tracking, and testing that centralization was designed to enforce were also resisted, and in fact school reform became a major political battleground in American cities of the late nineteenth and early twentieth century. Working people and particularly immigrant working people who often saw centralization as a means of eliminating ethnic culture from the schools[40] fought for a measure of control over the schools into which they would send their children. They sometimes also fought specifically against the stratifying reforms when they understood them for what they were. At the turn of the century, the American Federation of Labor took a strong stand against the efforts of the National Association of Manufacturers and other business groups to introduce vocational education into the schools.[41] And the Chicago Federation of Labor in 1924 bitterly attacked the use of intelligence tests. "[T]he so-called 'mental level' ascertained . . . corresponds in an astounding exactness with the social and economic status of the family," asserted the CF of L. It was a "brand of inferiority . . . placed upon all productive workers through the medium of propaganda emanating from the public schools."[42]

I do not want to overstate the strength or solidity of working resistance to education. Some among the working class, particularly better-off strata, believed in the promise of education as a route to occupational success and political power and believed this from the earliest phases of public education. Thus, at the very time that the New York Common Council was considering the refusal of poor relief to indigent workers who did not send their children to school, better-off artisans in the Workingmen's Party demanded, among other things, free public education for their children.[43] The governor of New York, who had been swept into office in 1838 with working-class support, expressed the workers' version of educational doctrine when he said that the power of the few "cannot be broken while the many are uneducated."[44]

But with the spread of public education, the pattern repeated itself and enlarged. People came to believe, as educators argued, that schooling was a solution to low status and hardship. Tyack writes that during the nineteenth century "every black voluntary group, almost all black politicians, rated the improvement of education near the top of priorities for their people."[45] It is not surprising, therefore, that when a protest movement finally emerged among blacks in the mid-twentieth century, it was educational advancement that figured so prominently in its objectives, first in the form of the demand for desegregated schools, later in the form of demands for improved schools and for greater community influence over the schools, and for increased black enrollments in the colleges. The most subjugated people in the United States had risen. Pressed by the hardships of agricultural displacement and forced migration, they had found the strength to defy the feudalistic terrors of the South and the massive prejudice of the North. And yet, when they rose up, they demanded not land reform or economic reform, but educational reform.

But blacks only shared the beliefs held by all Americans. By the end of the nineteenth century, the labor movement had come to stand "behind educational expansion as the only remaining path toward mobility, security, and social responsibility."[46] Even labor's opposition to vocational education had dissipated by World War I. And by 1973, 76 percent of the respondents to a Gallup poll said that they thought education was "extremely important" to "one's future success."[47]

This redirection of working-class politics from economic issues to educational issues in part reflected the gradual absorption by the working class of educational beliefs, of the doctrine that economic problems could be solved and advancement secured when individuals had the talent and opportunity to absorb literate knowledge, a doctrine whose origins preceded the schools but that had been vigorously promulgated by educational reformers and imposed on the entire population through the practice of compulsory schooling. In part, the shift in the pattern of protest also reflected the decentralized structural features of the schools. People had come to believe that education was a solution to their problems, but even if they did not, the structures in which economic decisions were lodged were remote and inaccessible. By contrast, school boards were visible parts of the local governmental structure, seemingly accessible to pressure by ordinary people, even encouraging participation by ordinary people. For these reasons, the shoemakers of Beverly, Massachusetts, who were being pressed hard by mechanization in the mid-nineteenth century, nevertheless rose up against the town high school in 1860[48] just as a century later the people of Harlem, pressed hard by unemployment, rose up against the teachers. Ralph Waldo Emerson may have been more prescient than he knew when he suggested that one day we would learn to supersede politics through education.

The most pervasive way in which education superseded politics was not, however, through the redirection of collective protest but by inhibiting collective protest and promoting individualized and self-destructive protest instead. Economic hardships and upheavals did not cease, and people did not cease to resist. But now resistance had been stripped of the strength it could gain from alternative interpretations of social life and driven into privatized and self-destructive forms consistent with the individualizing and self-blaming doctrines of the schools, doctrines that had been etched by school preaching and school practice into the minds of all children. The schools had taught that the economic and social circumstances experienced by people were the result of individual talent, industry, and merit in the pursuit of authoritative knowledge. The schools had taught that the race was open to all and that the many who failed had only themselves to blame. And the schools had engraved the shame of that failure by its treatment of its special deviants—its truants, its retarded, its handicapped.

All of this has to do with political democracy in a very fundamental way. It has to do with political democracy because it has to do with the capacities of people to interpret their situation, capacities that underlie their ability to act in political society. No doubt public education affected other aspects of American life as well, and perhaps many of these effects were beneficial in one way or another. But I have not tried to provide a comprehensive assessment of public education. I have tried only to probe its impact on political life by probing its impact on the ability of ordinary people to recognize their own interests. If the schools undermined that ability, they played a role in American politics that corroded the vision of political democracy that guided the statement of our rights in 1791.

NOTES

1. Public schools had been initiated earlier, but they were systematized and expanded in the nineteenth century. Massachusetts passed laws requiring that towns of one hundred or more households establish schools as early as the mid-seventeenth century, but the laws were implemented in a relatively informal and even chaotic way. Samuel Bowles and Herbert Gintis, *Schooling in Capitalist America* (New York: Basic Books, 1976), p. 153. The early schools in New York State, where the legislature made its first appropriations for common schools in 1795, were also haphazard, particularly in smaller cities and rural areas, where the schools were often run by the local community. See Diane Ravitch, *The Great School Wars: New York City 1905–1973* (New York: Basic Books, 1974), p. 7; David Tyack, *The One Best System* (Cambridge, Mass.: Harvard University, 1974), pp. 19–21.

2. Bowles and Gintis report a state-by-state study of the relationship between school attendance and industrialization for the period 1840–1860. School attendance was positively related to the percentage of the labor force employed in manufacturing, and negatively related to the role of slaves in the state economy. Bowles and Gintis, *Schooling in Capitalist America*, p. 176.

3. Ibid., pp. 153, 154.

4. Ronald Gross and Paul Osterman, eds., *High School* (New York: Simon and Schuster, 1971), p. 5.

5. Ravitch gives the social composition of the free school society of New York, all of whose members were extremely wealthy business men. Ravitch, *The Great School Wars*, pp. 8–9. The function of philanthropic educa-

tional efforts as laboratories for subsequent innovations in public education continued throughout the nineteenth century. Wealthy philanthropists, for example, "Founded private kindergartens for poor children in cities as far apart as Boston and San Francisco; in a number of cities they privately funded the first public trade schools and commercial high schools, as well as 'industrial schools' for the children of the poor; they supported the first program of vocational guidance; they created 'parental schools' and other institutions for truants and pre-delinquents; and they sometimes subsidized municipal research bureaus, which were the forerunners of research departments of the city school system." Tyack, *The One Best System*, p. 186.

6. Education was imposed, writes Michael Katz, in three senses: "In the first place . . . educational reform was imposed by the prominent upon the community. Second, the goals of that reform represented the imposition of upper and middle class fears and perceptions of social deficiencies. Third, the content of that reform represented an imposition of the values of communal leaders upon the rest of society." Michael Katz, *Class, Bureaucracy and the Schools* (New York: Praeger, 1971), p. 151.

7. Colin Greer, *The Great School Legend* (New York: Basic Books, 1972), p. 18.

8. Thus Jacob Riis argued centralization was needed in New York City because the ward system had failed to enforce compulsion: "A management which leaves 48,000 children . . . to roam the streets, deprived of school accommodation, sends truants to jail, and makes a laughing stock of the compulsory education law, is not fit to exist." Tyack, *The One Best System*, p. 151.

9. One advocate in support of abolishing ward school boards in New York City in 1896 stated quite candidly that local control was imprudent, "in a city like this so impregnated with foreign influence . . . where the mode of living is repugnant to every American," and where, at least in working-class wards, people are "incapable of judging the efficiency" of the school. Quoted in Tyack, *The One Best System*, p. 151. That elites perceived the problem as a class problem and not simply one of eliminating ethnic influence is clear from Katz's account of centralizing efforts in Massachusetts (1968) as well as the effort to centralize control in rural schools. Tyack, *The One Best System*, pp. 13–27.

10. Clearly, however, it was not politics but popular politics that was the problem in the view of educational reformers, for they sought to make membership on school boards appointive instead of elective and to specify the criteria for such appointments in class term. In 1891 a National Education Association committee went further, endorsing a proposal to limit the franchise by excluding the ignorant and vicious classes. Tyack, *The One Best System*, p. 132. This theme ran through the municipal reform move-

ments of the late nineteenth century, although expediency usually prevented its frank articulation. Katz makes a similar point in *Class, Bureaucracy and the Schools*, p. 75. In any event, the campaign succeeded. Scott Nearing's study of 104 city boards showed that by 1917 businessmen and professionals had come to constitute 79 percent of the membership of these school boards; see "Who's Who on Our School Boards of Education," *School and Society* 5, no. 108 (January, 1917): 89-90.

11. Katz says this also. "Perhaps the strongest impulse behind the founding of public education systems was what today we would call the urge for law and order." *Class, Bureaucracy and the Schools*, p. 108.

12. Raymond Mohl, *Poverty in New York, 1783-1825* (New York: Oxford University Press, 1971), pp. 16-17.

13. Ibid., p. 174.

14. Michael Katz, *The Irony of the Early School Reform* (Boston: Harvard University Press, 1968), p. 99.

15. Tyack quotes the educational historiographer Ellwood Cubberly as writing that when too many immigrants enter a community, "there is no longer enough of the older residential class" of "strong, opinionated, virile" Americans left to run the community. The immigrants, of course, were ignorant, and lacked the initiative and enterprise. Tyack, *The One Best System*, p. 11. John Cubberly was relatively gentle in his characterization of the problem. For example, the secretary of the Connecticut Board of Education thought that, "It is largely through immigration that the number of ignorant, vagrant and criminal youth has recently multiplied to an extent truly alarming in some of our cities. Their depravity is sometimes defiant and their resistance to moral suasion is obstinate." And a Boston schools committee member advocated corporal punishment in the schools in immigration wards explaining that "many of these children come from homes of vice and crime. In their blood are generations of iniquity." See Tyack, *The One Best System*, p. 75.

16. Mohl, *Poverty in New York*, p. 202.

17. Edward Thompson, "The Moral Economy of the English Crowd in the Eighteenth Century," *Past and Present* 50 (February 1971): 76-136.

18. Bowles and Gintis, *Schooling in Capitalist America*, p. 152.

19. Tyack, *The One Best System*, pp. 74-75.

20. Bowles and Gintis report that the Rockefeller-endowed General Education Board, the American Bankers Association, and at least four major railroad companies supported this reform effort. They also report a study showing that the states that had been the centers of the Populists revolt devoted significantly less resources to public education, a finding that they say, "invites a variety of interpretations." *Schooling in Capitalist America*, p. 177.

21. An 1874 pamphlet entitled "The Theory of Education in the United States," which was cosigned by 77 college presidents and city and state superintendents of schools stated: "Military precision is required in the maneuvering of classes. Great stress is laid upon (1) punctuality, (2) regularity, (3) attention, and (4) silence, as habits necessary through life for successful combination with one's fellow-men in an industrial and commercial civilization." Tyack, *The One Best System*, p. 50.

22. One might speculate that the nature of work in a capitalist society, where skill requirements change continuously as the division of labor advances and the techniques of scientific management elaborate, makes skills training in the schools impractical. Thus even when the schools do undertake occupational skills training, as in vocational education courses, the results are notorious for their irrelevance to the actual requirements of contemporary work.

23. I do not mean by this argument to entirely dismiss what is sometimes called the "human capital" perspective on education, although I would sharply qualify it. According to this perspective, the advancing technology of industrial capitalism generated new skill requirements and commensurately greater rewards for those with the requisite skills, with the result that people sought more education in response to these new incentives. This interpretation surely has validity for occupations involving technical and managerial skills, and it seems reasonable to think that the incentive to invest "human capital" thus generated did motivate middle-class families to seek education for their children. There is also substantial evidence that the middle class supported the introduction of high schools, which at the outset benefitted mainly their children, just as the young of the middle class were later the main beneficiaries of public colleges and universities. But the public schools did not begin as high schools, and the public school reformers did not begin with middle-class constituency. Rather the schools began as institutions for the children of the working class and the bottom of the working class at that. The human capital perspective provides little in the way of explanation of this aspect of educational history. Nor can it explain the continuing concentration of educational endeavor on the many for whom schooling had little direct bearing on occupation.

24. "Education" writes Katz in describing the emphasis on restraint, "was a substitution; and schoolmen agreed precisely on what was to be replaced and on its replacement." Thus schoolmen proposed not only the inculcation of obedience, but the inculcation of new personality traits, which would lead to the substitution of "higher" pleasures for "lower" pleasures. Katz, *Class, Bureaucracy and the Schools*, pp. 120–21.

25. Eric Hobshawn, "Religion and the Rise of Socialism," *Marxist Perspectives* 1, no. 1 (1978): 22.

26. Thompson, "The Moral Economy of the English Crowd," p. 26.

27. One of the most extreme exemplars of the perspectives was Richard Carlisle, whose radical publications earned him and his shopmen some 100 years in prison: "Let us then endeavor to progress in knowledge, since knowledge is demonstrably proved to be power. It is the power of knowledge that checks the crimes of cabinets and courts; it is the power of knowledge that must put a stop to bloody wars and the direful effects of devastating armies. . . . When the political principles laid down by Thomas Paine are well understood by the great body of the people, everything that is necessary to put them in practice will suggest itself, and then plots and delegate meetings will be wholly unnecessary. . . . In the present state of this country the people have no other real duty than to make themselves individually well acquainted with what constitutes their political rights." See Edward Thompson, *The Making of the English Working Class* (New York: Vintage, 1963), pp. 764–65.

28. Joseph White, Secretary of the Massachusetts Board of Education, writing about Massachusetts high schools, quoted Katz, *The Irony of Early School Reform*, pp. 44–45.

29. Tyack reports a 1909 study by the U.S. Senate's Immigration Commission of the rate of progress in the schools of different ethnic groups. Children who were two or more years older than the normal age for their grade were often defined as retarded, and the results showed that rates of retardation averaged 63.6 percent for southern Italian children, and 58.1 percent for Polish children. Overall, immigrant children showed retardation rates of 40.4 percent, compared to 30.4 percent for native-born children. See Tyack, *The One Best System*, p. 243. As Colin Greer points out, while the diverse cultural backgrounds of different ethnic groups may have influenced this pattern, its true significance is in the match between retardation rates and socio-economic status, which also varied by ethnic group.

30. Katz, *Class, Bureaucracy and the Schools*, p. 41.

31. Tyack reports that by 1932 three-fourths of the 150 large city school systems used intelligence tests in the assignment of pupils. See Tyack, *The One Best System*, p. 208.

32. This point is made by Colin Greer, *The Great School Legend*, pp. 8, 127; and Ronald Gross and Paul Osterman, *High School*, p. 48.

33. By processing truants as criminals, educators also gave symbolic credence to the doctrine that it was schooling that preserved society from crime and other ills. Moreover, since the overwhelming majority of truants were poor or immigrants, the processing of truants as criminals also served to confirm the school's definition of the criminal character of the lower orders.

34. Ravitch, *The Great School Wars*, pp. 9, 32.

35. Bowles and Gintis, *Schooling in Capitalist America*, p. 154.

36. Katz, *The Irony of Early School Reform*, p. 102.

37. Gross and Osterman, *High School*, p. 22.

38. For a review of some of the studies of resistance to compulsory schooling by immigrants and the poor, see Bowles and Gintis, *Schooling in Capitalist America*, p. 175.

39. Tyack, *The One Best System*, pp. 177–78.

40. The Irish understood public education to mean Protestant education, which they resisted. But other ethnic groups had sometimes managed to win concessions from the public schools, often in the form of the languages of their native countries. These concessions were eliminated with centralization.

41. Bowles and Gintis, *Schooling in Capitalist America*, p. 193.

42. Tyack, *The One Best System*, p. 215.

43. Ravitch, *The Great School Wars*, p. 23.

44. Ibid., p. 38.

45. Tyack, *The One Best System*, p. 110.

46. Bowles and Gintis, *Schooling in Capitalist America*, p. 186.

47. David Tyack, "Ways of Seeing: An Essay on the History of Compulsory Schooling," *Harvard Educational Review* 45, no. 3 (1976): 382.

48. Katz, *The Irony of the Early School Reform*, pp. 80–84. Katz ascribes the relative absence of machine breaking and physical assault in the United States to the opportunity provided working people to vent their anger in struggles over school issues. The shoemakers who voted to abolish the high school were suffering from rapid degradation of their status and their wages. Much of their anger, however, was redirected into a struggle over school policy, in this case against school expansion.

SECTION VII
Racial Justice

14

CHARLES V. HAMILTON

The Future and the Civil Rights of Minorities in America

In a speech on June 11, 1963, President John F. Kennedy referred to the civil rights issue as follows: "We are confronted primarily with a moral issue. It is as old as the Scriptures and is as clear as the American Constitution. . . . Now the time has come for this nation to fulfill its promise . . . those who do nothing are inviting shame as well as violence. Those who act boldly are recognizing right as well as reality."[1]

In a speech on May 22, 1964, President Lyndon B. Johnson stated: "The Great Society rests on abundance and liberty for all. It demands an end to poverty and racial injustice, to which we are totally committed in our time. . . . It is a place where the city of man serves not only the needs of the body and the demands of commerce but the desire for beauty and the hunger for community."[2]

And, then, in an opinion rendered on June 28, 1978, in *Regents of the University of California v. Allan Bakke*, Justice Lewis Powell wrote:

> We have never approved a classification that aids persons perceived as members of relatively victimized groups at the expense of other innocent individuals in the absence of judicial, legislative, or administrative findings of constitutional or statutory violations.
>
> . . . After such findings have been made, the governmental interest in preferring members of the injured groups at the expense of others is substantial since the legal rights of the victims must be vindicated. In such a case, the extent of the injury and the consequent remedy will have been judicially, legislatively, or administratively defined. Also, the remedial action usually remains subject to continuing oversight to assure that it will work the least harm possible to other innocent persons competing for the benefit. Without such findings of constitutional or statutory violations, it

cannot be said that the government has any greater interest in helping one individual than in refraining from harming another.[3]

At one time not too long ago, this country did not have to *admit* that it had a serious problem of racial segregation and discrimination. The signs were literally hanging or painted there for all to see: "whites only"; "Colored Waiting room" and so forth. Those signs are gone, substantially as a result of the struggles (legal and political) that culminated in the Civil Rights Act of 1964 and subsequent decisions and actions.

But there were other signs, however, that were less overtly racial but no less manifest. They depicted poverty and educational deprivation, poor health and housing conditions, and high unemployment rates.

These conditions (these signs, if you will) were not as vulnerable to the kinds of legal and political processes that attacked the *overt* racial ones. (Indeed, I toyed with the idea of entitling this chapter "The Future of Minorities in America: The Signs of The Times.")

Precisely because the "signs" are different now, we are faced with a new set of circumstances, and we are required to think in terms of different approaches to public policies. The "signs" today are different and conflicting. On the one hand, we are told that the problem is no longer one essentially of race, but of class. For instance, a black professor of Sociology at the University of Chicago, William Julius Wilson, in his recent book entitled *The Declining Significance of Race* writes:

> A consequence of the rapid growth of the corporate and government sectors has been the gradual creation of a segmented labor market that currently provides vastly different mobility opportunities for different segments of the black population. . . .
>
> Talented and educated blacks are experiencing unprecedented job opportunities in the growing government and corporate sectors, opportunities that are at least comparable to those of whites with equivalent qualifications. The improved job situation for the more privileged blacks in the corporate and government sectors is related both to the expansion of salaried white-collar positions and to the pressures of state affirmative action programs.
>
> The recent mobility patterns of blacks lend strong support to the view that economic class is clearly more important than race in predetermining job placement and occupational mobility.[4]

On the other hand, officials of the National Urban League and some other agencies question both the data and the conclusions. If, in fact, there is this newly developing black middle class, which is—as Professor Wilson states—a function in part, at least, of "pressures of state affirmative action programs," then are not these programs racially and minority-based? The consequences might well be to create a cadre of people earning higher incomes, but this is possible, is it not, precisely because they are identified as members of a *preferred* group.

If one concludes that economic class and not race is becoming more important in determining life-chances, then this would seem to suggest that special efforts should be predicated along class lines and not racial ones. But the data show that the "black underclass" is substantially below their white counterparts. Black teenage unemployment rates are at least three times those of white teenagers. Does this signify a black lower-class strategy or simply a lower class strategy?

However these kinds of questions are resolved, it is clear that the earlier focus of the civil rights struggle has shifted. That struggle, understandably, was concerned mainly with overcoming *de jure* segregation. A great deal of attention was focused on reinterpreting the "equal protection of the laws" clause of the Fourteenth Amendment for purposes of ending *overt* acts of racial segregation and discrimination. And to the extent that that struggle was successful, all blacks would benefit. *All* blacks, irrespective of socioeconomic status, were required to sit in the back of the bus, drink from water fountains marked "colored," denied entrance to Howard Johnson's, and prohibited from voting.

In one sense, the goals were simple and uncomplicated. Now, we seem not to be so sure of either the goals or the policies. It is not because we cannot see the *signs* of deterioration and deprivation. Rather, we seem not to know what caused them or how best to go about remedying them. We hear much more discussion now of the zero-sum effect of public policy. What sixteen minorities gain at the University of California—Davis Medical School, Allan Bakke will lose. What newly hired black policemen in Detroit gain, unhired white applicants will lose. And we hear sincerely put questions such as, "tell me, is affirmative action just?"

If, as I believe to be the case, "affirmative action" will be the focus of much of the minority struggle in the near future, it is this question of "justice" that must be broached. If we prefer one racial or minority group over another, is this not, in reality, "reverse discrimination"? Are we not penalizing some, who had no role in prior subjugation practices, in favor of others, who were not themselves the direct victims of previous discrimination? Are not the preferred ones and the penalized ones the objects of public policy solely on the basis of their racial identification? And is this not abhorrent to our notion of justice and equity? Is this not precisely what we wanted to overcome in that long struggle to do away with racial stigmas? Is not a color-blind, rather than a color-conscious, society preferrable?

Is it, in fact, *more* than rights that this future struggle over affirmative action portends? Perhaps.

I would have us focus for a moment on the concepts of "equity" and "justice." Frequently, we hear as the rationale for affirmative action, the necessity "to *compensate* for the effects of societal discrimination."

The term "compensate" is an important one. It refers to *repayment*, to settlement; it seeks to vindicate, to rectify a particular wrong or injustice. Indeed, note the language of Justice Powell, whom I cited earlier: "After such findings have been made [that is, findings of constitutional or statutory violations] the governmental interest in preferring members of the injured groups at the expense of others is substantial, since the legal rights of the victims must be *vindicated*"[5] (emphasis added). Compensation, then, aims to correct, and it is fundamental to the principle of *equity*.

Let me refer to Aristotle. And let us consult his *Nicomachean Ethics*:

> The equitable is just, despite the fact that it is better than the just in one sense. It is not better than the just in the sense of being generically different from it. This means that just and equitable are in fact identical (in genus), and, although both are morally good, the equitable is the better of the two . . . the equitable is not just in the legal sense of "just" but as a *corrective* of what is legally just.[6]

Equity, then, is corrective; it seeks to remedy. It recognizes that the *legally* just cannot fit all occasions; thus, equity seeks to correct what the legal cannot do. It is, if you will, justice in a particular form.

Does this mean that preferential-corrective policies for minorities seek *more* than rights? No, not really. Aristotle is not suggesting that in his discussion of equity.

There is another aspect of this matter, stemming from Justice Powell's opinion in the *Bakke* case, that ought to be raised here. One will recall that he said: "We have never approved a classification that aids persons perceived as members of relatively victimized groups at the expense of other innocent individuals in the absence of judicial, legislative or administrative findings of constitutional or statutory violations."[7]

The chairperson of the Equal Employment Opportunities Commission, Eleanor Holmes Norton, calls this the "Powell Test." Thus, where a governmental agency (court, congress, or executive) has made a finding of past discrimination and violation of rights, this will permit a reasonably wide approach to affirmative action programs.

This is, of course, Norton's reading of Powell—which may or may not be accurate, and even if so, Powell is only one justice on a reasonably divided Court.

At any rate, the near future will likely see concentration on issues of equity. What is the most equitable way to proceed to try to narrow the gap (mainly, economic and educational, I suspect) between the status of minorities and the "general public"? Considerable attention will be paid to numbers: income, school enrollment, ratios on the job, "guidelines" that suggest numerical "goals" but studiously avoid "quotas."

The Equal Employment Opportunities Commission (EEOC) and the Department of Justice can be expected to continue to prod private and public agencies to adopt and implement affirmative action plans. Shortly after the *Bakke* decision, the Justice Department filed an *amicus curiae* brief with the U.S. Court of Appeals for the Sixth Circuit in July 1978 supporting Mayor Coleman A. Young and Detroit's affirmative action plan, which sets strict numerical quotas for the promotion of blacks in the Detroit police department. The brief distinguished the Bakke and Detroit cases by arguing that the Detroit police department had admitted past discrimination against blacks. In its ninety-page brief, the Justice Department gave a long list of discriminatory practices, including the use of biased tests and highly subjective rating systems. As recent as 1967, the Detroit police force was less than 5 percent black although the city was close to becoming majority black.

Where past discrimination can be shown, it is likely that more numerically-oriented remedies will be allowed. Some observers believe that in most employment situations, it will not be too difficult to establish past discriminatory practices. At a recent meeting of the American Political Science Association, Attorney Nathaniel Jones, General Counsel of the NAACP, suggested that in very many instances it would even be appropriate for the court to take "judicial notice" that racial discrimination existed in the past.

Therefore, it will likely not suffice for an agency, institution, or company to assert that it *no longer* discriminates, that it *now* treats all applicants on their merits alone. In reviewing several federal regulations, Mr. Justice Brennan, dissenting in the *Bakke* case, wrote: "These regulations clearly establish that where there is a need to overcome the effects of past racially discriminatory or exclusionary practices engaged in by a federally funded institution, race-conscious action is not only permitted but required to accomplish the remedial objectives of Title VI."[8]

But Mr. Brennan was not convinced that *past* discrimination was the only problem. In his opinion, he stated:

> A glance at our docket and at those of lower courts will show that even today officially sanctioned discrimination is not a thing of the past.
>
> Against this background, claims that law must be "color-blind" or that the datum of race is no longer relevant to public policy must be seen as aspiration rather than as description of reality. This is not to denigrate aspiration; for reality rebukes us that race has too often been used by those who would stigmatize and oppress minorities. Yet we cannot . . . let color blindness become myopia which masks the reality that many "created equal" have been treated within our lifetimes as inferior both by the law and by their fellow citizens.[9]

It may be that some people will continue to see these issues in moral terms, as articulated by President Kennedy. But in a time of scarcity and retrenchment and with an ethos influenced by a Proposition 13 mood, one should not be sanguine that morality will be the motivating force behind action. Likewise, one might understand, and even be impressed by Aristotle's concept of "equity," but I suspect that many of these issues of race and civil rights will be dealt with more in terms of self-interest.

In a sense, many of the traditional issues of civil rights did not "cost" the country anything. There was no economic cost involved in permitting blacks to go to public accommodations unhampered by racial restrictions. There was no economic cost involved in ending voting denials in the South. Viewed in one sense, one might suggest that the traditional civil rights struggle was waged to *permit* minorities to *spend* their money in an open market.

Now the agenda is different. It will *cost* something to provide adequate jobs and decent housing and good education. If the language of President Johnson fourteen years ago is to be realized, we will have to pay. And this will be a major consideration in the future. If the 4 percent unemployment goal by 1983 contained in the recently passed Humphrey-Hawkins Full Employment bill is to be attained, the society will have to pay. I suggest that whether we are able and willing to assume such costs will depend largely on how we perceive the solutions in cost-benefit terms and the extent to which political forces can be mobilized in the process.

We do not have a long history of thinking about civil rights in such economic terms, but it seems to me that this is precisely what will be required in the future.

As long as we view these matters in the context of a zero-sum game, as long as we attempt to deal with these problems in the context of retrenchment and minimum expenditures, then I suspect we will not be able to be exceptionally optimistic about the outcome.

At any rate, a discussion of the future and the civil rights of minorities will have to take into account these economic concerns. Thus, as the earlier civil rights struggle caused us to grapple with questions of morality and conscience, sometimes articulated in Gunnar Myrdal's phrase, "American dilemma," I suggest that if we are to be concerned in the future, it will cause us to rethink some of our fundamental views on economics and the role of the public and private sectors operating in concert.

Notwithstanding the rather optimistic findings (in one sense, optimistic) of Professor William Wilson, we still receive reports from the Bureau of Labor Statistics showing persistent income lag among minorities. It has recently been noted that the earnings gap between whites and minority groups after narrowing in the late 1960s and early 1970s widened again in the late 1970s.[10]

Therefore, my point is that if we were discussing the topic of civil rights, say, in the late 1950s or the early 1960s, we would be discussing such things as the jury trial provision in the Civil Rights Act of 1957 (whether voter registrars charged with discrimination in the South should be tried by a jury). Or we would be discussing Mrs. Murphy's rights to exclude guests from her boarding house—perhaps you will recall that discussion in the 1963–1964 legislative debates.

Now, however, our focus is more on equity, on economic gaps, on stagflation, on how best to pursue policies that narrow economic and educational gaps. Is this a discussion that involves "more" than rights? Or is it a discussion, if you will, that reflects that we are now responding to different *signs* during these different times?

NOTES

1. *Public Papers of the Presidents: John FitzGerald Kennedy* (Washington, D.C.: U.S. Government Printing Office, 1964), p. 469.
2. *Public Papers of the Presidents: Lyndon Baines Johnson* (Washington, D.C.: U.S. Government Printing Office, 1965), p. 704.
3. *Regents of the University of California v. Allan Bakke*, 438 U.S. 265, at 307–309.
4. *The Declining Significance of Race* (Chicago: University of Chicago, 1978), pp. 151–52.
5. 438 U.S. 265, at 307.
6. Aristotle, *Nicomachean Ethics* 1137.
7. 438 U.S. 265, at 307.
8. 438 U.S. 265, at 344.
9. 438 U.S. 265, at 327.
10. Helen Dewar, "Earnings of Minorities Still Lag, Study Reveals," *Washington Post*, 19 October 1978, p. 7.

Selected Bibliography

BOOKS

Abelson, Philip H. *Energy for Tomorrow.* Seattle: University of Washington, 1975.

Bell, Daniel. "The Post-Industrial Society: A Prospectus." *Search for Alternatives,* edited by Franklin Tugwell. Cambridge: Winthrop, 1973.

Brubaker, Sterling. *In Command of Tomorrow.* Baltimore: Johns Hopkins, 1975.

Clark, Wilson. *Energy for Survival: The Alternative to Extinction.* New York: Doubleday, 1974.

Commoner, Barry. *The Closing Circle.* New York: Knopf, 1971.

Davis, Kingsley. "Zero Population Growth: The Goals and the Means." In *The No-Growth Society,* edited by Mancurs Olson and Hans Landsburg. New York: Norton, 1973.

Dumont, Rene. *Utopia or Else.* New York: Universal, 1975.

Forrester, Jay. *World Dynamics.* Cambridge, Mass.: Wright-Allen, 1973.

Fowles, Jib. *Handbook on Future Research.* Westport, Conn.: Greenwood, 1978.

Gappert, Gary. *Post Affluent America: The Social Economy of the Future.* New York: Franklin Watts, 1979.

Giark, Wilson. *Energy For Survival: The Alternative to Extinction.* Garden City, New York: Doubleday, 1974.

Gordon, T. J. "The Current Methods of Futures Research." In *The Futurists,* edited by Alvin Toffler. New York: Random House, 1972.

Heilbroner, Robert. *An Inquiry Into the Human Prospect.* New York: Norton, 1974.

Lang, Jean. *Resources and Decisions.* North Scituate, Mass.: Duxbury, 1975.

Lovins, Amory. *World Energy Strategies.* Cambridge, Mass.: Ballinger, 1975.

Mancke, Richard B. *The Failure of U.S. Energy Policy.* N.Y.: Columbia University, 1974.

McIlwain, Charles. *Constitutionalism: Ancient and Modern.* Ithaca: Cornell, 1958.

Meadows, Donella H. *Limits to Growth: A Report for the Club of Rome's Project on the Predicament of Mankind.* New York: Universe, 1974.

Mishan, E. *The Costs of Economic Growth.* New York: Penguin, 1969.

Ophuls, William. *Ecology and the Politics of Scarcity.* San Francisco: W. H. Freeman, 1977.

Rosenbaum, Walter. *The Politics of Environmental Concern.* N.Y.: Praeger, 2nd. Ed., 1977.

Schumacher, E. F. *Small is Beautiful.* N.Y.: Harper & Row, 1976.

Ward, Barbara, and Dubas, Rene. *Only One Earth: The Care and Maintenance of a Small Planet.* N.Y.: Norton, 1972.

Yannocone, Victor. *Energy Crisis: Danger and Opportunity.* St. Paul, Minn.: West, 1974.

JOURNALS

Bender, Tom. "Why We Need to Get Poor Quick." *The Futurist* 11 (August 1977).

Caldwell, Lynton. "Environmental Quality as an Administrative Problem." *Annals* 403 (March 1972).

Corning, Peter. "Toward A Survival Oriented Policy-Science." *Social Science Information* 14 (1975).

Hardin, Garrett. "The Rational Foundation of Conservation." *The North American Review* 259 (Winter 1974).

Higgens, Ronald. "The Seventh Enemy: The Human Factor in the Global Crisis." *The New Ecologist* 9 (January–February 1979).

Meadows, Dennis. "The Predicament of Mankind." *The Futurist* 5 (August 1971).

Milbrath, Lester, and Tobin, Richard. "Problems in a Society Experiencing Cessation of Growth." Unpublished manuscript.

Novick, David. "Facing Up to the World of Scarcities." *The Futurist* 11 (August 1977).

Ophuls, William. "The Scarcity Society." *Harper's* (April 1974).

Watson, Richard. "The Limits of World Order." *Journal of World Policy* 1 (1975).

Wildavaky, Aaron. "The Past and Future Presidency." *The Public Interest* 10 (Fall 1975).

Index

About the Contributors

HENRY J. ABRAHAM is James Hart Professor of Government and Foreign Affairs at the University of Virginia and was previously Professor of Political Science at the University of Pennsylvania. His principal research efforts have been in the fields of constitutional law, civil rights and liberties, and comparative judicial process. He has authored numerous books, including *The Judicial Process: An Introductory Analysis of the Courts of the United States, England, and France*, and *Justices and Presidents, A Political History of Appointments to the Supreme Court.*

HENRY STEELE COMMAGER is Simpson Lecturer at Amherst College. He is author of *Freedom, Loyalty and Dissent* and *The Defeat of America* and numerous other books. In recognition of his pioneering work in the field of civil liberties, the Sydney Hillman Foundation awarded him its first medal for a lifetime devotion to the cause of constitutional freedoms.

HERMAN E. DALEY is Professor of Economics at Louisiana State University. He has also taught at Vanderbilt University and worked as a research associate at Yale. His principal research efforts have been directed toward the study of economic development and population.

NORMAN DORSEN is Frederick I. and Grace A. Stokes Professor of Law and Director of the Arthur Garfield Hays Program in Civil Liberties of the New York University Law School. He has held appointments at the University of California at Berkeley and the London School of Economics. He has authored and co-authored numerous books on a broad range of legal topics, including *Political and Civil Rights in the United States.* He has also successfully argued a number of cases before the U.S. Supreme Court.

THOMAS I. EMERSON is Lines Professor of Law (Emeritus) at Yale University Law School. He has also held appointments at the London School of Economics and the Brookings Institution. He is the author of *Toward a General Theory of the First Amendment* and the co-author of *Political and Civil Rights in the United States.* He has previously served as principal attorney for the National Labor Relations Board and as general counsel for the U.S. Office of War Mobilization and Reconversion.

CHARLES V. HAMILTON is Sayre Professor of Government at Columbia University and has held academic positions at Roosevelt and Rutgers universities. His main fields of interest include judicial behavior, ethnic politics, and constitutional history. He is author of *The Bench and the Ballot* and co-author of *Black Power: Politics of Liberation.*

CHRISTOPHER LASCH is Professor of History at the University of Rochester. He formerly held appointments at the University of Iowa and Northwestern University. He is the author of many books, including *The New Radicalism in America*, *The World of Nations*, *The Culture of Narcissism*, and *Haven in a Heartless World.*

ALPHEUS THOMAS MASON is McCormick Professor of Jurisprudence (Emeritus) at Princeton University and formerly held appointments at the University of Virginia and Mercer Beasley School of Law. He has done extensive writing on the U.S. Supreme Court, authoring numerous books, including *American Constitutional Law*, *Security Through Freedom*, and *Harlan Fiske Stone: Pillar of the Law.*

PAUL L. MURPHY is Professor of History at the University of Minnesota. He previously was Assistant Professor of History at Ohio State University. His major research efforts have been directed toward the study of American constitutional and legal history and the history of civil rights. He is author of *The Meaning of Free Speech* and of *World War I and the Origin of Civil Liberties in the United States.*

SISTER MARIE AUGUSTA NEAL is Professor of Sociology at Emmanuel College and has been Visiting Professor at the University of California at Berkeley and the Harvard Divinity School. Her research interests have focused on the sociology of politics and religion. She is the author of *Values and Interests in Social Change* and *A Sociotheology of Letting Go.*

LEO PFEFFER is Professor of Constitutional Law at Long Island University. His principal research efforts have been in the fields of judicial behavior and political and constitutional history. He is the author of *Church, State and Freedom* and *This Honorable Court.*

FRANCES FOX PIVEN is Professor of Political Science at Boston University and previously held appointments at Brooklyn College and New York University Law School. She has been primarily concerned with urban politics and social movements. She is co-author of *Regulating the Poor: The Functions of Public Welfare* and *Poor Peoples' Movements: Why They Succeed and Why They Fail.*

DAVID ROTHMAN is Professor of History at Columbia University. His major areas of interest include American social history with an emphasis on the roles of public and private institutions. He is author of *Politics and Power* and *The Discovery of the Asylum*.

GERALD SIRKIN is Professor of Economics at City College of New York Graduate Center. His intellectual interests focus on the role of public power in regulating economic activity.

ALAN A. STONE is Professor of Law and Medicine at Harvard University. His major area of research is the study of personality and the law. He has co-authored several works, including *Longitudinal Studies of Child Personality* and is the author of *Mental Health and Law: A System in Transition*.

About the Editor

STEPHEN C. HALPERN is Associate Professor of Political Science at the State University of New York at Buffalo. He is the author of *Police Associations and Department Leaders*.